WITHDRAWN

FRENCH EXISTENTIALIST FICTION: CHANGING MORAL PERSPECTIVES

TERRY KEEFE

BARNES & NOBLE BOOKS
Totowa, New Jersey

© 1986 Terry Keefe

First published in the USA 1986 by
Barnes and Noble Books
81 Adams Drive
Totowa, New Jersey, 07512
Printed in Great Britain

Library of Congress Cataloging-in-Publication Data

Keefe, Terry.
    French existentialist fiction.

    Bibliography: p.
    Includes index.
    1. French fiction—20th century—history and
criticism.   2. Existentialism in literature.
3. Ethics in literature.   4. Camus, Albert, 1913–1960—
Ethics.   5. Sartre, Jean Paul, 1905–   —ethics.
6. Beauvoir, Simone de, 1908–   —ethics.   I. Title.
PQ673.K4   1986   823′.914′09384   86-3469
ISBN 0-389-20627-X

CONTENTS

Texts and Abbreviations
Preface

Introduction 1

PART I: THE 'PRE-WAR' STORIES

Chapter 1. Solitude and Metaphysical Discovery 11

Chapter 2. Lucidity and Self-Deception 31

Chapter 3. The Individual and Society 48

Chapter 4. Self-Justification and its Limits 65

PART II: THE 'WARTIME' NOVELS

Chapter 5. Collective Situations and Groups 87

Chapter 6. Problems of Responsibility and Action
.... 111

Chapter 7. Guidelines and Limits 140

PART III: POST-WAR STORIES

Chapter 8. Transition 163

Chapter 9. Marriage and the Family 176

Chapter 10. Work, Judgement and Self-Scrutiny 193

Chapter 11. Society and the Individual Conscience
.... 212

Conclusion 236

Bibliography 245

Index 248

TEXTS AND ABBREVIATIONS

Part I

BEAUVOIR: *Quand prime le spirituel*(QPS)
       : *L'Invitée*(Inv)

CAMUS: *La Mort heureuse*(MH)
    : *L'Etranger*(Etr)

SARTRE: *La Nausée*(LN)
    : *Le Mur* ('Le Mur'(Mur), 'La Chambre'(Cham),
'Erostrate'(Ero), 'Intimité'(Int), 'L'Enfance d'un
chef'(ECh))
    : *L'Age de raison*(AR)

Part II

BEAUVOIR: *Le Sang des autres*(SA)
       : *Tous les hommes sont mortels*(THM)

CAMUS: *La Peste*(LP)

SARTRE: *Le Sursis*(Surs)
    : *La Mort dans l'âme*(MA)
    : *La Dernière Chance* ('Drôle d'amitié'(DA),
'La Dernière Chance'(DCh))

Part III

BEAUVOIR: *Les Mandarins*(LM)
       : *Les Belles Images*(BI)
    : *La Femme rompue* ('L'Age de discrétion'(AD),
'Monologue'(Mon), 'La Femme rompue'(FR)

CAMUS: *La Chute*(LC)
    : *L'Exil et le royaume* ('La Femme
adultère'(FA), 'Le Renégat'(Ren), 'Les Muets'(LMu),
'L'Hôte'(Ho), 'Jonas'(Jon), 'La Pierre qui
pousse'(PP)

Details of all of these texts, and of the editions
referred to, are given in section (a) of the
Bibliography. Abbreviations to be used are bracketed
and underlined.

PREFACE

This is, of course, just one of the numerous types of book that might be written about the fiction of Sartre, Camus and Simone de Beauvoir. Focusing on a certain range of topics treated in their novels and short stories, the analysis it contains is thematic rather than stylistic and it owes little to modern critical theory.

The book is intended primarily for those who enjoy studying stories because they are about 'people', embody philosophical ideas and raise moral questions. Needless to say, I believe that this is a perfectly good reason for taking an interest in the books of these authors.

I am indebted to the colleagues and the many students with whom, over the years and in differing contexts, I have discussed almost all of the stories examined here. I only hope that the following pages will help them and others to gain further insights into the fiction and thought of three very important figures in modern French literature.

Leicester   Terry Keefe

For my mother, and in memory of my father

INTRODUCTION

For some considerable time now, the so-called 'existentialist' French writers have exercised a rather special fascination over those interested in modern literature and modern thought. Young people in particular have frequently entertained the general belief that existentialism has something to say that is relevant to the conduct of their lives. At the same time, it is clear that many of the readers concerned have not been examining the philosophical texts that would directly support or refute such an assumption. The popular conception of existentialism, at least in its ethical aspects, is derived partly from hearsay and partly from acquaintance with works of literature, perhaps especially novels. It would be easy to deplore this or to treat the matter lightly, but we do better to take very seriously the fact that some readers are expecting to draw moral insights of some kind from certain works of fiction. In any case, the question of the ways in which such an expectation is met or frustrated by the novels of particular writers is one of intrinsic literary interest.

Sartre, Camus and Simone de Beauvoir belong to the last identifiable group of French authors to have written fiction largely in order to express deep moral concerns, and it is the exact nature of those concerns as displayed in their novels and short stories that will be analysed in the present work. The justification for focusing on these three writers together is strong. All born within an eight-year period, before the First World War, they lived through the main historical events of the first sixty years of this century at roughly the same age and more or less the same stage in their careers. The reputations of all three were established just before and during the Second World

War; then in the post-Liberation period they mixed
in the same Parisian circles, being at the height of
their national and international fame together - a
fact directly reflected in Beauvoir's *Les Mandarins*
- and sharing, in addition to their interest in
literature and philosophy, an involvement in
journalism and politics. Because of this common
framework and certain unmistakable similarities in
their general views, it is perfectly understandable
that they should frequently be grouped together as
writers and thinkers, whether or not the label
'existentialist' as popularly employed is
appropriate on strict philosophical grounds.

All of this constitutes a perfectly adequate
reason for devoting a study to Sartre, Camus and
Beauvoir, provided that two additional points are
made clear. Firstly, there can be no question of
claiming that they are unique in their
preoccupations, or that other writers could not be
considered in the same light. More important still,
however, is the point that the central intention
here is to locate and examine the moral concerns
common to these three authors. This in no way
implies that there are no differences between them,
or even that such differences are less important
than the similarities. It simply rests on the belief
that the affinities are extensive and significant.
In this sense, the proof of the pudding can only be
in the eating. But what can be said in advance is
that the very notion of common moral concerns should
not be construed in an over-simple way. One is less
likely to find absolutely identical elements in the
novels than the famous 'complicated network of
similarities overlapping and criss-crossing:
sometimes overall similarities, sometimes
similarities of detail' that Wittgenstein saw as
characterising family resemblances.[1] Indeed, the
potential advantage of taking three authors and
systematically seeking such similarities is that it
forces one to look at each writer from a fresh
angle. As well as throwing into relief features of
the texts that might otherwise escape attention, it
can yield new insights into more familiar aspects of
the books.

This is something of considerable value in the
case of Sartre, Camus and Beauvoir, for a great deal
has been written about each and all three have
published non-fictional works which have often been
allowed to dictate the line of approach to their
fiction. Commentaries already available attempt to
show the ways in which our authors' novels

2

illustrate the ethical content of their philosophical essays and articles. The present inquiry, however, without seeking to question the validity of such work, is of an entirely different nature, a deliberate effort having been made to look at the novels strictly in their own right and to *avoid*, as far as possible, comparisons (or contrasts) between fictional and theoretical writings. The major justification for this procedure is that there are crucial differences of kind between the novel and the philosophical essay which have been clearly recognised and acknowledged by all three authors. They write what is essentially philosophical fiction, but each has maintained that while a discursive or ratiocinative work must, to some degree, generalise and systematise, a novel can record the singularity or particularity of events or situations, embody a variety of individual stances, and issue in questions rather than answers.[2] To this extent, they all accept that a writer's moral views will take on a slightly different shape or quality according to the genre that he or she is adopting, and this fact in itself is enough to legitimise an examination of the content of their fiction as such.

Moreover, there is every reason to suppose that, for those who wish to go further, approaching the theoretical writings of Sartre, Camus and Beauvoir through their fiction will prove at least as stimulating and fruitful as the reverse process. This is, after all, the direction followed by many readers, for whom novels constitute an excellent introduction to philosophical works, suggesting certain questions that a given theory needs to answer, certain criticisms that it needs to meet. And the considerable advantage of surveying the whole fictional output of writers over a long period of time is that this can serve as a corrective to the dogmatic, absolute, timeless quality that their doctrinal statements may take on at any particular stage. In fact, the careers of these authors as novelists dovetail quite neatly at the chronological level: Sartre wrote no novels after 1949, but is the only one to have actually published works of fiction (two) before the war; Beauvoir alone went on writing novels into the nineteen-sixties, but published nothing at all before the war; and she wrote no fiction between 1954 and 1966, whereas Camus's last stories appeared in 1956 and 1957. In short, provided we concede that any scrutiny of views based solely on fiction can do no more than make a *contribution* to a more general understanding of a writer's outlook, there are excellent grounds for according a certain autonomy to our authors' novels in this respect, and for consciously abstaining from seeing them in the light of their published philosophical theories. Looking at one author's stories in the light of another's is, in any case, a kind of substitute for this last process and one that is likely to produce rather different, even complementary, results.

Reasons for not also examining plays by these writers do not attach solely to the fact that this would involve considering half as many texts again and thereby necessarily dilute detailed comment on the novels to a marked degree. There is also the point that among the very obvious differences between fiction and the theatre as genres, one is of crucial significance for our present purposes. Because of the very nature of the reading process, a greater closeness is possible in the relationship between the reader and a character in a novel than between the spectator and a character in a play. The novel, therefore, is uniquely well suited to describing from the inside - or, better, to exemplifying - particular views of the world. It is in this way that the notion of an individual's moral *perspective* comes into prominence. In addition to asking what are the judgements, decisions or actions of moral agents on specific occasions or issues, we may also ask in what way they see the situation they are in; that is, which features of it they regard as important (and which unimportant), what alternative views and actions they consider to be available in those circumstances, what sort of criteria they consider it appropriate to use in deciding between those alternatives, and so on. In other words, moral perspectives are at least as much to do with what individuals have strong views *about* and how they finally arrive at them as with the views themselves. Provided, therefore, that we use the idea to cover all of these elements of an outlook, we shall have a conceptual tool that is especially useful in an analysis of the moral content of novels in particular - much more so, for instance, than that of a moral code.

The significance to be attached to the qualification 'moral' when applied to the concept of a perspective is general rather than specific, for the whole question of what is or is not a moral issue constitutes, in itself, an important part of what is at stake. That is, one aspect of an individual's perspective is that in any given

situation it may involve seeing a moral problem
where another person sees none. If one talks of
'moral' perspectives at all, this is essentially to
signal that one is considering what, in general
terms, is of most fundamental concern to individuals
with regard to the conduct of their own lives. This
in itself is helpful when looking at a collection of
books like the present one, since it makes it
possible to touch on metaphysical, political or
historical, and social matters without having to
dwell upon them in their own right. These may be
seen as having considerable (and changing) relevance
to the individual's very deepest concerns, whilst
not being identical with them.

Most of these points, of course, apply with
just as much force at the level of the writer as at
that of characters in a story. It is possible for
novels to tell us little, or nothing, about their
authors' positive moral views, but it is not
possible (at least in the case of writers like the
present ones) for novels to tell us nothing about
their authors' moral perspectives; about the sort of
issues that concern them, the sort of considerations
that they take into account morally, and the general
ways in which they try to sift such considerations.
Admittedly, reaching the moral perspectives of
authors through those of their protagonists is no
easy matter. It is exceedingly doubtful whether
there is a single case in these books where it would
be plausible simply to identify the writer's own
outlook with that of one of his or her fictional
figures. And this in spite of the fact that Sartre
and Beauvoir share a narrative principle of
'coinciding' with one of the characters in a story
at any given point, at least in the sense of
exhibiting only the knowledge and thoughts that that
character might have had at the time.[3] (Nearly all
of Camus's stories, too, are written from the
standpoint of one of the characters.) Yet short of
giving up the search altogether, the best that one
can do is to examine, compare, and contrast the
different individual perspectives described in a
story and, taking into account the relevant
aesthetic factors, hope to arrive at some notion of
the author's own outlook. Like any process of
literary evaluation, this is a delicate enterprise,
producing results that are likely to be
controversial. But it is also an activity that is
subject to the usual rules of evidence – however
difficult they may be to apply – and the texts
themselves are always there to provide checks and

balances. If taking more than one book and more than one author is, in principle, to add layers of difficulty to such an analysis, the very fact of seeking only perspectives *common* to certain writers correspondingly simplifies matters somewhat. Once the legitimacy of taking an author's fiction as in some way displaying aspects of his or her own moral thinking is conceded, then the particular force of the present study can be seen to reside in the juxtaposition of the fiction of Sartre, Camus and Beauvoir, and in the emphasis on the notion of perspectives as such.

Finally, it scarcely needs to be pointed out that individuals develop and their moral perspectives change accordingly. Changes of outlook on the part of characters in books are usually of special interest, but over a period of some thirty years, in the process of writing thirty-three separate stories that vary greatly in length, subject-matter and style, our authors changed too. It is virtually impossible to avoid seeing the Second World War as the principal turning-point in the lives and thought of all three, and our treatment of the moral perspectives they have shared will reflect this point by dividing their works of fiction into three groups: the 'pre-war' stories, the 'wartime' novels, and post-war stories. Their books do not always fit easily or automatically into one or other of these categories and the division is in no way intended to produce watertight compartments. This is, however, a grouping of the stories that corresponds, in broad terms, to the general evolution of our writers' thought and provides a convenient as well as instructive framework for the delineation of their changing perspectives. It has validity only in so far as it helps to cast light on the moral content of the books themselves, which is, when all is said and done, the overriding aim of the whole analysis.

NOTES

1. L.Wittgenstein, *Philosophical Investigations*, pp. 31-32.
2. Beauvoir has expressed these points in 'Littérature et métaphysique' (in *L'Existentialisme et la sagesse des nations*, pp.89-107), as well as in her memoirs (see, for instance, *La Force des choses*, II,62). Sartre developed them most clearly in an interview in 1960 ('Entretiens avec Jean-Paul

Sartre, par Alain Koehler'). And Camus defends the same views in the section of *Le Mythe de Sisyphe* entitled 'La Création absurde', as well as in his 'Introduction aux *Maximes* de Chamfort'
   3. Beauvoir, *La Force de l'âge*, II,386.

PART ONE

THE 'PRE-WAR' STORIES

Chapter One

SOLITUDE AND METAPHYSICAL DISCOVERY

There are seven works by Sartre, Camus and Simone de
Beauvoir that may be classified and examined as
their 'pre-war' fiction: Sartre's novels, *La Nausée*
and *L'Age de raison*, and his collection of stories,
Le Mur ('Le Mur', 'La Chambre', 'Erostrate',
'Intimité', 'L'Enfance d'un chef'); Camus's *La Mort
heureuse* and *L'Etranger*; Beauvoir's interlinked
tales, *Quand prime le spirituel* ('Marcelle',
'Chantal', 'Lisa', 'Anne', 'Marguerite'), and her
novel, *L'Invitée*. Of the five not actually published
before the Second World War we know, thanks to
Camus's *Carnets* and Beauvoir's memoirs, that *La Mort
heureuse* was written between 1936 and 1938, *Quand
prime le spirituel* between 1935 and 1937, and that
the other three were all conceived, and indeed were
at an advanced stage in their composition, by the
outbreak of war. There is, therefore, a perfectly
straightforward sense in which all are pre-war
works. Because of the particular timing of their
composition and a definite overlap in their
subject-matter, *L'Invitée* and *L'Age de raison* might
be thought to form a sub-group within this category,
yet for reasons that will become apparent they
belong quite clearly to the general class of pre-war
stories.
    The term 'pre-war' is suggestive as well as
appropriate, since it encourages us to consider what
kind of perspectives the stories of this first
period exclude. There is no doubt that one negative
characteristic of this group of works is that they
convey little impression of history or politics
impinging upon the freedom of the individual. This
is self-evidently true of *La Nausée*, *Quand prime le
spirituel*, *La Mort heureuse*, *L'Etranger* and also,
in spite of the first story in the collection, of *Le
Mur*. The story 'Le Mur' itself is no more than an

11

apparent exception, for it is the study of a man's reactions in the face of imminent death (somewhat in the manner of the second part of *L'Etranger*), where the historical setting and occasion of the threat - actually the Spanish Civil War - might just as well have been quite different and is of no thematic importance in its own right.

With *L'Invitée* and *L'Age de raison*, of course, the situation does not appear to be quite the same. They were the last two of all of these books to be completed (the former was written between October 1938 and summer 1941; the latter between July 1938 and May 1941), and some of the major political events of the end of the nineteen-thirties do, admittedly, figure in them. Yet they are quite essentially books about the pre-war period and atmosphere, or at least essentially *set* in that period and atmosphere. Sartre himself summed up the ethos concerned in a comment on his novel: 'Pendant la bonace trompeuse des années 37-38, il y avait des gens qui pouvaient encore garder l'illusion, en de certains milieux, d'avoir une histoire individuelle bien cloisonnée, bien étanche' (1911). When *L'Invitée* and *L'Age de raison* were completed in 1941, large-scale, catastrophic events had of course just taken place in France, so that both authors found themselves looking back with some wonderment to a period when they were scarcely aware of history or politics at all. In her memoirs Beauvoir makes the points that even before *L'Invitée* was finished it was already for her 'de l'histoire ancienne', and that by the time it was published (August 1943) she was quite detached from it.[1] The fact that there are references in both works to the troubles in Europe in the late thirties is much less noteworthy than the scarcity and relative insignificance of such references. What is remarkable about these two books, considering that they were both finished after the defeat of France, is that politics and history play no substantive part in them at all; far from invalidating it, they actually confirm the point about the non-historical and non-political character of this group of works as a whole.

In spite of the fact that the story takes place in the twelve months preceding the outbreak of war, political events form no more than the flimsiest backcloth to the highly individual and personal plot of *L'Invitée*. References to the political circumstances of the time are uncommon and mostly inconsequential, usually being sandwiched between other topics in the conversations of the main characters (for instance, 111-12; 144; 291-92). There are only two sequences of any substance relating to the imminence of war. In the first, written from Gerbert's standpoint, the characters discuss in theoretical terms why Pierre will feel obliged to go and fight if war comes (322-28). And in the second, narrated partly from Elisabeth's viewpoint and partly from Françoise's, we see Pierre leaving after his call-up (468-80). Elisabeth's attitude by this stage is entirely different from that of Françoise and Pierre, who are still far from regarding themselves as being caught up in history and see the situation in wholly personal terms (477). Indeed, Beauvoir herself has claimed that the war merely provided her with a pretext for Pierre's departure, and has implied that bringing it into the book at all was a mistake:

> Quand je commençai *L'Invitée*, je préméditai de situer le meurtre de Xavière pendant une absence de Pierre: sans doute serait-il en tournée. La guerre me fournit un excellent prétexte pour l'éloigner ... mais il est impossible que l'énormité du drame collectif n'arrache pas Françoise - telle que je l'ai montrée - à ses soucis individuels ... Le dénouement paraîtrait plus plausible s'il se produisait en province, pendant la paix. [2]

In *L'Age de raison* (which takes place in June 1938), the role played by major historical events and by political circumstances is equally secondary. Once more, what is striking is the astonishing paucity of references to the prevailing situation in Europe. Brunet is the only figure of any importance in the novel who is visibly concerned by events in Germany and it is significant that he appears (briefly) in only two of the eighteen chapters. In fact, the rise of Nazism is touched on only six times in the whole book: in five cases it is merely a question of a passing mention, and when Brunet warns Mathieu of the imminence of war, 'discussion' of the matter takes up fewer than ten lines of the text (522). It is true that the novel contains a dozen or so references to the Spanish Civil War, including a memorable sequence on the bombing of Valencia (512-15), but the crucial point about the possibility of going to Spain to fight for the Republican cause is that, like the possibility of joining the Communist Party in order to help halt the spread of Nazism in Europe, it represents one more opportunity for commitment that Mathieu *misses*. Marcelle tells him very early on, '"Ta vie est pleine d'occasions manquées"' (401), and the whole book can be seen as a record of the various possibilities of commitment that Mathieu, for one reason or another, turns down. Some of these opportunities, of course, are purely personal ones, but it is fitting, if the reader is to have a complete picture of Mathieu's dilemma, that there should be political chances too. While Spain is perhaps an opportunity that Mathieu has already missed, Brunet's invitation for him to join the Communist Party is one that we actually see him refuse, but neither of these political situations in the background has intrinsic importance in the book. Just as Beauvoir might have used a theatrical tour instead of the war as a means of removing Pierre from Paris, so Sartre could, without loss, have taken quite different political situations as typical of those where Mathieu fails to commit himself. The significant point is that political circumstances do not yet bear so heavily upon Mathieu that he *has* to become involved.

It would be an obvious exaggeration to say that the personal dramas in the stories of this first phase are shown as taking place in a vacuum. In some of them period, place and social background are of considerable importance. Nevertheless, it is manifest that here, in contrast with later works by each of our authors, the pressures and constraints of broad political and historical forces are almost negligible. The emphasis falls heavily upon the particular thoughts and actions of the main characters in their immediate circumstances. Such threats and pressures as individuals face arise, for the time being, either from within themselves and the narrow confines of their private lives, or from within the society around them (or both). The basic question is not what demands a certain historical or political situation makes of individual characters, but what demands they make of themselves (or fail to make), and with what success and what consequences. Added dimensions are provided to this question, firstly by the existence and presence of other identifiable individuals (What bearing does this have upon the individual's personal ideals and efforts?), and secondly by the existence of a society embodied in particular institutions and representing certain values (What effect does this have upon the individual's life and attitudes?). Yet in the end these factors serve, above all, to

14

emphasise the isolation of the individual.

In fact, when we seek a common thread in the situations of the main characters in the pre-war stories, the concept that virtually imposes itself as a starting-point is that of solitude. This, however, is just the first of a number of key notions that we shall encounter which have an attractive but wholly spurious simplicity about them and require much more careful analysis than they are commonly accorded. Solitary figures most of the protagonists may be, but we need to be sure about the senses of 'solitude' that permit us to apply the term to such different cases as, on the one hand, Mathieu or Françoise, both of whom have a host of friends and acquaintances and certain very close relationships, and, on the other hand, Paul Hilbert in 'Erostrate', who apparently has none whatever, or Meursault, who for half of *L'Etranger* is entirely cut off from the few people he knows at all well.

Two basic clarifications of the idea of solitude will help us to ensure that it is employed in as meaningful a way as possible. Firstly, it is of course a relative and not an absolute notion: none of the main figures is, in the literal sense, a hermit, and some are more solitary than others. It is true that a degree of sequestration or physical isolation is at stake in some of the stories: Meursault in *L'Etranger* and Pablo Ibbieta in 'Le Mur' are both imprisoned (although Pablo, unlike Meursault, shares his condemned cell with two comrades); and like Eve in 'La Chambre' (as well as her husband Pierre and her mother Madame Darbédat), Marcelle in *L'Age de raison* lives virtually confined to her own room. But while Hilbert undoubtedly leads the most solitary life of any of the characters (especially after abandoning his job), certain others have regular and serious contacts with a number of people, and *all* of the rest maintain some such contacts at various times. This enables us to make a second point about solitude, which is that it is as much a matter of a mental attitude as of a measurable degree of seclusion. This must eventually raise the quesion of what exactly 'solitude' amounts to in the case of characters freely mixing with their friends and associates.

With these cautions in mind, however, we can say quite uncontroversially that there are strong senses in which the predominant state of the protagonists in the pre-war books is that of solitude. No further justification of the point is necessary in the instances of sequestration and isolation, although one can strengthen it in most cases. Even before his imprisonment, Meursault leads what can in some respects be described as a solitary sort of life, in spite of his liaison with Marie and the nascent 'friendship' with Raymond: the second chapter of *L'Etranger* is dominated by a relatively long description of how Meursault spends a whole boring Sunday alone in his flat. Almost identical comments may be made about Mersault in *La Mort heureuse*, whose life is at least as solitary as that of Meursault. Both of Camus's heroes on their balconies looking down on the street scene, furthermore, remind us of Hilbert at his window at the beginning of 'Erostrate', for although he is an altogether different sort of character with different motives, his brand of solitude has more than a little in common with theirs. And all are solitaries in roughly the same way as Roquentin in *La Nausée*, whose early statement is an obvious exaggeration, but gives an indication of the type of existence that is his: 'Moi je vis seul, entièrement seul. Je ne parle à personne, jamais; je ne reçois rien, je ne donne rien' (11). Eve's solitude in 'La Chambre' bears a certain similarity to these cases, but also has its own distinctive character. She lives with the man she loves and is in constant contact with her parents, yet because of her husband's madness finds herself stranded, alone, between two worlds:

> Elle pensa soudain avec une sorte d'orgueil qu'elle n'avait plus de place nulle part. 'Les normaux croient encore que je suis des leurs. Mais je ne pourrais pas rester une heure au milieu d'eux. J'ai besoin de vivre là-bas, de l'autre côté de ce mur. Mais là-bas, on ne veut pas de moi.' (250)

Over and above this, there is discernible in virtually all of the examples touched on so far a pattern that will help us to understand the particular nature of the solitude experienced by those characters who live in noticeably closer contact with their fellows. The movement of the pre-war stories is almost invariably towards an ever greater solitude rather than away from that state. Main characters are progressively stripped of their more important relationships in the course of the events and, often for a variety of reasons, end the story considerably more alone than they were at the beginning. This is manifestly true of *La Nausée*, in the course of which Roquentin loses Anny, the Autodidact and any other acquaintances he has in Bouville; of *Quand prime le spirituel*, where by the end of each of the stories the central female character has in some way lost relationships that were particularly important to her; of *La Mort heureuse*, where Mersault is alienated from Marthe and breaks with his friends of 'la Maison devant le Monde'; and of *L'Etranger*, where, in addition to hoping for 'des cris de haine' at his execution, Meursault recognises his changed attitude towards Marie - 'en dehors de nos deux corps maintenant séparés, rien ne nous liait et ne nous rappelait l'un à l'autre' (1206-07) - just as clearly as Pablo, in 'Le Mur', recognises that he has lost his desire to see his mistress (226).

The same pattern also prevails in the case of three of the four 'narrators' in *L'Age de raison* (there being little change in Daniel's essentially solitary stance throughout the book): by the end Boris is less close to both Mathieu and Lola (who he suggests is 'encore plus seule peut-être depuis qu'elle l'aimait'; 417); Marcelle has lost her lover of seven years' standing (only to gain the homosexual Daniel); and Mathieu, finding most of the pressures that have been bearing down upon him removed at the very last, and having lost both Marcelle and Ivich, sees himself in a new state of solitude: 'Mathieu vit disparaître Daniel et pensa: "Je reste seul." Seul, mais pas plus libre qu'auparavant' (729). For both Rirette and Lulu in 'Intimité', moreover, their solitude is just a little greater by the close of the story, for in addition to having upset her husband Lulu risks losing her lover, while Rirette realises that she will not be able to take Lulu's place. Nor should one by misled into believing that the direction of Lucien Fleurier's evolution in 'L'Enfance d'un chef' is away from solitude. As a slavish imitator, he is exceedingly dependent upon others in his youth, but his relationships are rather puerile ones of near-idolatry and much of the story traces the disillusionment that he comes to experience with those he knows (his parents, Riri, Berliac, Bergère, Maud), often feeling more alone than ever as a result. Certainly, he eventually finds his place in the world - that of 'un chef' - but this betokens no commitment to authentic personal relationships. As soon as he accepts his role, he is impatient for his father to die (388) and, in general, the sort of relations with others that he finally envisages seem likely to turn him into a powerful and bullying, yet essentially solitary, figure.

This leaves the case of *L'Invitée*, where the movement towards greater solitude requires careful delineation. It is easy to ignore those parts of the novel centring on Gerbert and Elisabeth, and this is perhaps justified in the former instance, since Gerbert has only a single chapter (Part II, chapter 3). But Elisabeth's position is seen to change for the worse in the course of the book: she is forced to recognise that her lover, Claude, will never divorce his wife, and by the time her brother Pierre goes off to war she is a very lonely figure indeed, acutely conscious that she has lost her opportunity of a close relationship with him (472). Françoise's own ties with Pierre are, of course, the main centre of interest in the book and, contrary to what is sometimes implied, this relationship is anything but destroyed by the end. However, it does take what is, at least aesthetically, very much a secondary place in the crucial final chapter. Early on Françoise was proud to agree with Pierre's remarks about the symbiotic nature of their relationship (61), but the advent of Xavière very soon calls the closeness of the union into question. Françoise comes to be more and more sceptical about her earlier assumptions and stage by stage is brought to a painful awareness of her real separateness from Pierre. By the end harmony and stability has been re-established in her personal relationship with Pierre, but the near-identification that she saw as prevailing before has gone for ever. In the final pages, with Pierre away at the war and Françoise committing her irrevocable act of murder, the emphasis is on Françoise's solitude:

> Il n'y avait plus personne. Françoise était seule.
> Seule. Elle avait agi seule. Aussi seule que dans la mort. Un jour Pierre saurait. Mais même lui ne connaîtrait de cet acte que des dehors. (503)

These cases taken together show that solitude is not seen in the pre-war books as a wholly static situation, and that far from being a simple 'quantitative' matter of lack of relations with others, it is one inseparably bound up with complex qualitative questions concerning what is expected of relationships, and their adequacy or successfulness. They also bring out the point that it would be an oversimplification to regard solitude as a condition that is simply forced upon the individual, as opposed to being self-imposed in some measure or other. In more than one instance there is - as one ought perhaps to expect - the suggestion that positive pleasure is to be derived from solitude. Meursault, in prison, eventually adjusts to it with considerable success, discovering the delights of memory and of looking up at the sky. Françoise at one point in her story actively (though unsuccessfully) seeks it and distinguishes between 'délaissement' and 'solitude' in a way that implicitly attributes value to the latter (Inv 216); in fact, from the beginning she notes the loss of solitude that has resulted from her relationship with Pierre (13), in much the way that Mathieu expresses a tinge of regret at the 'pensées de solitude' lost since his commitment to Marcelle (AR 402). Yet although the example of Meursault is an impressive one, he has little alternative but to make the most of his isolation; and the slight regrets of Françoise and Mathieu scarcely constitute a strong case in favour of the merits of solitude. Solitude is far from being advocated as a desirable state in its own right in these works.

This, however, does not entirely answer the question of whether our authors regard it as a blessing or a curse, for the fact is that individuals are almost always portrayed as *learning* something as a result of their solitude. Minimally, they learn more about the nature of solitude itself: either, like Mersault, that it is rather worse than expected (MH 157), or, like Françoise, that it is something that needs to be carefully cultivated or mastered (Inv 217). But much more important is the point that solitude is seen as associated with certain discoveries that individuals make about themselves, the nature of life and of human relations, and their place in the world; in a word, metaphysical discoveries. This link is always a particularly close one, but since it takes different forms in different cases we do well to examine it first in relation to a small number of relatively straightforward major examples, which will also begin to provide an outline of the exact metaphysical discoveries involved.

There is no doubt that it is the discoveries of Roquentin in *La Nausée*, the first-published and most overtly philosophical of these books, that are the most obvious and most explicitly formulated. As we have already seen, he is more alone at the end of

the story than at the beginning, but it is because
he is a solitary from the start that he discovers
the metaphysical truths that form the central
philosophical core of the novel. His intellectual
evolution in the story, we are given to understand,
would have been inconceivable in someone living a
less lonely and more sociable life. This fact is
stressed near the end, after Roquentin's revelations
in the park, when we are shown the Autodidact
embarking upon 'l'apprentissage de la solitude'
(190), and where the grotesque changes that
Roquentin imagines coming over the inhabitants of
Bouville are seen as having the effect of forcing
them into his state of isolation: 'On en verra
d'autres, alors, plongés brusquement dans la
solitude' (188). Although there is some suggestion
that he has rather over-indulged in it himself, by
the end of the story Roquentin still clearly regards
solitude as an indispensable condition of the kind
of metaphysical insight he has experienced.

The exact nature and content of Roquentin's
philosophical intuitions in *La Nausée* are well-known
and require no detailed examination here. Their
semi-technical formulation is not confined to the
major sequence beginning in the restaurant with the
Autodidact and ending with Roquentin's reflections
on the revelation in the park (144-60). In an
earlier passage, following the abandonment of his
Rollebon project, Roquentin (like Pablo in 'Le Mur')
makes discoveries concerning the essentially
embodied nature of consciousness (117-22); and in a
later one he comes to understand a little more
clearly the absolute freedom or 'nothingness' of
consciousness itself (199-202).[3] As far as the main
sequence is concerned - 'je comprenais que j'avais
trouvé la clé de l'Existence, la clé de mes Nausées,
de ma propre vie' (152-53) - it is sufficient to
summarise it very briefly indeed in Roquentin's own
terms. He refers to the 'absurdité fondamentale' of
everything that exists, and contrasts it with the
world of ideal constructs, like geometrical figures:
'le monde des explications et des raisons n'est pas
celui de l'existence' (153). In short:

L'essentiel c'est la contingence. Je veux dire
que, par définition, l'existence n'est pas la
nécessité. Exister, c'est *être là*, simplement;
les existants apparaissent, se laissent
rencontrer, mais on ne peut jamais les *déduire*.
(155)

Roquentin has discovered that he himself, like
everything else in the world, is 'gratuit', or 'de
trop', and that the world as a whole has no purpose:
'On ne pouvait même pas se demander d'où ça
sortait, tout ça, ni comment il se faisait qu'il
existât un monde, plutôt que rien. Ça n'avait pas de
sens' (159). Not surprisingly, in 'L'Enfance d'un
chef' Lucien Fleurier also lights upon fundamental
'truths' about the human condition, most of which
overlap with Roquentin's intuitions. He discovers
our inability to coincide with ourselves ('tout le
monde jouait'; 317); the breakdown of our terms and
categories in the face of contingency (320-21); the
redundancy of the concept of God (323-24); and so
on.

Before drawing further parallels between
Roquentin's insights and those of other characters,
however, it is worth emphasising that his
metaphysical discoveries are momentous ones only
when set against the background of Christianity or
some other religious framework within which life is
seen as having a purpose. Immediately after
registering the view that contingency is the essence
of his 'illumination', Roquentin makes the following
comment:

> Il y a des gens, je crois, qui ont compris ça.
> Seulement ils ont essayé de surmonter cette
> contingence en inventant un être nécessaire et
> cause de soi. Or aucun être nécessaire ne peut
> expliquer l'existence: la contingence n'est pas
> un faux semblant, une apparence qu'on peut
> dissiper; c'est l'absolu, par conséquent la
> gratuité parfaite. (155)

He thereby underlines the point that much of the
force and impact of his metaphysical insight is
drawn from its radical incompatibility with the
received body of Christian beliefs that allegedly
underlies Western civilisation. This is not to say
that characters in the pre-war books are shown as
hesitating between a Christian and a non-Christian
perspective. At least three (Fleurier in 'L'Enfance
d'un chef'; Marcelle and Marguerite in *Quand prime
le spirituel*) are actually seen losing their belief
in God, but for the most part the central figures do
not have the faith to begin with. Often we are left
to infer this from the total absence of references
to religion on the part of the characters, but some
openly express anti-Christian views. The two
important points to be retained, however, are that

most protagonists are open to metaphysical insights precisely because they are not convinced Christians with a wealth of doctrine and dogma to rely upon; and that it is by *contrast* with Christianity that the insights concerned stand out as significant. Thus a good measure of Meursault's development in the second part of *L'Etranger* is that while he reacts relatively calmly to having a crucifix thrust under his nose by the examining magistrate just after his arrest, he has an unaccustomed outburst of anger at the end when the prison chaplain offers to pray for him. It is essentially in opposition to the Christian perspective that he now asserts his own: 'j'ai tenté de lui expliquer une dernière fois qu'il me restait peu de temps. Je ne voulais pas le perdre avec Dieu' (1210).

In fact, even though the more articulate Meursault of the last few pages of *L'Etranger* is still much less explicitly philosophical than the narrator of *La Nausée*, his stated views are usefully complementary to those of Roquentin in some respects. There is a problem over whether Meursault's beliefs as expressed at the end are, or are not, ones that he has held and been acting upon for a number of years,[*] but in either case his enforced isolation and his death-sentence cause him to *spell out* such beliefs (to someone else and to himself), perhaps for the first time. The most fundamental of these are undoubtedly metaphysical in character and bear strong resemblances to Roquentin's in their attribution of an insignificant and contingent place in the universe to the individual: 'je m'ouvrais pour la première fois à la tendre indifférence du monde' (Etr 1211). But there are important differences of emphasis too: by the end, in addition to being less interested in the existence of material objects than Roquentin, Meursault is understandably more concerned with death and all of its implications, although it seems that like Pablo in 'Le Mur' he finds the implications a more fruitful topic for meditation than the idea itself. Pablo has no more imagination than Meursault for what is not life on earth, yet he too is sufficiently struck and changed by the supposed imminence of his own death to generalise his fate and look at others around him through different eyes (Etr 1211; Mur 230). Since the idea of personal immortality is a part of Christianity, it is to be expected that characters in these books will sometimes - by contrast - be preoccupied with the very finality of death, for if extinction as such rarely seems to worry them, there is always the knowledge that death affects an irrevocable summation of all the actions in the life of an individual and perpetuates indefinitely any doubts that may attach to that life. This comes out particularly well in a revealing sequence in *L'Age de raison*, where Boris mistakenly takes his mistress Lola for dead and involves Mathieu in his error:

> nul ne saurait jamais si Lola eût fini par se faire aimer de Boris, la question n'avait pas de sens. Lola était morte, il n'y avait plus un geste à faire, plus une caresse, plus une prière ... 'Si je mourais aujourd'hui, pensa brusquement Mathieu, personne ne saurait jamais si j'étais foutu ou si je gardais encore des chances de me sauver.' (624)

If solitude and certain metaphysical truths are *forced* upon Meursault and Pablo, the same cannot be said of Mersault in *La Mort heureuse*. When he makes a deliberate break with Marthe and his Algerian acquaintances, it is difficult to know to what extent he is consciously cultivating solitude and to what extent his flight is a necessary precaution after his crime. In any case, his subsequent isolation brings him certain insights into life and death and he comes to see solitude as a necessary means to his end of personal happiness, knowing that he will eventually have to struggle with the temptations of companionship and comfort (122). Hence he leaves the 'Maison devant le Monde', although he has obviously found some kind of happiness there, and he categorically refuses to let his wife Lucienne live with him (161). The last two to three years of his life are spent in his house on the Algerian coast, where he leads a solitary though not entirely secluded existence and finally finds exactly the kind of acceptance of life that he has been seeking. Death is just as important in this book (as the titles of the work and its two parts, 'Mort naturelle' and 'La Mort consciente', suggest) as in *L'Etranger*, and by a certain self-imposed solitude Mersault arrives at a stoical attitude towards it very similar to Meursault's (MH 197).

Enforced or self-imposed, then, solitude provides opportunities for, and constitutes a spur to, fundamental metaphysical discoveries relating to the individual's place in the world, contingency, body and mind, and death. It is certainly not a sufficient condition of such discoveries, but whether it is seen as a necessary one (as appears to be the case in *Quand prime le spirituel*) is not easy to say, since in a number of cases we need to assume that some of the 'truths' involved were discerned before the story begins. And this is only one reason why the relationship between solitude and metaphysical discovery is a more complicated one than it first seems to be, for a further cluster of metaphysical insights gained by characters in the books actually concerns the existence of other people. While certain obvious aspects of these insights run counter to the experience of solitude, other aspects serve to reinforce and intensify it.

It scarcely needs emphasising that the very core of *L'Invitée* is Françoise's painful recognition of the existence of others as independent centres of consciousness. Like Roquentin's intuition of contingency, Françoise's realisation develops gradually but inexorably in the course of the story. It is touched upon in the very first chapter (14), but grows in importance as she comes to understand more and more the impact that the presence of Xavière is having on the lives of Pierre and herself. It reaches its height when Xavière deliberately burns her own hand in a night-club: 'le scandale éclatait, aussi monstrueux, aussi définitif que la mort' (363). The discovery and Françoise's reactions to it are described in fairly simple terms when she explains to Pierre why she has cried:

> 'C'est parce que j'ai découvert qu'elle avait une conscience comme la mienne; est-ce que ça t'est déjà arrivé de sentir comme du dedans la conscience d'autrui?' De nouveau elle était tremblante, les mots ne la délivraient pas. 'C'est inacceptable, tu sais.'
> Pierre la regardait d'un air un peu incrédule.
> 'Tu penses que je suis soûle, dit Françoise. Par ailleurs je le suis, c'est vrai, mais ça ne change rien. Pourquoi es-tu si étonné?' Elle se leva brusquement: 'Si je te disais que j'ai peur de la mort, tu comprendrais; eh bien, ça, c'est aussi réel et aussi terrifiant. Naturellement chacun sait bien qu'il n'est pas seul au monde; ce sont des choses qu'on dit, comme on dit qu'on crèvera un jour. Mais quand on se met à le croire ...'
> (369)

The analogy with an awareness of death in these two

passages (and in a later one) is interesting from a number of viewpoints, but above all it shows that the basic ontological discovery of the existence of the Other is very much on a par with the various aspects of the discovery of contingency already discussed.

Françoise's discovery, of course, is not just an acknowledgement that there really are other people in the world: it is the realisation that others exist, as it were, *opposite* oneself. She and Pierre eventually agree that such an insight was much less likely to arise out of their own relationship than out of the presence of someone as unpredictable and hostile as Xavière. The fact is that Françoise's discovery is tantamount to the recognition of deep and basic *conflict* between individuals, and Beauvoir's Hegelian epigraph to her novel ('Chaque conscience poursuit la mort de l'autre') is exactly parallel to Sartre's famous claim that 'l'essence des rapports entre consciences n'est pas le Mitsein, c'est le conflit'.[5] The brute fact of conflict between Françoise and Xavière and the resulting hostility between Françoise and Pierre are obvious enough, but the exact nature of the conflict between the two women is worth dwelling upon. Whatever Xavière wants from the trio, it is made clear from the first that Françoise's aim is somehow to take over the consciousness of Xavière, to 'possess' her metaphysically ('rien ne donnait jamais à Françoise des joies si fortes que cette espèce de possession'; 23). Such an aim is almost bound to meet with resistance and, in common-sense as well as Sartrean terms, is doomed to failure. There is even another struggle in *L'Invitée* with a roughly similar outcome, for Elisabeth would dearly love somehow to 'tame' Françoise's independent existence: 'c'était idiot; elle ne pouvait ni devenir Françoise, ni la détruire' (87).

Such personal struggles for ascendancy or domination are easy to find in *L'Age de raison* and Sartre's other stories. What Mathieu wants of Ivich is perhaps to 'annex' her in much the way that Françoise wishes to absorb Xavière, and this is possibly not so different from what Marcelle wants of him. Lola is certainly doing her best to take over Boris body and soul and, interestingly, both Mathieu and Lola are shown as needing to know what is going on in the minds of their 'victims' in order not to lose control over them (415; 455). In 'Intimité' Lulu enjoys a certain kind of sexual power that she exercises over her husband (280), but objects strongly to the very similar power that her lover wants to wield over her (286). This in turn reminds one of Lucien Fleurier's close association of sex with material possession (ECh 365; 387); and of the very strange relationship between Roquentin and Anny in *La Nausée*. Allusions to the form previously taken by this last relationship bring out clearly that Anny's aim was to dominate Roquentin, and in the course of their one meeting in the book she expresses annoyance that she can no longer possess him and use him in the way she wants (178).

Although Camus's philosophical framework is certainly less formal and rigorous than that lying behind Sartre's stories and *L'Invitée*, examples are to be found in both *La Mort heureuse* and *L'Etranger*, too, of failed attempts to 'annex' another consciousness. Meursault agrees to marry Marie, but she cannot get him to say he loves her, nor to give up any of the freedom associated with his way of life as a somewhat eccentric individual. Similarly, Mersault marries Lucienne, but only on condition that they live apart and that she joins him whenever he needs her. Perhaps more significantly, Mersault's earlier attempt to assign precisely the place and importance to Marthe that suited him - he liked to display her in public (MH 51) and later thinks back to 'cet étonnement du début à posséder un corps particulièrement beau, à le dominer et à l'humilier' (124) - had broken down because of his jealousy (53). The point to be stressed in connection with these and earlier cases is that any failure or inadequacy in the relationship is not finally to be attributed to external pressures, or even to psychological factors in the narrow sense. Both doubtless have a part to play, but at a more general level problems are seen within the context of a certain broad view of human relations that emphasises the need for personal freedom and the consequent conflict that is *bound* to ensue between individuals.

We may now begin to see that much of the solitude experienced by main figures in these pre-war books has less to do with physical isolation than with what is sometimes called 'la séparation des consciences'. *L'Invitée* is such an excellent example of this because Françoise more or less simultaneously becomes aware that she and Pierre are not one unit but two separate beings, and that relations with others in general are characterised by hostility, or at least by regular failure of communication. These are not discoveries made *as a result of* solitude so much as discoveries of particular facets of solitude itself, and much the same point could be made about all of the stories in *Quand prime le spirituel*. Not that characters in the books of this period are always brought to see such things for the first time in the course of the story. A number perhaps never understand them at all, and those who have some grasp of the fact of separation from the first receive further confirmation of their view, or find themselves forcibly reminded of how definitive is their separation from one particular person or from people at large. The stories reveal that the barriers, tensions and gaps between individuals can take on an almost inexhaustible variety of forms.

There are a few outstanding cases of outright malevolence in these books, where the characters concerned have no particular, or at least no justifiable, reason for wishing their 'friends' harm: Daniel will not help Mathieu and deliberately interferes in the relationship between Mathieu and Marcelle, just as Elisabeth uses Gerbert to disturb the trio of Françoise, Pierre and Xavière; and perhaps Rirette, trying to persuade Lulu to leave her husband in 'Intimité', would come into the same category. But mostly the hostility illustrated, in Sartre's stories in particular, is of a rather more diffuse and innocuous kind. Examples abound in *L'Age de raison* and *Le Mur*, where characters are frequently thinking to themselves how much they hate or detest those to whom they are ostensibly close, although precisely similar phenomena can be found in *Quand prime le spirituel*: '"Ma seule amie", pensa Lisa avec angoisse ... Et pourtant elle ne pouvait s'empêcher d'empoisonner cette amitié par le doute, l'envie et parfois une espèce de haine' (113-14). An especially fine chapter in *L'Age de raison*, when four of the main characters are together in the Sumatra night-club (chapter XI), constitutes a long and continuous depiction of the subtle and half-hidden in-fighting that can take place among intimate acquaintances.

Moreover, all hostility apart, no one – and this is as much a part of the message of Camus's novels as of the other books of the period – can know, let alone control, other people's private thoughts if they do not wish to divulge them. And even if a serious effort is made to express these thoughts, there are still a number of obstacles – sometimes insurmountable – to any understanding and sharing of them. Thus in 'La Chambre', to take just one case, Eve is quite unable to enter into her husband's madness, partly because it is in any case impossible for her to share his state of mind and partly because she is not entirely sure how 'sincere' he is. The same story also shows how Eve's mother and father are utterly unable to understand anything of her attitude towards Pierre, and indeed how they fail to make real contact with each other. Madame Darbédat's dream of mystical communion with selected others is one treated with evident irony. The intuitive understanding that appears to exist, in *L'Age de raison*, between Boris and his sister Ivich is taken rather more seriously, yet even here cracks are visible enough to the attentive eye:

> Il était entendu qu'ils se disaient tout, mais de temps en temps on pouvait faire exception à la règle ... Il se demandait ce qu'Ivich avait voulu dire, mais il n'en laissa rien voir: ils devaient se comprendre à demi-mot, sinon le charme eût été rompu. (637)

Their relations constitute no real exception to the failure of communication between individuals that is generally predominant in these stories, and Boris's impression that they are one (641) is seen to be as illusory as Françoise's similar belief about herself and Pierre.

Central to the conflict that is seen to characterise human relations is individuals' recognition that the Other can think about them and judge them at will, quite independently of their own judgement or wishes. This is certainly a crucial aspect of the discoveries that Françoise makes after the arrival of Xavière ('elle était incapable de porter aucun jugement sur cette inconnue. Et pourtant Xavière la jugeait'; Inv 184), and it is what directly precipitates the final act of murder. Mathieu, too, comes to a realisation of the full extent to which he is judged by others (AR 528), but it is perhaps Daniel who best expresses the fear of being judged in his absence:

> Ils l'avaient jugé par derrière, ils l'avaient démonté, disséqué, et il était sans défense ... ça fait deux personnes pour qui j'existe et puis trois et puis neuf, et puis cent ... il se promène en liberté avec son opinion sur moi au fond de la tête et il en infecte tous ceux qui l'approchent. (AR 556-57)

Early in *La Nausée*, too, Roquentin refers to the way in which those living in society learn to see themselves as others see them (24), and by the end of the book the whole matter of how he will be seen after his death seems to be of some importance to him (210). It is no accident, of course, that one talks in this connection of 'seeing' people in a certain way : 'le regard' figures prominently in Sartre's stories as an indication of the manner in which one individual classes and judges another. Daniel is truly obsessed with the question of how others see him ('Ha! si l'on pouvait vivre au milieu d'aveugles'; AR 556), and there is a classic incident in an amusement arcade, where he is trying to 'reify' an old queen by looking at him, only to be caught in the same trap himself when unexpectedly accosted by a former lover (533-38). A character like Lulu in 'Intimité' is almost equally sensitive to being looked at, especially when she is not in full control of a situation.

It would be a mistake to believe that these last considerations have no relevance to Camus's early novels. They are, admittedly, of little importance in *La Mort heureuse*, although even there Mersault is greatly disturbed by the look of one of Marthe's ex-lovers in the cinema (52-54). But discovery of what Sartre calls our 'being-for-others' has a vital role to play in *L'Etranger*. One aspect of this is the shattering of Meursault's conviction that he is 'un homme ordinaire'. From the very beginning he shows signs of an uncomfortable awareness of the gaze and judgement of others, but from early in the second part of the book he begins to realise that others see him as a criminal (1171; 1175-76), and this feeling reaches its height during his trial: 'pour la première fois depuis bien des années, j'ai eu une envie stupide de pleurer parce que j'ai senti combien j'étais détesté par tous ces gens-là' (1189). One of the crucial changes that comes over Meursault in the course of the book is precisely this full recognition that others see his life and values in an entirely different perspective from his own. He eventually draws strength from this discrepancy – which is as much a result of his long-term solitude as of his crime – and this brings about the final state of exhilaration that he attains at the end of the novel.

If we look at the whole collection of cases just touched on, it is clear that the pressure of others' judgement is just one fragment of a gloomy and pessimistic picture of personal relations in general presented in these stories. The dominant pattern is that of breakdown or discontinuation, or at least of attenuation or falling off in the quality of relationships. It is true that the bonds between Eve and Pierre in 'La Chambre' and between Françoise and Pierre in *L'Invitée* appear to be unweakened at the end of those stories, but question-marks or threats hang over both (because of the husband's fast-encroaching mental disintegration in 'La Chambre', and the war and the murder that Françoise has committed in *L'Invitée*). Again, there are a few unemphasised examples of relationships that do not seem to have deteriorated by the end, but where these have not been terminated by death we are left with the impression that they are of no particular importance.

In any case, all of these instances are swamped by the flood of those discussed earlier where relations have either irretrievably broken down or have degenerated very seriously. There is scarcely an example, in these early books, of an on-going relationship that is actually stronger at the end than it was at the beginning (perhaps the friendship between Françoise and Gerbert is an exception, but Françoise's willingness to 'give back' Gerbert to Xavière casts some doubt on the depth of this; Inv 499); scarcely an example of a new and continuing bond built up during the events of the book (during his trial Meursault responds with a new-found affection to his Algerian acquaintances, but by this time he is cut off from them in almost every sense). The movement, as we have seen, is invariably towards the greater solitude and isolation of the main characters. And recognition of what underlies this movement constitutes one way in which they may make some of the metaphysical discoveries that also characterise the pre-war stories.

NOTES

1. *La Force de l'âge*, II,619 and II,637.
2. Ibid., II,392.
3. See R.Goldthorpe, 'The presentation of consciousness in Sartre's *La Nausée* and its theoretical basis'.
4. See, for instance, B.T.Fitch, *L'Etranger d'Albert Camus. Un texte, ses lecteurs, leurs lectures* pp.97-103.
5. *L'Etre et le Néant*, p.502.

Chapter Two

LUCIDITY AND SELF-DECEPTION

Granted that, at a certain level of generality, the
main metaphysical truths that Camus, Sartre and
Simone de Beauvoir all see their characters as
facing are the same - contingency, the essential
embodiment of consciousness, the finality of death,
the deep divide between individuals - we now need to
consider more carefully where the main characters in
these stories stand in relation to those truths. But
since there are marked discrepancies in how much
different figures are shown to know or to discover,
some preliminary questions impose themselves
concerning the effort that characters make to
perceive the truth and their immediate reactions to
such perceptions as they have.

It is obvious that one may react to a glimpse
of the light either by trying to hold it in focus,
even by looking harder at it, or by attempting to
block it out in some way or other. If we take a
synoptic view of the pre-war stories, we are first
struck by the possibility, or even the necessity, of
placing virtually every main character somewhere
along a continuous line or scale that runs from what
we shall call 'lucidity' at one extreme to
self-deception at the other. This is not the only
line along which characters could be situated, but
it is undoubtedly one of the most important. It does
not mean, as we shall soon see, that there are only
two camps, that of the lucid and that of the
self-deceived. Nor does it mean that any character
can be firmly assigned one place and one place only
on the scale. But it does mean that whatever else
these stories may do, above all they show us
characters reacting to the metaphysical truths
outlined earlier with varying degrees of lucidity
and self-deception, and various combinations of the
two. One main element common to our authors' moral

perspectives in this period – however vague or
vacuous it may seem – is the belief that we should
face up squarely and unequivocally to our
metaphysical state and somehow come to terms with
it, rather than try to evade it or cover it up in
some manner. We may immediately illustrate the
importance of lucidity by taking one major example
from each author.

Roquentin's determination to see things clearly
is precisely his reason for beginning to write a
diary: 'Tenir un journal pour y voir clair' (LN 5).
As we would expect, the notion of lucidity for him
is necessarily bound up with that of solitude, with
facing up to things alone. First of all, facing up
to the fact that one *is* alone – he says of the
Autodidact: 'Au fond il est aussi seul que moi;
personne ne se soucie de lui. Seulement il ne se
rend pas compte de sa solitude' (144) – but,
subsequently, facing up to the truths that one's
solitude enables one to see: 'Quand on veut
comprendre une chose, on se place en face d'elle,
tout seul, sans secours' (83-84).

Mersault speaks in very similar terms:
'"J'avais besoin de partir et de gagner cette
solitude où j'ai pu confronter en moi ce qui était à
confronter"' (MH 178). Although he is dominated much
less by a passion for truth than by his 'volonté de
bonheur', the two drives are ultimately inseparable,
for by the end he has come to recognise that 'la
lucidité elle aussi était une longue patience'
(196). 'Lucide' and 'lucidité' are unquestionably
key terms in *La Mort heureuse*, and in the second
half of the book in particular it is rare for many
pages to go by without some crucial use of one or
the other. There is also a rather remarkable example
of the ideal of lucidity in the last few pages,
where Mersault is determined not to die in a state
of 'inconscience' and persuades his doctor to give
him adrenalin to keep him conscious up to the very
last moment: '"Je ne veux pas finir dans une
syncope. J'ai besoin de voir clair, vous comprenez"'
(198).

The case of Françoise in *L'Invitée* is already a
slightly more mixed one, although instructively so.
She states the ideal of lucidity quite as clearly as
either Roquentin or Mersault: 'Elle avait toujours
refusé de vivre parmi des rêves, mais elle
n'acceptait pas davantage de s'enfermer dans un
monde mutilé. Xavière existait et on ne devait pas
la nier' (207). And she, too, sees clearly that it
involves facing things alone: 'il fallait se

ressaisir, elle avait besoin de s'entretenir avec
elle-même' (214-15). She has a rather more complex
set of truths to face than the other two, yet in
relation to Pierre as well as to Xavière she is
determined to look at the facts honestly, unlike
Elisabeth, whom she sees as self-deceived: 'Il
allait trouver de beaux arguments et ça serait si
commode d'y céder. Se mentir, comme Elisabeth,
Françoise ne voulait pas, elle y voyait clair'
(200). But Françoise's lucidity seems, as it were,
to slumber from time to time. She is periodically
lulled, or perhaps allows herself to be lulled, into
a false sense of security, and she seems in general
to need at regular intervals the shock of
particularly unpleasant circumstances to remind her
that lucidity is what Mersault calls 'une longue
patience'.

This is helpful, because once we realise that
the linear pattern of more or less constant lucidity
and progressively increasing insight (of, say, *La
Nausée* and *La Mort heureuse*) is not the only one,
then we can see that lucidity is not
self-generating, since effort is needed to reach and
maintain the state. We can also see that it may be
an ideal that certain characters awaken to and
pursue only under the pressure of adverse
circumstances, yet be none the less strong for that.
Apart from Françoise herself, a number of major
characters recognise and illustrate the value of
lucidity in precisely this way. Pablo in 'Le Mur'
acknowledges that he cannot but think about death in
the situation he finds himself in, and rather
resents the fact that Tom apparently attempts to
evade such thoughts by consoling Juan (217). More
positively, he wants to understand death and his own
reactions to it, and comes to assert, like others,
that there is definite virtue or value in
confronting things in a state of lucidity:

> Si j'avais voulu, je crois que j'aurais pu
> dormir un moment: je veillais depuis
> quarante-huit heures, j'étais à bout. Mais je
> n'avais pas envie de perdre deux heures de vie:
> ils seraient venus me réveiller à l'aube, je
> les aurais suivis, hébété de sommeil et
> j'aurais clamecé sans faire 'ouf'; je ne
> voulais pas de ça, je ne voulais pas mourir
> comme une bête, je voulais comprendre. (225)

Once more, Meursault has an identical reaction in
his prison cell:

> C'est à l'aube qu'ils venaient, je le savais.
> En somme, j'ai occupé mes nuits à attendre
> cette aube. Je n'ai jamais aimé être surpris.
> Quand il m'arrive quelque chose, je préfère
> être là. C'est pourquoi j'ai fini par ne plus
> dormir qu'un peu dans mes journées et, tout le
> long de mes nuits, j'ai attendu patiemment que
> la lumière naisse sur le vitre du ciel. (Etr
> 1205)

Indeed, the first part of the last chapter of
L'Etranger is a striking testimony to lucidity, with
Meursault concentrating all his energies on facing
up, in a surprisingly systematic and thorough way,
to the facts of his situation.

A much more complicated case, but where
lucidity still manifests itself only some of the
time, or where it might be said to be only partial,
is that of Mathieu in *L'Age de raison*. As a
philosopher, he apparently has no difficulty in
accepting contingency and many of its implications,
but he is obsessively concerned with preserving his
freedom, and it is not altogether clear with what
degree of lucidity he pursues his goal. Very early
on, Marcelle talks of his 'fameuse lucidité', and
although Mathieu is unhappy about the word, he
espouses it to the extent of agreeing that his
primary aim is to avoid lying to himself, and of
describing his relationship with Marcelle in terms
of it ('Il ne pouvait aimer Marcelle qu'en toute
lucidité: elle était sa lucidité'; 402). This last
point is important, since if there is one area where
Mathieu may well be lacking in lucidity, it is
certainly in his relations with Marcelle. At one
stage he suggests that if by any chance Marcelle
wanted to have the baby that they have 'agreed' to
have aborted (as of course she does, unbeknown to
him), everything would look very different:

> Et si elle voulait l'enfant? Alors là, tout
> foutait le camp, il suffisait de penser ça une
> seconde et tout prenait un autre sens, c'était
> une autre histoire et Mathieu, Mathieu
> lui-même, se transformait de la tête aux pieds,
> il n'avait cessé de se mentir, c'était un beau
> salaud. (512)

The problem here lies in knowing whether Mathieu is
being too hard on himself, since we have only very
limited information about his past with Marcelle.

And in general it is difficult to know how one could possibly push investigation into Mathieu's honesty with himself further than he does, or pursue it more rigorously; difficult to see how anyone, for instance, could hope to fare better than he in his attempt to detect one possible layer of self-deception underlying lucidity, then another below the next level of lucidity or the one after that:

> Mais ça n'était pas vrai, il n'était pas sincère: au fond il voulait plaire à Ivich. Il pensa: 'Alors, j'en suis là?' Il en était à profiter de sa déchéance, il ne dédaignait pas d'en tirer de menus avantages, il s'en servait pour faire des politesses aux petites filles. 'Salaud!' Mais il s'arrêta effrayé: quand il se traitait de salaud, il n'était pas non plus sincère, il n'était pas vraiment indigné. C'était un truc pour se racheter, il croyait se sauver de l'abjection par la 'lucidité', mais cette lucidité ne lui coûtait rien, elle l'amusait plutôt. Et ce jugement même qu'il portait sur sa lucidité, cette manière de grimper sur ses propres épaules ... (579)

One final 'mixed' case that is worth examining is that of Eve in 'La Chambre', who is required, in very special circumstances, to face up to 'la séparation des consciences'. She unquestionably confronts certain aspects of living with her demented husband bravely and honestly, but falls somewhat short of acknowledging reality in all respects. This comes out in her dialogue with her father:

> 'Tu veux vivre uniquement par l'imagination, n'est-ce pas? Tu ne veux pas admettre qu'il est malade? Tu ne veux pas voir le Pierre d'aujourd'hui, c'est bien cela? Tu n'as d'yeux que pour le Pierre d'autrefois ... Il n'y a rien de tel que de regarder les choses en face, crois-moi.'
> 'Tu te trompes, dit Eve avec effort, je sais très bien que Pierre est ...'
> Le mot ne passa pas. (245-46)

She is clear-headed about the fact that within three years Pierre will be completely insane (246), yet she is verging on self-deception in her attempt to join him in his madness. Quite apart from the point

that she suppresses certain doubts about his
sincerity, she cannot even devote her whole
attention to what is happening in his room (258),
and eventually acknowledges: 'ce n'était qu'un jeu,
pas un instant je n'y ai cru sincèrement' (259). As
with Mathieu, the question is whether her moments of
lucidity about her self-deception somehow cancel out
that self-deception itself. But in any case she is a
far more admirable figure than her parents and we
are reluctant to see her attempt to join Pierre in a
wholly unfavourable light.

With both Mathieu and Eve we are discussing
phenomena that are highly complex psychologically
and philosophically. Hence the ideal of facing up to
metaphysical truths with lucidity is not presented
as being an easy one to follow, nor as one whose
attainment by others can be measured by use of a
clear and straightforward criterion. But none of
this undermines the ideal as such. By and large, the
characters in these stories meet with our approval
and sympathy to the extent that they are visibly
trying to understand and face the truth about
themselves, others and the world; and with our
disapproval or scorn to the extent that they are
obviously trying to evade such truth, or hide it
from themselves. It is worthwhile examining,
therefore, the direction in which the ideal of
lucidity begins to be developed in these books.

While still on the level of individuals'
relations with themselves, we can go just a fraction
further than the ideal of lucidity on the basis of
these texts. The characters held up, in one measure
or another, for our approval or admiration often
have quite explicitly as a further ideal, or at
least as a task in hand, the gaining and exercising
of *control* over themselves and their lives, although
not unnaturally the exact nature of the control
sought after varies a great deal, according to the
particular situations in which the characters find
themselves. In a comment to Xavière in *L'Invitée*,
Pierre points out the alternative to exercising
control over one's life and suggests that the
prerequisite of the latter is lucidity: '"si
vraiment vous avez horreur d'être écrasée dans le
monde, si vous ne voulez pas être un mouton, il n'y
a pas d'autre moyen que de commencer par penser bien
clairement votre situation"' (295).

Whatever Mathieu's success in achieving
lucidity, there can be no doubt that he is
preoccupied with the idea of threats to his personal
freedom, and wants above all to keep a grip on his

own life: '"je voudrais ne me tenir que de moi-même"' (AR 403). This is something explained in the very first chapter of the book, and when he later refers to his 'pari' (the determination to be free that goes back to when he was seven), he makes it clear that this amounts to a struggle for maximum control over himself and his life: '"Etre libre. Etre cause de soi, pouvoir dire: je suis parce que je le veux; être mon propre commencement"' (445). It is true that, at least momentarily, he now claims to regard these as 'des mots vides et pompeux, des mots agaçants d'intellectuel', but again there is no reason for being quite so pessimistic as he is and seeing him as having failed entirely in his quest. When, later still in the story, he is tempted to believe that the whole matter of Marcelle is now out of his hands, he quickly pulls himself up and regains his lucidity:

'Non, non, ce n'est pas pile ou face. Quoi qu'il arrive, c'est *par moi* que tout doit arriver.' Même s'il se laissait emporter, désemparé, désespéré, même s'il se laissait emporter comme un vieux sac de charbon, il aurait choisi sa perdition: il était libre ... il n'y aurait pour lui de Bien ni de Mal que s'il les inventait. (664-65)

Nor is Mathieu the only character in *L'Age de raison* who is concerned to have control of his own life. Boris, naturally enough as he is Mathieu's 'disciple', is seeking the same, in his youthful way. His horror when he makes love with Lola, for instance, is that he may lose consciousness: 'On ne sait plus ce qu'on fait, on se sent dominé' (429). And his sister Ivich - though we are never given her inner thoughts - shows every sign of struggling (often in an infantile and pointless way) to prevent others from controlling her life: '"Je dépends des autres, c'est avilissant"' (453).

Mersault, Meursault and Pablo show the same desire for control, too. Mersault is as preoccupied with the notion of personal happiness as Mathieu is with that of personal freedom, but evidently sees the determination of his own life as a prerequisite: 'il voulait seulement tenir sa vie entre ses mains' (MH 124). This is the basis of his need to stop working for eight hours a day in an office, and Mersault does not shrink from the awesome consequences of his eventual freedom: 'On ne naît pas fort, faible ou volontaire. On devient fort, on devient lucide. Le destin n'est pas dans l'homme mais autour de l'homme' (196). Both Pablo and Meursault, on the other hand, are in extreme circumstances and need to establish and exercise control over themselves at the most basic level. Pablo not only wants to understand what is happening to him, he wants to keep control over his own body and is determined to ensure, so far as is possible, that things happen in a way acceptable to him: 'Moi j'étais buté, je voulais mourir proprement et je ne pensais qu'à ça' (Mur 228). Similarly, Meursault's struggle for control over himself spans the whole of his long period of imprisonment. This does not come at all easily to him, but he wins the fight and by the end is exercising a very marked degree of control, even over his thoughts (Etr 1206). Moreover, in a general, if somewhat obscure, way Meursault is now in control of his life and values as never before. In his outburst against the prison chaplain, he claims:

> Moi, j'avais l'air d'avoir les mains vides. Mais j'étais sûr de moi, sûr de tout, plus sûr que lui, sûr de ma vie et de cette mort qui allait venir. Oui, je n'avais que cela. Mais du moins, je tenais cette vérité autant qu'elle me tenait. (1210)

The extent to which Françoise and Roquentin are successful in taking a grip on their lives is more open to debate, but once more the fact that they are attempting to do so is beyond dispute. The point is that both start, as it were, with a deficit: they are trying to catch up on certain sorts of control over their lives that they have lost or are losing. Perhaps Françoise never succeeds in recouping very much, but she struggles particularly hard for lucidity and control when she realises that changes are coming about in her situation:

> Il faudrait qu'elle se décide une bonne fois à regarder en face tous les changements qui s'étaient produits ... Il ne fallait pas faire comme Elisabeth.
> 'Je veux voir clair,' se dit Françoise. (Inv 192)

Her tragedy consists in the fact that what she really needs to control seems to be the life and character of another being, Xavière, and if she finally does win through to some kind of possession

of her changed life - 'Elle avait enfin choisi. Elle
s'était choisie' (503) - this is only by permanently
suppressing that alien consciousness (and thereby
going back on her pledge not to 'mutilate' the
world). Interestingly, of the central figures in
Quand prime le spirituel, which belongs to a
slightly earlier stage in Beauvoir's thought, only
Marguerite, at the very end of the last of the
stories, approaches the realisation that she must
face up to the world and choose her own way of life:
'j'ai voulu montrer seulement comment j'ai été
amenée à essayer de regarder les choses en face,
sans accepter d'oracles, de valeurs toutes faites'
(249).

Roquentin, like Françoise, is trying to pin
down a change that he is undergoing and this is why
he begins writing a diary: 'Il faut déterminer
exactement l'étendue et la nature de ce changement'
(LN 5). But whereas Françoise somewhat powerlessly
watches things happen outside herself, Roquentin is
much more in the grip of something: 'Alors la Nausée
m'a saisi ... elle me tient' (25). In fact, an
urgent need for control - even a certain desperation
- underlies a great deal of the book. From very
early on Roquentin fears that, as a result of his
'nausea', he is losing his freedom, losing control
over himself and his life:

> Si je ne me trompe pas, si tous les signes qui
> s'amassent sont précurseurs d'un nouveau
> bouleversement de ma vie, eh bien, j'ai peur.
> Ce n'est pas qu'elle soit riche, ma vie, ni
> lourde, ni précieuse. Mais j'ai peur de ce qui
> va naître, s'emparer de moi - et m'entraîner
> où? ... Je voudrais voir clair en moi avant
> qu'il ne soit trop tard. (10)

Understanding what is happening to him, then, is the
first stage in the process whereby he hopes to
regain control of his life, and although in the
course of his revelation in the park Roquentin
acknowledges that he is not necessarily immune from
further attacks of nausea, he undoubtedly goes some
way towards achieving his aim ('je comprenais la
Nausée, je la possédais'; 155). By the end of the
book, at least the worst of his crisis appears to be
over.

In any case, success or failure apart, lucidity
and some basic kind of control over oneself and
one's life definitely constitute the main common
ideals in the stories of this period. It is no

accident that in some of the examples that we have
considered characters refer to these ideals by
contrasting them with the conduct of others around
them, for, as is so often the case, a clearer idea
of lucidity and control can be gained by a grasp of
their polar opposite, namely self-deception. If we
ignore the temptations of the much-abused terms
'mauvaise foi' and 'bad faith' in order to turn our
attention, however briefly, to the phenomena of
self-deception, we shall find that the notion is of
considerable importance to the moral perspectives of
this period and that certain characters in the books
who illustrate it particularly well confirm the
centrality of the values of lucidity and control in
so doing.

Lucidity, we have suggested, consists not just
in discovering or knowing certain truths, but also
in consciously admitting or facing up to them. There
is already some significance in this way of putting
things, for we do not talk of having to 'face up' to
truths that are pleasant or comforting. We only need
to face up to truths that are unpleasant and which
we would prefer not to have to face at all. In these
stories the unpalatable truths concerned are
metaphysical ones concerning contingency and the
'scandalous' aspects of the existence of others. For
our purposes, self-deception – which is quite
distinct from lying to others, and ought to be kept
equally distinct from simple error [1] – consists in
knowing these facts but hiding them from oneself;
that is, thinking and acting as if they are not
facts at all. It is a forbiddingly complex and
paradoxical phenomenon, to describe which we have to
say apparently absurd things, such as that the
person at one and the same time knows and does not
know something, or is at the same time conscious and
not fully conscious of it.[2] But paradoxical or not,
the process is undeniably a real one, one that is
well exemplified in a number of these stories, and
one that throws the ideals of lucidity and control
into sharp relief. Sartre's 'prière d'insérer' to *Le
Mur* brings this out especially clearly:

> Personne ne veut regarder en face l'Existence.
> Voici cinq petites déroutes – tragiques ou
> comiques – devant elle, cinq vies ... Toutes
> ces fuites sont arrêtées par un Mur; fuir
> l'Existence, c'est encore exister. L'Existence
> est un plein que l'homme ne peut quitter.
> (1807)

Even if this formula is in fact too neat and
convenient to encapsulate accurately the different
themes of the five stories, it gives an indication
of the significance and importance of self-deception
in the pre-war books. (In her brief preface to the
stories of *Quand prime le spirituel*, Beauvoir also
stresses this theme.)

The best theoretical insights into the process
come, predictably, from Roquentin, who is the most
explicit about the metaphysical truths that he
discovers in the first place. Immediately after
stating the core of his discovery in the park and
suggesting that some people have tried to overcome
contingency by inventing God, he makes these
observations:

> Or aucun être nécessaire ne peut expliquer
> l'existence: la contingence n'est pas un faux
> semblant, une apparence qu'on peut dissiper;
> c'est l'absolu, par conséquent la gratuité
> parfaite... voilà ce que les Salauds - ceux du
> Coteau Vert et les autres - essaient de se
> cacher avec leur idée de droit; ils sont
> entièrement gratuits, comme les autres hommes,
> ils n'arrivent pas à ne pas se sentir de trop.
> Et en eux-mêmes, secrètement, ils *sont trop*,
> c'est-à-dire amorphes et vagues, tristes. (LN
> 155)

The 'salauds', then, try to hide the fact of
contingency from themselves, either by recourse to
the concept of God, or to that of Rights. Roquentin
constantly comes back to the notions of rights and
duties, stressing that to know of contingency and
yet claim some kind of right to life is one of the
most basic forms of self-deception (99; 121). And
claiming the 'right' to immortality, of course, is
just one way of attempting to evade the fact of
death. But self-deceivers like Pacôme often claim
rights over others too:

> Il avait toujours fait son devoir, tout son
> devoir, son devoir de fils, d'époux, de père,
> de chef. Il avait aussi réclamé ses droits sans
> faiblesse: enfant, le droit d'être bien élevé,
> dans une famille unie, celui d'héritier d'un
> nom sans tache, d'une affaire prospère; mari,
> le droit d'être soigné, entouré d'affection
> tendre; père, celui d'être vénéré; chef, le
> droit d'être obéi sans murmure. (101)

41

All of this is bound to remind us of one outstanding case of self-deception in these stories, that of Lucien Fleurier in 'L'Enfance d'un chef' ('Lucien Fleurier est le plus près de sentir qu'il existe mais il ne le veut pas, il s'évade, il se réfugie dans la contemplation de ses droits'; 1807). Late in the story, he cannot prevent the metaphysical truth about his own nature from striking him with its full force: 'Son existence était un scandale et les responsabilités qu'il assumerait plus tard suffiraient à peine à la justifier' (364). But unlike most of the characters we have looked at so far, Lucien is not concerned to maintain his lucidity and tries to hide his discoveries from himself, first by means of a new all-embracing concept ('je suis un déraciné'; 372), then by joining 'L'Action Française', then by striking the posture of an Anti-Semite. Finally, at the end of his 'childhood', Fleurier is ready to accept his heritage and become one of the 'salauds' castigated in *La Nausée*: 'Et voilà que Lucien, justement, c'était ça: un énorme bouquet de responsabilités et de droits ... "J'existe, pensa-t-il, parce que j'ai le droit d'exister"' (387).

Fleurier is a doubly useful illustration of self-deception, for just as it consists in denying that which lucidity would lead the individual to accept, so it may also take the form of denying the possibility of that control which the lucid individual is trying to exercise over his life. Fleurier is a slavish imitator who passes from one mentor to another and in the end explicitly gives up direct control over what he is, in order to find himself in others' eyes: 'Le vrai Lucien - il le savait à présent - il fallait le chercher dans les yeux des autres' (386). But Lulu, in 'Intimité', represents an even clearer case of this form of self-deception. There is a fine little scene where she hangs limp - 'molle comme un paquet de linge' (302) - between Henri and Rirette, who are trying to pull her in different directions. And above all there are Lulu's own continual references to the 'fact' that she has played no active part in the turn events have taken: '"Vous savez, je n'ai rien décidé, dit Lulu modestement, ça s'est décidé tout seul"' (293). Towards the end of the story she adopts a whole pseudo-philosophy of fatalism in order to shuffle off her responsibility for all that has happened (308-10). In this respect, Lulu gives way to a temptation that Daniel (who is himself the most fascinating mixture of lucidity and self-deception) experiences from time to time - 'On n'y pouvait rien, c'était comme ça. Quelque chose dans ce ciel, dans cette lumière, dans cette nature en avait décidé ainsi' (AR 541) - and one that we have seen Mathieu resisting: 'Non, non, ce n'est pas pile ou face ...' (AR 664).

It would be possible to pursue this detailed and instructive investigation of Sartre's treatment of self-deception very much further: if *La Nausée* explains its theoretical basis, *Le Mur* and *L'Age de raison* almost constitute case-books, where the phenomenon is exemplified in many diverse forms, and where few, if any, characters can be said with certainty to be completely free of it. And very much the same can be said of Beauvoir's stories *Quand prime le spirituel*: Marcelle visibly deceives herself about her sexuality and her commitment to social work; in the story 'Anne', Pascal Drouffe's attitude towards love and Madame Vignon's claim to be an instrument in the hands of God clearly display self-delusion; and Marguerite eventually recognises that she has been blinding herself about her beloved Denis. *L'Invitée*, too, contains at least one fairly well-developed case of self-deception, that of Elisabeth. In fact, as with Fleurier it is her image in the eyes of others that she is most concerned with and dependent upon. And here as in other cases, once we leave the territory of metaphysical truths as such, we find Elisabeth a rich source of examples of self-deception in less abstract matters, like her relations with Pierre, her attitude towards war and her commitment to art. Moreover, in trying to persuade herself that she does not need her lover Claude (90), she becomes one more in a long line of women characters in Beauvoir's fiction who palpably deceive themselves about their men.

Now, although there are no central figures in Camus's first two novels who could be said to be self-deceived without over-straining that term, this is not to say that the concept has no relevance at all to those novels, or that there are no minor examples closely similar to some of those just discussed. It is, admittedly, hard to see how self-deception is important to the story of *La Mort heureuse*, but it does have an indirect but none the less strong relevance to *L'Etranger* in the figures of the examining magistrate and the prison chaplain. Since these two characters are seen only from the outside, it may seem illegitimate or somewhat harsh to regard them as self-deceived, but the same could be said, after all, about the 'salauds' of Bouville in *La Nausée*. One of the major difficulties with the notion of self-deception (as we glimpsed in the case of Mathieu) is that the only person who can be certain that it is taking place (or, more strictly, that it *has taken* place) is, precisely, its victim. It is something that we should accuse others of only with the greatest reluctance and the surest grasp of a great deal of evidence about them. And the fact is that, even allowing for the fiction genre, it is far from clear in these pre-war books that Sartre, Camus and Beauvoir exercise the appropriate degree of caution in their treatment of certain categories of people. Even if we grant, for instance, that Christian beliefs are wrong, there is still every reason to go on trying to distinguish between error and self-deception; between those genuinely believing something that we regard as mistaken and those agreeing with us deep down but achieving some success in hiding the truth from themselves.

The signs are that our authors fail to make this important distinction in their early works. Without discrimination, the believers of Bouville are accused of self-deception in *La Nausée*, as are, in a more oblique way, those in *Quand prime le spirituel*. And Camus's two Christian figures in *L'Etranger* are also implicitly charged with this fault. The examining magistrate reacts to Meursault's clear answer that he does not believe in God in a less-than-rational way that betrays some insecurity in his own beliefs:

> Il m'a dit que c'était impossible, que tous les hommes croyaient en Dieu, même ceux qui se détournaient de son visage. C'était là sa conviction et, s'il devait jamais en douter, sa vie n'aurait plus de sens. 'Voulez-vous, s'est-il exclamé, que ma vie n'ait pas de sens?' (Etr 1175)

The prison chaplain also tries to persuade Meursault that he cannot *not* believe in God ('on se croyait sûr, quelquefois, et, en réalité, on ne l'était pas'; 1207), and claims that it is not possible to face up to the 'terrible épreuve' of death without such a consoling belief (1208). Like the examining magistrate he becomes emotional in trying to convince Meursault, eventually crying in the face of the latter's heated outburst (1211). This is less direct than the accusations that Roquentin levels at the 'salauds', but there can be little doubt that

Camus is implicitly charging his two Christian
figures with self-deception simply by virtue of
their religious attitudes – even to the point of
caricature – and strongly contrasting their unstable
state with Meursault's lucidity.

Another aspect of this point is that one of the
rights or duties that the 'salauds' of Bouville and
those like them take upon themselves is that of
instructing, or imposing their views upon, others.
Thus Madame Vignon in Beauvoir's 'Anne' gives
herself this right: 'c'était atroce de torturer
cette enfant, mais il fallait penser à son salut,
non à son bonheur' (QPS 145). And whatever the
differences between these characters and the two
Christian figures in *L'Etranger*, they all certainly
have this characteristic in common. They go beyond
what might reasonably be considered the bounds of
their responsibilities or professional duty and
attempt to force their religious views upon their
victims. The examining magistrate (who perhaps
deliberately arranges to see Meursault without his
lawyer; 1173) aggressively thrusts a crucifix under
Meursault's nose in order to intimidate him, and
shouts 'd'une façon déraisonnable': '"Moi, je suis
chrétien. Je demande pardon de tes fautes à
celui-là"' (1175). Similarly, the chaplain imposes
himself upon Meursault, visiting him in spite of the
fact that Meursault has refused to see him; trying
to tell him what he really believes; and finally
expressing an uncalled-for and unwittingly insulting
determination to pray for him, which provokes
Meursault's outburst.

For our purposes, in fact, it is perhaps less
important that these 'oppressors' seem,
unjustifiably, to be seen by Sartre, Camus and
Beauvoir as necessarily self-deceived because they
are Christians than that they represent a particular
kind of opposition to the ideals of lucidity and
control. It is no longer a question of an opposing
tendency within individuals themselves, but of
forces external to them militating against the
achievement of those ideals. Or perhaps one ought to
say *potentially* militating against them, for
Roquentin and Meursault both resist strongly. It is
not without significance that Meursault is brought
to his highest point of lucidity and self-awareness
by coming up against a perspective sharply opposed
to his own, for when we look at these stories as a
whole it is almost as if characters are crucially in
need of a point of opposition to kick against,
before they can attain a degree of lucidity and

control; as if the very existence of contrary
external forces is a condition of the individual's
articulating, sharpening and affirming his own
awareness and values. The opposition can take a
variety of forms, but in many cases individuals have
to resist a deliberate attempt to impose certain
values upon them. Beauvoir says that when she wrote
Quand prime le spirituel, 'J'étais en révolte contre
le spiritualisme qui m'avait longtemps opprimée'
(QPS VII), and, certainly, all of the heroines in
those short stories are seen as severely constricted
by their pious upbringing. Meursault, as we have
noted, is under pressure from the religious, but
Roquentin, too, constantly feels under attack from
the Bouville dignitaries, even dead ones like
Impétraz and Jean Pacôme ('son jugement me
transperçait comme un glaive et mettait en question
jusqu'à mon droit d'exister'; LN 101). Also in *La
Nausée*, the Autodidact has obviously given in to
such pressures, for he has absorbed the abstractions
and values thrust at him to the extent of even
sharing the complacency and smugness that go with
them (140). Lucien Fleurier, too, (unlike Eve in 'La
Chambre', who stubbornly rejects her parents'
values) eventually absorbs the world-view that has
sustained his father in his beliefs. Paul Hilbert in
'Erostrate', on the other hand, is consciously
opposed to the values that he sees as being foisted
upon him, and it is to him that we owe the most
far-reaching description in these books of the way
in which 'Humanist' beliefs, by their very
all-pervasiveness, may be seen as an intimidation of
the unwary individual:

> 'Je suis libre d'aimer ou non le homard à
> l'américaine, mais si je n'aime pas les hommes,
> je suis un misérable et je ne puis trouver de
> place au soleil. Ils ont accaparé le sens de la
> vie ... Les outils mêmes dont je me servais, je
> sentais qu'ils étaient à eux; les mots par
> exemple: j'aurais voulu des mots *à moi*. Mais
> ceux dont je dispose ont traîné dans je ne sais
> combien de consciences; ils s'arrangent tout
> seuls dans ma tête en vertu d'habitudes qu'ils
> ont prises chez les autres.' (271)

He sees that Humanists have a way of assimilating
anything, including misanthropy, into their scheme
of things, and he deliberately sets out to see if
something can be achieved 'against' men. (Mersault
also talks about the relationship between being

happy and being 'contre', but he is perhaps vaguer about what exactly he is against.) Hilbert is doubtless an extreme case, and his own particular form of reaction against Humanism is thoroughly repulsive. Yet there are certain respects in which his tragedy resembles that of Meursault, at least to the extent that we agree to see him as in some measure the victim of those who 'oppress' in the name of humanity and normality.

What emerges in general from a consideration of self-deception as well as certain external obstacles to the individual's quest for lucidity and control is that this quest, if consistently pursued, is shown as generating a degree of independence and individuality that is bound to increase solitude and isolation. Individuals, struggling to be clear-headed about the metaphysical truths they have discovered and to take a grip on their own lives within the context of those truths, receive no encouragement at all from the outside world. On the contrary, they will often need to resist not only the constant temptation of self-deception, but also the attempts of others less lucid than themselves to draw them along well-worn, easier, and ostensibly more comfortable tracks. Such resistance, on our authors' view of the world, will almost certainly involve going against the crowd in some measure, and although there is the hope that the outcome will be a bracing and ultimately fruitful one, the extenuating effort required carries no guarantee to that effect. The individual's reward for coping honestly with an added dimension of solitude is, at best, one with a painful as well as an exhilarating aspect.

NOTES

1. See my own 'Simone de Beauvoir and Sartre on *mauvaise foi*'.
2. See, for example, H.Fingarette, *Self-Deception*.

Chapter Three

THE INDIVIDUAL AND SOCIETY

By this time, of course, we are touching upon the general question of where individuals stand in relation to society. Broadly speaking, it is clear that our authors' pre-war fiction is strongly marked by the fact that main characters are not in any full sense in tune with, and frequently do not easily fit into, the society to which they nominally belong. In one or two stories – 'Le Mur' and perhaps 'Intimité' – this matter may be considered as largely irrelevant, and it crops up in a characteristically inverted form in 'L'Enfance d'un chef' (that is, the point of the story is to show how Fleurier *does* eventually allow himself to become absorbed by 'society' and, precisely, to make us feel some kind of moral revulsion when he does so). In virtually all other cases, however, the ways in which protagonists are shown to be less than fully incorporated into society constitute highly significant features of the texts.

Beauvoir's *Quand prime le spirituel* is a special and revealing case, since the central figures of all of the stories are young women at extremely formative stages of their development, who in one way or another are still undergoing the effects of early attempts to 'socialise' them. Like Lisa, Anne appears not to have sufficient strength to resist ('incapable d'accepter les préjugés de son milieu et la vie que Mme Vignon lui destinait, elle n'avait pas encore la force de secouer toute contrainte'; 155), and both characters are seen to suffer as a result. Chantal considers herself something of a rebel, but in fact has manifestly not broken free of her upbringing, any more than the self-deluded Marcelle, who believes herself to be so different ('"Je ne suis pas comme les autres"'; 7). Marcelle's sister Marguerite looked like succumbing

48

to the same pressures – in particular, those associated with 'une éducation chrétienne' – until she glimpsed the possibility of genuine independence, a process described at the very end of the collection: 'il a fallu tout réinventer moi-même' (249).

By contrast, in *L'Invitée* and *L'Age de raison*, as was the case with political matters, it is the more or less complete absence of social pressures that is so noticeable. There is little suggestion in *L'Invitée* that the social background of the five main characters is of any significance, and in the time-span of the events of the story they are all notably free from constraints upon the ways in which they use their time and energy. Their work – Françoise is a writer, Pierre a theatrical producer, Elisabeth an artist, Gerbert an actor, and Xavière has no regular job – leaves them considerable freedom of movement and they live out their private lives, as Françoise sees, in a kind of magic circle that cuts them off from the rest of the world (345). It is essential to the novel that the reader should virtually ignore the society within which the characters exist, in order to concentrate upon the deep 'ontological' aspects of their relationships. Similar considerations apply to *L'Age de raison*. The few links that characters are seen to have with their family background are ones that they are trying to sever (with the exception of Boris's relations with Ivich). And, as critics have pointed out, all of the main figures again have basic situations or jobs that place them on the fringes of society rather than squarely within it: Daniel is a homosexual, Marcelle a 'séquestrée', Lola a night-club singer, Ivich and Boris students, and although Mathieu has a teaching post, he is on holiday throughout the story and we never see him at work or even giving any thought to his classes. All of the emphasis falls once more upon individuals as independent agents and on their relations with other individuals; society as an entity has only the most shadowy existence in the novel.

It is valuable to look at works where society is effectively absent as a force, since this acts as a corrective to the not-uncommon but over-simplified view that the crux of the pre-war books is open conflict between the individual and society. Not that anyone could possibly deny that such conflict is to be found in these stories. If we take what must presumably rank as its paradigm, that is criminality, we are bound to be struck by the abundance of examples presented. The central figures of *L'Etranger*, *La Mort heureuse*, and *L'Invitée* all actually commit murder, and Paul Hilbert in 'Erostrate' is at least a would-be murderer. Lucien Fleurier takes part in a near-murderous attack upon a man in the street ('L'Enfance d'un chef') and Eve in 'La Chambre' is determined to kill her husband before his condition deteriorates much further. Although there is no murder or planned murder in *L'Age de raison*, Marcelle and Mathieu are quite prepared to procure a criminal abortion (what Jacques calls 'un meurtre métaphysique'). Mathieu, in any case, steals money from Lola (who is a drug-addict), and Boris regularly steals books and other articles from shops. In *La Mort heureuse*, when Mersault commits murder he too steals money, and it is also suggested that his victim Zagreus had come by the money partly by criminal means in the first place (77).

Yet although this is a very impressive list of criminal acts or intentions in these stories, and although in certain circumstances any one of them would be enough to bring the individual concerned into conflict with the law, we do well to hesitate for a moment before putting all of the cases mentioned into the single, and simple, category of open conflict with society. For one thing, there is an important distinction between actual and potential conflict. We have already seen that society with its rules and restrictions is accorded little importance at all in *L'Invitée* and *L'Age de raison*, so that, whatever criminal acts may be committed by the characters there, the crucial point cannot be to show the latter brought into direct conflict with society by their criminality. Indeed, Mathieu and Marcelle do not, in the end, procure an abortion; the money that Mathieu steals from Lola is returned; Lola is shown as getting away with her drug-taking and Boris with his thieving; and at the end of *L'Invitée* we are given reason to suppose that Françoise will escape the legal consequences of her murder of Xavière (503). Similarly, in *La Mort heureuse* Mersault's act of murder (like his victim's shady dealings) goes undetected and unpunished, as do many of the minor criminal acts in these books.

The only two criminal acts that actually bring main characters into immediate conflict with the law are those of Meursault and Paul Hilbert, and the contrast between these two cases is very striking. Hilbert's murder, or attempted murder, is deliberate and pre-meditated, while this is the very thing that

Meursault's murder of the Arab is not. And yet the ensuing conflict with the law is dwelt upon in the latter's case but not in the former's. At the beginning of Hilbert's tale he explains briefly how he was ill-treated by the police after his capture, but the story actually ends with his surrender and we learn no more about his fate or the legal consequences of his action. In the case of Meursault, on the other hand, conflict with the law clearly constitutes a central feature of the second half of the book. He is condemned to death by the official representatives of society because society feels itself *threatened* by him. Camus spelled this out in his preface to the American edition of the book: 'le héros du livre est condamné parce qu'il ne joue pas le jeu ... la société se sent menacée' (1928). But the point is perfectly clear in the text itself, when the prosecutor sums up his case and describes Meursault's heart as 'un gouffre où la société peut succomber' (1197). Meursault, then, is eventually presented as being in direct and desperate conflict with the whole of 'regular' society through the law. Yet this conflict, the only fully developed example of its kind in all of these stories, is, on his part, a wholly unintentional one.

In fact, the sense of the term 'conflict' has to be taken rather loosely for it to help us to recognise any overall pattern in this period as far as the individual's relations with society are concerned. We need to look beyond situations and acts as such, to motivation. The important point is that while there is certainly divergence or opposition of *values* in this area, only rarely in the stories do the contrasts issue in open battle. Perhaps only in 'Erostrate' is such a battle actively sought by the individual, for Paul Hilbert, as we noted earlier, sees himself as opposed to men in general and deliberately sets out to discover 'si l'on peut réussir quelque chose *contre eux*' (272). Even so, his particular manoeuvre has the air of a means to an end, since his deepest wish is to draw attention to himself: '"Voilà ce que je voudrais, les étonner tous"' (267). Hence his love of guns and his admiration for Herostratus, who burned down the Temple of Diana at Ephesus in order to become famous (269). In other words, any actual conflict that Hilbert may eventually engage in with society is of less interest than what lies behind it, or what it represents in philosophical terms. The same might even be said of *L'Etranger*, where society's mistaken

judgement on Meursault takes its place as a spur to
the main character's full discovery of himself and
his own values.

It is the exact nature and underlying
principles of divergence in values that are
important to our authors. A subtle illustration of
this point is the case of Boris in *L'Age de raison*.
It cannot be said that by his systematic and
non-profit-making thieving - 'Le profit du vol était
tout moral' (546) - Boris, like Hilbert, is going
out of his way to generate a conflict with society,
for he is careful not to be caught or to flaunt his
criminal activities. There is an occasional hint
that he may be avenging the oppressed (546), but,
however this may be, he regards theft as essentially
a kind of duty. Once more conflict with society is,
in itself, of less significance than the personal
and philosophical factors that motivate the
individual. And yet, in conformity with the emphasis
throughout the book on the youth of Boris and his
sister Ivich, Sartre hints that they are both a
little too concerned with the business of rebelling
for the sake of rebelling: 'Elle dit d'un ton
canaille: "Moi je m'en bats l'oeil, de la morale. Je
m'en bats l'oeil"' (636). He has them rather
foolishly agreeing on the positive virtue of taking
heroin (422), and explicitly contrasts their
somewhat immature stance towards theft with the more
sober attitude of Mathieu (548). This is not to say
that they are clearly presented as being in the
wrong and Mathieu in the right. When Mathieu first
has the opportunity to overcome his problems (and
Marcelle's) by stealing money from the apparently
dead Lola but fails to overcome his scruples in
order to do so, he is not shown in a particularly
favourable light. Nor does he improve matters by
changing his mind almost immediately and going
through with the theft. His stance in relation to
society's rules is perhaps no more satisfactory in
the end than that of Boris and Ivich. There can be
no doubt, however, that interest in the book focuses
on the analysis of complex situations, principles
and motives, rather than on the simple fact of
divergence from society's norms and its
consequences.

A related point is that genuine discussion or
debate confronting society's point of view with that
of the individual is as rare in these stories as
open conflict. Eve Darbédat takes no more active a
part in the 'discussion' with her father about the
rights and wrongs of her attitude towards Pierre

than does Meursault at his trial; and while Roquentin and the Autodidact exchange a few points that might be seen in this light, the Autodidact is by no means an authentic mouthpiece for society, being as much of an outsider as Roquentin himself is. Only the scene in *L'Age de raison* between Mathieu and his brother Jacques (500-10), where Mathieu is effectively called upon to justify his departure from bourgeois standards, contains argument of any substance. There Mathieu - although in the eyes of the reader he does not emerge from the contrast with great credit - is confronted by a character with whom it is very difficult indeed to sympathise (needless to say, neither this scene nor any other part of the book is narrated from Jacques's standpoint). The actual quality of the arguments used on each side is rather overshadowed by the clash of personalities and our general attitude towards the characters involved. In other words, nowhere in the pre-war books is there a really serious attempt to present the point of view that society might oppose to that of the individual. These books are for the most part one-sided, expounding and developing at length only the individual's case. Thus, for instance, the murders committed by Mersault and Françoise are committed without significant reference at all to society's norms and laws. The characters are obviously aware that what they are about to do is illegal and contrary to the very spirit upon which social life must be based, and yet this is a consideration that simply fails to weigh with either of them. It is not that they do what they do *because* it runs counter to the values of society, but that, given their own particular preoccupations and motives, this fact is of no importance to them. They have aims or ends, however vague or metaphysical, and the only question is that of how to achieve them. This is no more than another way of putting the point that while their values are essentially at variance with those of society, any actual conflict between the two frameworks is in a sense accidental, and certainly secondary.

However, having emphasised that open conflict between individual and society is not what these stories are most centrally about, we need to stress equally strongly that it *is* essential to the books that the individual's values and patterns of behaviour should be at odds with those of society. Apart from anything else, this throws the main issues that our authors wish to consider into strong relief. Indeed, from the literary point of view the major achievement of many of these early works is precisely to make us sympathise for the duration of the story with views and characters that go beyond, or are opposed to, the 'normal'. We understand how Françoise and Mersault can be in the position of simply discounting society's laws and restrictions in the pursuit of their own ends; we understand how Mathieu can be unmoved by the illegality of abortion and the severity of the punishments; we see how Meursault can find himself committing murder without any prior intention of doing so; and so on.

If we look at less dramatic areas of morality in these stories, we can easily confirm that divergence of values has the effect of making us think through certain basic issues afresh with individual characters. We find, for instance, that the attitudes of main figures towards sex and marriage are almost always unorthodox in relation to society's norms at the time. Marcelle's marriage in *Quand prime le spirituel* is an unmitigated disaster because the outlook with which she enters into it is (like that of her husband) a bizarre and unstable one. And Lulu's marriage in 'Intimité' is also a rather miserable affair, similarly based upon thoroughgoing self-deception. We have more sympathy with Mersault in *La Mort heureuse* and Eve in 'La Chambre', but, as we have already seen, their marriages are both highly unusual ones: Eve's simply because Pierre is mad and does not, in any real sense, regard her or treat her as his wife, and Mersault's because he does not claim to love Lucienne and in any case will not live permanently with her. All other marriages shown here are portrayed through the eyes of those with unorthodox views, so that we are encouraged to regard them as forming part of, or resting upon, a reprehensible or contemptible 'bourgeois' system of values. This is what is implied in the case of the marriage between Claude and Suzanne in *L'Invitée* and that between Jacques and Odette in *L'Age de raison*, although neither of these relationships is dwelt upon at length. In instances of this kind marriage is considered as no more than an aspect or extension of the systematic views on rights, property and possession that Roquentin castigates in *La Nausée*. Mathieu suddenly grasps this side of his brother's marriage ('Cette femme discrète et pudique sentait la possession'; AR 499), and the point is brought out particularly well at the end of 'L'Enfance d'un chef':

> Quelque part en France, il y avait une jeune
> fille claire dans le genre de Pierrette, une
> provinciale aux yeux de fleur, qui se gardait
> chaste pour lui ... Il l'épouserait, elle
> serait *sa* femme, le plus tendre de ses droits
> ... Son plus tendre droit; son droit le plus
> intime: le droit d'être respecté jusque dans
> sa chair, obéi jusque dans son lit. 'Je me
> marierai jeune', pensa-t-il. (387-88)

Even where the matter of possession and rights is
not explicitly broached, the whole value-system of
which it forms a part is there in the background, as
with the Darbédat couple in 'La Chambre'. In their
case we are also given to suppose that bourgeois
marriage rests mostly upon day-to-day habit, with a
certain underlying hostility between the partners.

   That there is, in general, a certain kind of
anti-marriage stance in these stories is confirmed
by the distinct lack of enthusiasm for the
institution on the part of Mersault and Meursault,
and perhaps above all by the examples of Pierre and
Françoise in *L'Invitée* and Mathieu and Marcelle in
L'Age de raison. Both of these last couples have
been together for seven or eight years but have
refused, as a matter of principle, to marry. There
is an interesting discussion of the topic between
Jacques and Mathieu which serves to remind us - and
both because we are successfully projected into the
lives of 'unorthodox' characters and because the
moral climate has changed, we *need* to be reminded
from time to time - that the relations between
Mathieu and Marcelle, like those between Françoise
and Pierre, are illicit or immoral by conventional
social standards of the thirties and forties.
(Madame Darbédat, for instance, is shocked at her
husband's daring suggestion that their daughter
would be better off taking a lover; Cham 239.) It is
an important point to be reminded of, since so many
of the heterosexual relations portrayed in these
works fall into this category and therefore either
are, or would be, disapproved of by society.
Sometimes the characters are breaking their own or
others' marriage vows in their sexual relations
(Lulu in 'Intimité', Elisabeth in *L'Invitée*), but
more often we have examples of non-marital affairs
of greater or lesser duration (Roquentin and the
café *patronne*, Boris and Lola, Mersault and Marthe,
Meursault and Marie). The example of Meursault is
the one that illustrates most clearly that, even if
in all of these cases society is not in a position

to act upon its disapproval, the potential moral censure is always there and could, in particular circumstances, become a powerful weapon against the individual:

> Le procureur s'est alors retourné vers le jury et a déclaré: 'Le même homme qui au lendemain de la mort de sa mère se livrait à la débauche la plus honteuse a tué pour des raisons futiles et pour liquider une affaire de moeurs inqualifiable.' (Etr 1193)

It goes without saying that an area of still greater potential conflict is that of what society might call 'perverted' sexual behaviour. There is at least one instance of this in Beauvoir's *Quand prime le spirituel* and examples abound in Sartre's stories, where some attention is given to homosexuals, possible lesbians, exhibitionists, male prostitutes, masochists, sadists, rapists and child-molesters.

In general, then, after *Quand prime le spirituel*, which is, broadly, about bourgeois society's damaging attempts to indoctrinate young women, the pre-war stories are dominated by a whole range of what we might call 'non-conformers', characters whose values and patterns of conduct diverge in some significant way from those of society at large, and who consequently cannot be regarded as having a full or entirely regular place within society. The list extends from deliberate murderers and those who are quite consciously independent in their moral views at one end of the scale, to merely odd or 'different' people at the other end; and along the way it takes in thieves, perverts, the mentally disordered, and so on. Our authors' theoretical reasons for writing more about abnormal than normal people are evidently linked with their reasons for dwelling upon characters in a state of solitude. Beauvoir records in her memoirs that she and Sartre were quite clear very early on in their careers about their interest in criminals and any extreme cases concerning individuals - 'nous pensions que pour comprendre quelque chose aux hommes il faut interroger les cas extrêmes'[1] - and a similar principle operates with Camus. It is he who brings out most sharply, in *L'Etranger*, the point that, given divergence in values between the individual and society, the potential for painful and even mortal conflict is always present. This is perhaps the real significance of his slightly strange comment on the book:

> J'ai résumé *L'Etranger*, il y a longtemps, par
> une phrase dont je reconnais qu'elle est très
> paradoxale: 'Dans notre société tout homme qui
> ne pleure pas à l'enterrement de sa mère risque
> d'être condamné à mort.' Je voulais dire
> seulement que le héros du livre est condamné
> parce qu'il ne joue pas le jeu. (1928)

That he is not talking specifically of criminals is
clear from the presence in the book of the 'bizarre
petite femme' or 'femme automate' who appears first
at Céleste's restaurant and then at Meursault's
trial. She is simply strange or faintly ridiculous
and, from society's point of view, perfectly
harmless. She stands at the opposite end of the
scale from Meursault, yet she *is* on the same scale,
for the ridiculous eventually merges into the
criminal in society's eyes and, as Meursault himself
points out during the trial (and as his case as a
whole illustrates), the distinction can be a
difficult one to draw: 'ce n'était pas le ridicule
qu'ils cherchaient, mais le crime. Cependant, la
différence n'est pas si grande' (1185).

Yet in spite of all of this, when we seek
further elucidation of the nature and significance
of the dissonance between individual and society in
these books, we find it surprisingly difficult to
register it with precision and to express it in
terms that are not metaphorical. However independent
characters may be in their moral outlooks, there is
little question of their definite exclusion from
society. (Monsieur Darbédat would have his
son-in-law shut away with his own kind, but has no
way of bringing this about.) Their dissent does not
cause them to live entirely outside society in the
way that Robinson Crusoe was accidentally forced to
do; nor are they 'drop-outs' who deliberately sever
as many links with it as possible. As we have seen,
the individuals of *L'Age de raison* and *L'Invitée*
might be said to be oblivious of society, but they
are heavily dependent upon it in material and other
ways. And even those characters whose solitude is
most apparent are similarly dependent, at least for
some of the time. Hilbert and Meursault both have
regular office jobs until disaster begins to
overtake them, as does Mersault until his revolt
enables him to escape; even Roquentin's solitary
life-style depends upon such social 'institutions'
as hotels, cafés, and public libraries. The most
appropriate single formula to fit the main

characters is perhaps the one that Camus used of Meursault in saying that 'il est étranger à la société où il vit, il erre, en marge, dans les faubourgs de la vie privée, solitaire, sensuelle' (1928), although even this is metaphorical. At best it appears to be certain aspects of life in society that characters disapprove of, or at least maintain an edgy indifference towards.

When the matter is posed in this way, it becomes clear that earlier statements about the relations between the individual and 'society', while accurate at a certain level of generality or as a pointer, would need careful qualification in order to stand as more precise outlines of the moral perspectives of this period. Since individuals continue to live, as it were, on the fringes of society, we evidently need to ask *which* are those aspects of it that they disapprove of, and which are those of its values that they reject. The answer to these questions will ultimately take us back to the discussion of lucidity and self-deception, but an obvious possibility to examine first is that it is simply the bourgeoisie and bourgeois values that are being challenged, explicitly or implicitly, by most main figures in the stories. Indeed, we have already suggested, for example, that it is the bourgeois conception of marriage that is under attack; we have seen Roquentin scorning what would have to be classified as the bourgeois stratum of society; we have noted that it is essentially bourgeois upbringing that is censured in *Quand prime le spirituel*; and we know in general that *all* of the sympathetic main characters have only contempt for the ethic of conformism, material success and ambition that is traditionally associated with the French bourgeoisie. Although the main preoccupations of, and the authors' main interests in, some of the major characters lie elsewhere, with the result that the anti-bourgeois strain of certain stories is not especially prominent (*L'Invitée, La Mort heureuse*, 'Le Mur', 'Intimité'), in a number of major cases the individual manifestly stands in overt opposition to the bourgeoisie. Nevertheless, as brief examination of a number of examples will show, caution is needed even at this point when one is seeking to formulate general characteristics of the outlooks displayed in these books.

As far as *L'Etranger* is concerned, it is doubtful whether the most helpful or accurate thing to say about Meursault is that his unorthodox values come into conflict with those of the bourgeoisie.

Certainly, those nameless representatives of society who resent his life-style and threaten his life may be described as bourgeois. It is also true that the friends and acquaintances who in one way or another rally to Meursault at some stage in the book are equally clearly *not* bourgeois figures. But we have to remember that it is a jury of 'ordinary' people that condemns Meursault in the end and that virtually *all* of the spectators in the courtroom are depicted as being against him (1189). Moreover, there are *national* differences at stake in the book. Meursault, an Algerian in Algeria, is nonetheless condemned 'au nom du peuple français', and this fact is one very important aspect of the conflict of values involved.

Now, since there is little in *L'Invitée* that casts direct light on this topic, and since those heroines in *Quand prime le spirituel* who find the bourgeois principles on which they were raised inadequate are still heavily influenced by them and are too young or too weak to go far beyond them, it is in fact only in the fiction of Sartre that we have a strong and definite impression that the authentic individual's values clash squarely with those of the bourgeoisie as such. Roquentin seems to associate self-deception specifically with the bourgeois class, and we have clear examples of the rather odious things that the bourgeois are thought to stand for in the figures of the Darbédat couple in 'La Chambre', the whole Fleurier family in 'L'Enfance d'un chef', and Jacques in *L'Age de raison*. All of these are, in different ways, incontrovertible cases, yet at least in the two novels the question of their exact significance needs to be approached with care.

In *L'Age de raison* Mathieu's brother Jacques is portrayed as a pompous, materialistic and rather objectionable representative of the bourgeoisie. He utters foolish platitudes that Sartre has condemned elsewhere, and he is pathetically proud of his 'rebellious' youth, which creates a close parallel between his character and values and those of Lucien Fleurier. So much is obvious, but what is less so is the extent to which there is substance in his claim that Mathieu himself, for all his independence of thought, is 'un bourgeois honteux' (506). It is true, after all, that Mathieu is a *fonctionnaire*; and, as Lola points out to Boris, he lives in a rented flat, has a fixed salary, a pension to come and a permanent relationship with Marcelle. Even Brunet comes to see Mathieu in this light: '"tu es

moins dégagé de ta classe que je ne croyais"' (526).
Mathieu is clear-headed enough to see that he cannot
simply dismiss this sort of charge out of hand and,
in fact, never decisively rebuts it in the course of
the book. Yet the implications of these points are
difficult to measure. Do they somehow soften
criticism of bourgeois values in the story or, on
the contrary, do they make them seem all the more
odious because they are so pervasive and
insinuating? In any case, in so far as the reader
feels sympathy for Mathieu and his broad aims in
life, this feature of the novel makes it impossible
to regard the values in the book as polarised in a
perfectly simple way which makes the bourgeoisie as
such the individual's most important adversary.

Furthermore, although it is an almost
irresistible temptation to see such a polarisation
in *La Nausée*, even there the matter deserves
slightly closer scrutiny. Roquentin's attack on the
Bouville dignitaries in the portrait gallery is, in
its way, quite merciless, as is that on the
characters whom he classifies elsewhere in more or
less exactly the same way (Impétraz, Docteur Rogé).
But his attitudes during the well-known scene of the
walk along the rue Tournebride and his subsequent
observation of a typical Bouville Sunday are
considerably more complex. In the rue Tournebride
itself ('le rendez-vous des élégants et des notables
... l'élite'; 53), he is undoubtedly talking about
the bourgeoisie, as his story concerning the origins
of the church of Sainte Cécile shows. Yet his
attitude towards them at this point is by no means a
particularly harsh or aggressive one. He finds the
élite rather silly and snobbish, but gives no sign
of considering them in the least harmful. He is
evidently detached from them, looks at them from the
outside, and gains some amusement from so doing, but
his tone is a rather kindly one and any criticism
there may be is only implicit and is very muted. By
the afternoon Roquentin finds himself no longer
observing just the bourgeoisie, but the crowd as a
whole:

Elle était plus mêlée que le matin. Il
semblait que tous ces hommes n'eussent plus la
force de soutenir cette belle hiérarchie
sociale dont, avant déjeuner, ils étaient si
fiers. Les négociants, et les fonctionnaires
marchaient côte à côte; ils se laissaient
coudoyer, heurter même et déplacer par de
petits employés à la mine pauvre. Les

> aristocraties, les élites, les groupements
> professionnels avaient fondu dans cette foule
> tiède. Il restait des hommes presque seuls, qui
> ne représentaient plus. (63)

He goes on to express sympathy for all those for
whom Sunday is the only day of rest and is drawn to
the Bouvillois in general as nowhere else in the
book, having eventually to remind himself that he is
not one of them (65). Near the end of the book,
where Roquentin looks down on Bouville from up on a
hill, a scorn for the bourgeoisie in particular is
readily discernible, but his sense of detachment
from *everyone* is now accentuated and what was, for
an instant, a generalised tenderness towards the
inhabitants of the town as a whole is now a
generalised contempt: 'Il me semble que j'appartiens
à une autre espèce' (186).

The images of 'tamed', civilised life that
Roquentin uses at this last point indicate that we
are back on specifically philosophical territory,
rather than that of class-warfare. What is most
fundamentally at issue is criticism of all of those
who fail to acknowledge the contingency that lies at
the basis of their organised lives and who insist
that there are absolute standards of Good and Evil
which men have no alternative but to recognise. Such
people, as we have seen, are accused of
self-deception, and this charge is at the very heart
of all of Roquentin's attacks on any conforming
members of Bouville society. None of this prevents
him from feeling sympathy towards them as human
beings on occasions (as he does for the Autodidact),
but it does mean that his basic objection to the
values that he opposes is a philosophical and not a
class one. Clearly, Roquentin believes that
self-deception is most characteristic of the middle
classes, and perhaps especially of the élite that
governs them, but the focal point of his disapproval
is the self-deception rather than the class itself.

This fact receives a certain kind of
confirmation in the story of Paul Hilbert in
'Erostrate'. Although, just like Roquentin, Hilbert
at times seems alienated from the whole human race,
the root of his alienation is a philosophical
objection to the attitudes of those with certain
beliefs, his particular target in the crucial letter
that he writes before committing his crime being
Humanists. Only the emphasis of his attack is
different from that of Roquentin, since he appears
less concerned with contingency and self-deception

as such than with the related tendency on the part
of Humanists and the like to try to *impose* their
moral and social values on others. The point again
is that this is a not a class matter: had Hilbert
been centrally opposed to the bourgeoisie as such,
it is difficult to see why he should have sent his
letter to one hundred and two French *writers*. Here
as in *La Nausée* we have a conflict or divergence of
values and life-styles which, at least in its most
fundamental and authentic form, transcends class
differences in themselves and therefore goes far
beyond the familiar desire to bash the bourgeoisie.

This is not necessarily to say that the
appropriate distinctions are sufficiently clearly
drawn in these books. It might very well be argued
that in so far as Sartre allows his philosophical
views proper to merge with more general objections
to the bourgeoisie in his stories, he is thereby
allowing the former to be weakened. We noted earlier
that it is a mistake to blur the distinction between
error and self-deception, and there is no doubt that
to go further still and accuse one whole class (as
opposed to others?) of self-deception is to open
oneself to still more serious objections. Neither
move, as we saw, is made quite explicitly in
L'Etranger, but similar implications could be said
to be carried by that book. There is something more
than a little unsatisfactory, on the philosophical
level, about the way in which Camus depicts and
treats the representatives of 'official' society in
the story. In almost every case what we have is not
a convincing portrayal but something approaching a
caricature. Moreover, this is just one of a number
of extreme measures that Camus is obliged to adopt
to illustrate his rather silly claim that anyone who
fails to weep at his mother's funeral risks being
condemned to death.[2]

In short, the fact that reference to social
classes in this connection is potentially misleading
and not, in any case, of critical importance is
simply one aspect of the general point that society
does not receive particularly careful or fair
treatment in the pre-war stories, and that the whole
matter of the relations between individual and
society is left in a somewhat vague, unresolved
state. We have no detailed or fully coherent account
of individuals' grievances against society, nor even
a definite impression of the precise extent of their
alienation. We know that differences of values are
at stake, and we know, at a fairly high level of
abstraction, what underlies these differences. Yet

in spite of their dissent and their relative solitude, most of the characters here seem perfectly content to go on depending upon society in various ways, to go on living on its fringes. With some exceptions, they seem genuinely uninterested in society as an entity and happy to go their own way within it for as long as they are allowed to do so; the important issues lie elsewhere. In fact, in discussing earlier the value and significance attached to solitude in these books - the metaphysical discoveries made by the individual and the basic ideals of lucidity and control - we were already considering the central factors and the main parameters of the moral perspectives of this period. The way in which these factors place the individual in opposition to a certain stereotype of the self-deceived bourgeois, as well as on the fringes of society itself in certain respects, is, philosophically and morally speaking, a secondary matter.

This alignment of forces in the books only takes on its full significance when we remember that we are dealing with works of fiction and not with philosophical treatises. The novel is an excellent vehicle for presenting characters and forms of conduct that are to be disapproved of, and such portrayals here have the function of showing us clearly and graphically what the non-conforming individual stands *against*, what sort of way of life we have to contrast with his. The outlooks that main characters repudiate are associated or identified with certain particular positions in, and sections of, society and our authors may well be guilty of distortion and over-simplification in this matter. Yet all such opposition serves to heighten individuals' perceptions of their own values and helps the reader to focus still more sharply upon the individual's standards and their implications.

Lucidity and personal control are ideals that society in no way helps the individual to pursue, but this fact may even strengthen the individual's determination to pursue them. In any event, provided that individuals are firm and independent enough, society cannot ultimately stand in their way either. Many of the central figures in these stories realise this sooner or later and shift all of their attention away from social rules and restrictions towards moral issues that concern them more deeply. If their movement, on the whole, is away from society rather than towards it, and if the lessons that they learn from enforced involvement with society are essentially negative ones, then what needs further elucidation is the general nature of their own preoccupations and the 'positive' outcome of their moral reflections upon them.

NOTES

1. *La Force de l'âge*, I,60.
2. See R.Girard, 'Camus' Stranger Retried'.

Chapter Four

SELF-JUSTIFICATION AND ITS LIMITS

Since in the pre-war stories the adoption of
ready-made and socially approved values - including
the whole framework of Christianity - is generally
repugnant to individuals, the question arises of
where they are to find something sufficiently
important to justify their own existence, to base
their life upon and to die with, or perhaps for. The
discovery that the Other, on both the personal and
the social levels, is on the whole hostile adds
urgency to this question, so that personal salvation
or self-justification may be described as the
predominant concern of main characters in these
books. At the same time, the discovery of separation
and hostility is bound to impose severe limitations
upon the communicability and general application of
any self-justifications arrived at. Individuals are
presented here as encountering limits beyond which
they are entirely unable to pass; as finding that
the solitude that has enabled them to make their
discoveries about life also prevents them from
sharing in any significant way with others their
reactions to those discoveries.

'Personal salvation' is not, of course, to be
understood in any religious sense, although the
characters' particular angle of approach to
fundamental metaphysical and moral problems is
doubtless dictated in some measure by the fact that
their notional starting-point is the demise of
Christianity. The crux of the matter is that in the
face of contingency individuals, often somewhat
desperately, seek some kind of justification for
their own existence, and while this sounds highly
theoretical, the search is seen to be inseparably
bound up with the matter of choices and conduct.
Consequently, if 'action' is primarily a matter of
means rather than ends, of a continuous process that
is basically instrumental in character, much of the

emphasis now falls upon the notion of the *act*, upon particular deeds that somehow symbolise, crystallise, or are otherwise inextricably linked with, the justification that the individual needs. Like Marguerite in *Quand prime le spirituel*, Mathieu discovers that this is very different from the 'gratuitous' act. His own deepest wish is to be able to perform honestly an act that will definitively commit him in some way, 'un acte irrémédiable' (AR 728). His own position is contrasted with that of Brunet, who Mathieu believes has found his salvation: 'Entrer au Parti, donner un sens à sa vie, choisir d'être un homme, agir, croire. Ce serait le salut' (524). Even as different a character as Elisabeth in *L'Invitée* can desire the same thing as Mathieu, in her own slightly twisted way: 'Quelque chose à faire; un acte authentique qui ferait couler de vraies larmes' (283). There is, in fact, no shortage at all of such acts in these books, which are dominated by examples like those of the acts of murder committed by Françoise, Meursault and Mersault ('à cause d'un seul geste calculé en toute lucidité, sa vie avait changé'; MH 123); Hilbert's attempted murder ('un crime, ça coupe en deux la vie de celui qui le commet'; Ero 273); Pablo's practical 'joke'; and so on.

Another notion that emphasis on the momentous act brings to the fore, though in a sketchy and rudimentary form, is that of the *responsibility* that individuals bear for what they are. Indeed, it is tempting to see this as a further ideal espoused by main characters and to argue that in addition to pursuing lucidity and struggling for control over their lives, most of them are also in the process of accepting or assuming responsibility for their own lives. With Françoise at the end of *L'Invitée*, for instance, the point is perhaps not simply that she has at last taken a grip on her life – however misguidedly – but also that she has finally done something, or become something, for which she is willing to answer: 'Elle avait enfin choisi. Elle s'était choisie' (503). In this sense, she is very close to Meursault's position at the end of *L'Etranger*: he at last considers himself fully justified in the choice of his way of life, and is ready to take the consequences of that choice. This is part of the reason for his final wish in the book, that there may be many people at his execution, greeting him with cries of hatred, for its fulfilment would somehow confirm the individuality and distinctiveness of his own

life-pattern. Again, the cases of Meursault and
Françoise are both, in this respect, parallel to
Mersault's, for he never tries to evade
responsibility for the killing of Zagreus. On the
contrary, he sees that it is what has enabled him to
achieve his goal of happiness, and regards it as an
integral part of his total choice of himself:

> Celui qui avait donné la mort allait mourir ...
> et ce choix que dans l'homme crée le destin il
> l'avait fait dans la conscience et le courage.
> Là était tout son bonheur de vivre et de
> mourir. (MH 199-200)

Sartre's characters constitute rather more
sophisticated cases as far as responsibility is
concerned: Roquentin may be just reaching this point
at the end of *La Nausée*, but no more; Pablo Ibbieta
thinks he can perform harmless, 'irresponsible' acts
but is proved wrong; Daniel (like Lulu in
'Intimité') is entirely unable to assume
responsibility for his life and delights in 'les
situations fausses' (AR 495); Lucien Fleurier, at
the end of 'L'Enfance d'un chef', might seem to be
accepting responsibility for himself in espousing
his father's way of life, but in fact is manifestly
failing to create his own individual pattern of
conduct and values; and Mathieu, as ever, presents a
somewhat complicated picture. Mathieu's ideal of
control over his own life certainly encompasses that
of assuming responsibility, and his disciple Boris
recognises this in describing Mathieu's aim as 'de
n'être responsable que devant soi-même et de
remettre en question, constamment, tout ce qu'on
pense et tout le monde' (AR 544). Mathieu sees
himself, however, as falling well short of this
ideal. Thus one part of him envies someone like
Brunet for having achieved it ('Son âge, sa classe,
son temps, il avait tout repris, tout assumé ... "Je
suis un irresponsable", pensa-t-il'; 523). And yet
for apparently respectable reasons his more strictly
intellectual side is still not quite ready to be
committed to any particular position.
Mathieu's case, like the others, shows that the
link between the ideal of control and that of
responsibility is so close as to make them virtually
inseparable, even for theoretical purposes. And
although referring to the notion of responsibility
as a goal may add a little to our understanding of
what characters are seeking, we have to weigh this
against possibly misleading factors. It is perhaps

significant, for example, that this concept figures only rather rarely in the texts, for it needs to be understood in a very restricted sense - that of taking responsibility for oneself, for what one is - and bears none of the more common connotations of public ascription of responsibility, or those carried by such a phrase as 'one's responsibilities' (indeed, we have seen that this last idea is attacked by Sartre). Hence it is at best a very private or personal guideline for some of the characters, and it brings us directly back to the central issue of self-justification through choice and act.

A useful point here is that in Sartre's stories in particular (although both Marcelle and Chantal in Beauvoir's *Quand prime le spirituel* also come into this category) there are some good examples of what we may uncontroversially regard as false or wholly inadequate self-justifications. Lucien Fleurier's return to the bosom of his family is, as he recognises in his moments of lucidity, not enough to fully justify his existence ('Son existence était un scandale et les responsabilités qu'il assumerait plus tard suffiraient à peine à la justifier'; ECh 364). Boris occasionally feels justified when he is with Lola (AR 418), but Roquentin bitterly exposes the futility of such attempts at self-justification as he watches two lovers in a restaurant (LN 132), even though he himself succumbs for some time to a slightly more sophisticated version of this temptation in his relations with Anny ('j'avais compté sur Anny pour me sauver, je le comprends seulement maintenant'; 185). And both Boris and Daniel also seek justification in other directions that are shown as unproductive, the latter in attempted acts of masochism and of malice which serve no purpose at all, and the former in a rather silly cult of youth (AR 595). However, with these general bearings in mind, to gain a clearer idea of the light in which self-justification is presented in the pre-war period we first need to look in detail at some major cases.

The best starting-point is probably the case of Mersault in *La Mort heureuse*, since his particular goal - that of personal happiness - is not only a definite and clear one, but also one of the most obvious general aims for the individual. If a man cannot accept transcendent values, nor yet social goals, should he not concern himself simply with his own happiness? It is in the key dialogue with Zagreus that Mersault seems to become convinced that his own 'volonté de bonheur' must constitute the overriding value in his life. One of the first things that Zagreus says is that he never likes to talk seriously, '"parce qu'alors, il n'y a qu'une chose dont on puisse parler: la justification qu'on apporte à sa vie"' (MH 69). Yet it is apparent that in his eyes 'l'exigence du bonheur' is justification enough for anything, and the eventual outcome of the discussion is that Mersault decides to revolt against the drudgery of his office job and to go all out for his own happiness. He subsequently murders Zagreus himself as a means to that end and comes to regard the impulse to happiness as 'sa seule justification' (167). Indeed, at the end of the story we have to see Mersault as having found self-justification in the attainment of his goal: 'Car lui avait rempli son rôle, avait parfait l'unique devoir de l'homme qui est seulement d'être heureux' (202). And in this respect we are bound to compare him with Meursault. Although the hero of *L'Etranger* does not set out to attain the goal of personal happiness, or at least does not do so nearly so consciously and determinedly as Mersault (and does not deliberately override society's rules), he is in a very similar state of mind by the end of the book. He too talks of self-justification ('C'était comme si j'avais attendu pendant tout le temps cette minute et cette petite aube où je serais justifié'; 1210), and even of happiness (1211). At the last, like Mersault, he feels able to look back on his life with a certain degree of satisfaction, and believes that it has all been justified. These two are perhaps the only characters in these books who find some kind of general salvation or justification for their lives by the end. It is perhaps not without significance that they are also the only two main figures to die or be about to die, and can therefore look back over their lives as a whole.

The only other major character who appears to come anywhere near to finding 'salvation' is Roquentin in *La Nausée*. In listening for the last time to the Negress singing *Some of These Days* and in thinking about the composer, he has a sudden insight into the possibility of some kind of self-justification: 'La Négresse chante. Alors on peut justifier son existence? Un tout petit peu?' (247). But he certainly has not found a way of justifying his own life by the end, even if he has caught a glimpse of what may possibly be one. Critics have talked as if Roquentin is definitely

going off to write a novel, yet in fact he has made
no decision by the end ('Je m'en vais, je me sens
vague. Je n'ose pas prendre de décision'; 247), and
it is very noticeable that everything is in the
conditional tense after he first mentions a novel.
The very possibility of success is hedged around
with all sorts of qualifications, and it may be
that, since the 'Avertissement des éditeurs' makes
no mention of a novel by Roquentin, we are meant to
assume that his project never came to fruition.[1]

In any case, even if we were to assume the
contrary, if we were to take it that *La Nausée* stops
at a point where Roquentin is actually on the way
towards a justification of his life as clear and
firm as those found by Mersault and Meursault, there
would still be some strong incentives for asking how
satisfactory his solution is; just as there are for
asking the same question about theirs. It is true
that, since these works of fiction are outstandingly
successful in projecting us into the minds of
non-conforming and somewhat odd characters, any
process that resembles judging their moral standards
from the outside (as the court judges Meursault)
requires careful explanation and defence, especially
as such a process takes us a little beyond textual
analysis of the kind performed so far. But, in fact,
a number of good reasons prevent us from abstaining
altogether from some sort of evaluation of the final
moral outlooks of Meursault, Mersault and Roquentin,
not least of which is the simple point that they
represent the most prominent 'positive' positions
adopted by any characters in these stories over and
above the assent to the broad ideals of lucidity and
control recorded earlier. The moral earnestness of
our authors is such that it seems a betrayal to fail
to react in any way to their fictionalised
perspectives. After all, they themselves, as we
shall see, were prepared to express views on the
attitudes of their protagonists, either at the time
or after the pre-war period. Moreover, certain
features of the texts encourage the process of
evaluation: while the markedly fragmentary and
tentative character of the ending of *La Nausée*
necessarily provokes further speculation, the very
extreme nature of the steps by which both Mersault
and Meursault find self-justification is bound to
generate debate. At the very least, the novels must
be said to raise, in however indirect a way, the
question of the *cost* of the solutions associated
with these three characters. In the present context,
therefore, we can appropriately touch upon the

potential flaws or inadequacies in the final stances
of the heroes concerned: it is less a matter of
showing their outlooks to be defective than of
drawing attention to some of their unmistakable
limitations.

Some critics have been inclined to see Sartre's
attitude towards Roquentin's thoughts of 'salvation
through art' at the end of *La Nausée* as essentially
an ironical one. Now, while the internal evidence
for this view is exceedingly slight (if it exists at
all), what is true is that any detached view of
Roquentin's final position is bound to expose the
obvious but severe limitations of the course of
action that he is contemplating. Not everyone -
indeed, not many people at all - can become a
novelist, a jazz singer or a composer; or even find
personal salvation in any other branch of the
creative arts. Roquentin's 'solution' is at the very
best one that might work for him on a personal
basis, for it has little general appliction and is
apparently not even suitable for someone with views
as similar to his own as those of Anny. This may be
part of what Sartre had in mind when he chose as the
epigraph for his book a quotation from Céline:
'C'est un garçon sans importance collective, c'est
tout juste un individu', and it is certainly what he
believed by 1975: *'La Nausée* est l'aboutissement
littéraire de la théorie de "l'homme seul" et je
n'arrivais pas à sortir de là, même si j'entrevoyais
déjà les limites de cette position' (1700).
Roquentin seems to be setting out on another utterly
solitary journey, towards some kind of personal
'immortality', and renouncing any attempt to make
direct contact with his fellow human beings.

Very similar comments apply to Mersault and
Meursault. They only 'progress' by cutting
themselves off more and more from their fellows, and
the solitude that might have looked like a necessary
means to a particular end comes to colour the end
itself unfavourably. Meursault's conclusions have
two faces: they appear to have general implications
for others, but, curiously, at the same time are
highly personal and self-centred:

> Que m'importaient la mort des autres, l'amour
> d'une mère, que m'importaient son dieu, les
> vies qu'on choisit, les destins qu'on élit,
> puisqu'un seul destin devait m'élire moi-même
> et avec moi des milliards de privilégiés qui,
> comme lui, se disaient mes frères. (Etr
> 1210-11)

And what we remember most about the last sentence of the book is the isolation and hatred that it points to:

> Pour que tout soit consommé, pour que je me sente moins seul, il me restait à souhaiter qu'il y ait beaucoup de spectateurs le jour de mon exécution et qu'ils m'accueillent avec des cris de haine. (1211-12)

Furthermore, whatever personal salvation Meursault achieves at the end is gained - albeit accidentally - at the expense of the life of a perfectly innocent Arab, about whose death he expresses no trace of regret whatever.

In all of these respects, the parallels with *La Mort heureuse* are very strong. Of course, Mersault knows his victim personally and even comes to feel a kind of 'fraternité sanglante' with him near the end (199). But again there is no suggestion that he comes to regret his act of murder, and in so far as he thinks of it at all, he still appears to regard it as thoroughly justified. Hence in its final stages the story raises far more questions than it solves:

> Il avait pris conscience de cette vérité essentielle et immorale que l'argent est un des moyens les plus sûrs et les plus rapides pour conquérir sa dignité ... Cette malédiction sordide et révoltante selon laquelle les pauvres finissent dans la misère la vie qu'ils ont commencée dans la misère, il l'avait rejetée en combattant l'argent par l'argent, avec la haine la haine. (184)

Again the stress on hatred is disquieting, and one is left puzzled by the implications of Mersault's use of the concept of immorality, as well as by the suggestion that he may somehow have acted on behalf of the poor in general. We are bound to take very seriously the fact that in a number of ways Mersault has deliberately used others as means to his own personal ends. Like Meursault, he is finally quite cut off from other people. If in the case of Roquentin and Meursault one was inclined to believe that the perspectives they eventually adopt are so personal and particular to their own situations as to lack universalisability, it is difficult to brush aside the feeling that Mersault is a rather different case and has actually taken the further step into the realm of egoism and callousness. In any case, it is indisputable that Mersault's life benefits no one but himself and that certain others pay dearly for the personal salvation that he apparently finds.

The problem is that, just as there is dispute over the attitude of Sartre towards Roquentin's views at the end of *La Nausée*, so any internal evidence that Camus disapproved of the final perspectives of Mersault and Meursault is slender in the extreme. There are few signs that he is detached from his main characters as we read these books, and yet once more it is impossible to conceive that he was entirely insensitive to the kind of limitations in, and reservations about, the conclusions of his heroes that we have sketched out. In fact, a comment in his *Carnets* which unmistakably prefigures the theme of *L'Etranger* also has relevance to the aspects of *La Mort heureuse* that we have been discussing: 'Récit - l'homme qui ne veut pas se justifier. L'idée qu'on se fait de lui lui est préférée. Il meurt, seul à garder conscience de sa vérité - Vanité de cette consolation.'[2] And another comment dating from just after the outbreak of war underlines and develops this view:

> De plus en plus, devant le monde des hommes, la seule réaction est l'individualisme. L'homme est à lui seul sa propre fin. Tout ce qu'on tente pour le bien de tous finit par l'échec. Même si l'on veut toutefois le tenter, il est convenable de le faire avec le mépris voulu. Se retirer tout entier et jouer son jeu. (Idiot.)[3]

Setting out to examine what positive moral conclusions individual characters draw from the metaphysical discoveries they make, we have so far - on the basis of three major examples - had cause to suggest that the very conditions for the making of those discoveries preclude or militate against the individual's concern with anything beyond his own private salvation, whatever may be the way in which he conceives it. We might say that metaphysical discoveries constitute the *gain* afforded by relative solitude or isolation, whilst one of the definite *losses* it results in is the individual's incapacity either to take morality as having to do with the nature and quality of our relations with others, or to deal with others in a satisfactory way. We can now go on to see that all of the other stories bring

out these points still more clearly by portraying
individuals who are much less 'successful' in their
search for personal self-justification than
Mersault, Meursault and Roquentin.

Mathieu stands as a major example here. He is
fully aware from the first of the basic metaphysical
truths that others have to awaken to in the course
of the stories, and has already passed on to more
characteristically ethical preoccupations (there is
a suggestion that he was conceived as a kind of
continuation of Roquentin in precisely this
respect).[4] Yet he is, in his own way, just as
centrally concerned with self-justification as the
characters previously discussed. His overriding aim
(which he traces back to his youth: '"Je ferai mon
salut!"'; AR 455) is to exercise his lucidity and
control in such a way as to make the best use of (or
preserve - part of his dilemma is to decide which of
these two things is at stake) his freedom. But he
entirely fails to justify himself in his own eyes,
since he cannot find a cause to which he is
completely convinced that he should commit himself,
in spite of the fact that he acknowledges to Brunet:
'"Je pense comme toi qu'on n'est pas un homme tant
qu'on n'a pas trouvé quelque chose pour quoi on
accepterait de mourir"' (525). Moreover, whenever he
tries to do something decisive, the consequences of
his actions seem somehow to be 'stolen' from him
(727-28). He wishes to communicate with others, but
so long as the fundamental problem of the meaning of
his life is unresolved, he is quite unable to build
up and sustain lasting and sincere relationships. In
the course of *L'Age de raison* he may actually lose
ground in his search for self-justification. Since
he is aware of the flaws in his personal
perspectives, but apparently able to do little about
them, this continually accentuates his pain:

> 'Beaucoup de bruit pour rien.' Pour rien: cette
> vie lui était donnée pour rien, il n'était rien
> et cependant il ne changerait plus: il était
> fait ... Déjà des morales éprouvées lui
> proposaient discrètement leurs services: il y
> avait l'épicurisme désabusé, l'indulgence
> souriante, la résignation, l'esprit de sérieux,
> le stoïcisme, tout ce qui permet de déguster
> minute par minute, en connaisseur, une vie
> ratée. (729)

Perhaps Françoise in *L'Invitée* may be seen as a
kind of cross between Mersault and Mathieu in the

final position she reaches. Like Mersault, she has
deliberately committed murder in order to satisfy
her own personal desires and aims (negative though
these seem to be in her case), and also like him she
claims, in the very last paragraph, to have obtained
some kind of deep satisfaction from the exercising
of her will. But it is clear that Françoise is
permanently conscious from an earlier point in the
book onwards of being, rather more like Mathieu, in
a position of complete defeat in certain key
respects. Quite apart from her failure to 'annex'
Xavière, there is the question of the disruption of
her earlier relationship with Pierre. Although
harmony has been re-established between them by the
end, the fact remains that Françoise loses in the
course of the story what she had previously taken to
be the justification of her life: that is, a
uniquely close relationship actually seen in terms
of identity. This loss is the hinge of the whole
book, and it is definitely presented as the
discovery of a mistake on Françoise's part:

> Le tort qu'elle avait, c'était de reposer sur
> Pierre de tout son poids; il y avait là une
> véritable faute, elle ne devait pas faire
> supporter à un autre la responsabilité
> d'elle-même (138);

> mais Pierre n'était pas en faute, il n'avait
> pas changé. C'était elle qui pendant des années
> avait commis l'erreur de ne le regarder que
> comme une justification d'elle-même (166).

Interestingly, this is the very mistake that
Mersault warns Catherine against in *La Mort heureuse*
(156); it may well be Marcelle's problem in *L'Age de
raison*; and Marguerite in *Quand prime le spirituel*
also comes to recognise that she has been
over-dependent upon her husband (246).

Yet the important question in *L'Invitée* is what
Françoise does once she discovers her mistake. It
could be argued that her gravest error is simply to
swap over-dependence upon Pierre for over-dependence
upon the whims of Xavière: 'c'était une vraie
angoisse de dépendre à ce point dans son bonheur et
jusque dans son être même de cette conscience
étrangère et rebelle' (299). It is very significant
that Françoise, who is in some respects so lucid
about the hollowness of seeking external guarantees
of one's existence (147; 170-71), should again fall
so comprehensively into this trap. She fails to draw

any positive moral conclusions about her relations with others from the earlier error of her ways, and even stands in self-contradiction at the end: having claimed that she could not live in a mutilated world, she deliberately mutilates it by killing Xavière. If common sense is sufficient for an awareness of the limitations of Roquentin's final position, how much more is this true of the ending of *L'Invitée*! Beauvoir's own later remarks on the ending are revealing. She admits that 'supprimer la conscience d'autrui, c'est puéril',[5] and comments as follows:

> Françoise a renoncé à trouver une solution éthique au problème de la coexistence; elle subit l'*Autre* comme un irréductible scandale; elle s'en défend en suscitant dans le monde un fait également brutal et irrationnel: un meurtre.[6]

We need to remember, of course, that Beauvoir set out to explain Françoise's deed and to make us believe in it (the original title of the book was *Légitime Défense*), but it is a little surprising to find her apparently allowing the possibility that Françoise's action may be permissible ('Peu m'importe qu'elle ait tort ou raison').[7] Nevertheless, Beauvoir's observations serve to confirm much of what has been said about the limits of any positive conclusions reached in the pre-war books, since they mark the acknowledgement of a moral impasse and an appeal to literary as opposed to ethical considerations.

In the case of two of Sartre's stories from this period one may easily detect built-in reservations about the crucial attitudes and decisions of the central figures. Pablo Ibbieta in 'Le Mur', in similar circumstances to Meursault, is unable to find any self-justification and adopts what we might call a 'death perspective': 'la mort avait tout désenchanté'; 'Je ne tenais plus à rien'; 'rien n'avait plus d'importance'. But the events of the story (however implausibly) expose the foolishness of this stance by a twist of fate that thwarts even his purely gratuitous and malicious action of sending his captors off on a wild goose chase. And Paul Hilbert's attempt to find his own salvation in 'Erostrate' by adopting 'une supériorité de position' over all of his fellow men and achieving something *against* them is palpably exposed as impossible by the pathetic outcome of his

act: 'Alors j'ai jeté le revolver et je leur ai
ouvert la porte' (278). As far as the other stories
in *Le Mur* are concerned, they add little to the
picture already described. Lucien Fleurier's
self-justification, as we saw, is an inadequate one
by his own admission. The general stance and final
decision of Eve in 'La Chambre' are by no means
lacking in consistency and dignity, but even if we
ignore her failure to join Pierre in his madness,
her sympathy and tolerance again have strictly
personal targets and could scarcely be seen as moral
options of any scope. Finally, Lulu and Rirette in
'Intimité' also illustrate, in a deliberately
trivial way, the point that characters here never
entirely escape from the private and selfish
concerns that their metaphysical solitude imposes
upon them.

   That a review of the moral content of these
particular books should both begin and end with an
emphasis on the theme of solitude is neither
surprising nor fruitless. It is as if our authors
have pushed the question of the isolation of the
individual to its extreme limits. They set off from
a starting-point and assumptions that in themselves
inexorably set severe restrictions upon how far the
development of a positive ethic could possibly go.
Answers to the question of what individuals are to
do when irremediably cut off, either by choice or
otherwise, from their fellows can only ring slight
changes on the advice to face up squarely to what
solitude teaches them about themselves and the
world, and to try to find salvation in their own
way. All of the variety will come from the extent to
which this advice is followed; the exact manner of
any attempt to follow or ignore it; and the outcome
of the situation as a result of these and other
quite different factors, such as chance. It is as
much what is absent from the moral attitudes here as
what is present that is most characteristic of them
as a whole. And what is most noticeably absent is
any significant *sharing* of moral perspectives by the
individuals portrayed. Even where, in particular
cases, certain potentially generalisable moral
principles show signs of emerging, no thought is
given by the individual moral agents involved to the
need for, or consequences of, so generalising them.
Moreover, these principles are themselves either so
rudimentary or so vague and undeveloped as to
constitute little more than broad pointers in the
direction of morality. The ideals of lucidity and
control fall into this category, but it is worth

looking briefly, by way of illustration of these general points, at a possible extension of the first of these.

If lucidity - as opposed to self-deception - consists in being truthful to oneself about what one knows, then being truthful *to others* about what one knows suggests itself as a desirable and universalisable moral principle. And this principle is of especial interest in the light of certain comments that Camus himself made about *L'Etranger*, when he pointed out that Meursault refuses to lie and described the book as 'l'histoire d'un homme qui, sans aucune attitude héroïque, accepte de mourir pour la vérité' (1928). The latter formulation is potentially misleading, but the observation that Meursault 'refuse de mentir' is a more fruitful one. Even if there is reason to doubt his total truthfulness in relatively trivial matters, Meursault is indeed outstandingly truthful in certain major respects (not only with representatives of the law, but also, for instance, with Marie or his boss). The point is, however, that his truthfulness has little to do with a desire to communicate the right things to other people. It is a markedly private, self-enclosed kind of honesty that is much more fundamentally connected with being true to oneself than with being truthful with others. If Meursault believed in telling the truth as a moral principle, he would wish to see the principle generally accepted, or at least be interested in the question of whether others are honest or not. Yet these issues are ones that he is not in the slightest concerned about, as the whole episode of the story that Raymond tells him about his ex-mistress shows. Whatever Meursault's personal preferences may be regarding telling the truth, or not lying, he is simply indifferent to whether others are honest or not, apparently regarding it as none of his business. His own honesty, in the last analysis, is as much a purely private matter as the self-justification that he finds at the end, and with which it is intimately bound up.

Interestingly enough, honesty is a characteristic of Mersault and Roquentin, too. Mersault is generally frank and truthful in his relations with, say, Marthe, Zagreus, his 'amies' and Lucienne; and Roquentin sets himself very high standards of honesty in the writing of his diary. Indeed, Roquentin's case bears out very strongly our general view of Meursault's refusal to lie. Like Meursault (though perhaps more deliberately and self-consciously throughout), he is determined not to say more than is the case: 'il ne faut pas mettre de l'étrange où il n' y a rien. Je pense que c'est le danger si l'on tient un journal: on s'exagère tout' (LN 5). Even more obviously than Meursault's, however, Roquentin's honesty has nothing to do with a desire to communicate properly with others. As we have seen, it is a feature of his struggle for lucidity and for control over himself. He makes a principle out of honesty in the writing of his diary, but his diary is manifestly not intended for publication and is written entirely for his own personal benefit ('Tenir un journal pour y voir clair'; 5). And it is equally difficult to find any generalised message in favour of truthfulness towards others in *La Mort heureuse*, where Mersault keeps a great deal to himself and is almost exclusively preoccupied with his own happiness.

It could not be said, therefore, that truthfulness, which might have been held up as a principle which provides the link between the individual's relations with himself (lucidity, self-control) and his relations with others, is presented in precisely this way in these books. In addition to the fact that, where certain characters are unusually truthful, this is more for their own sake than for the sake of honest communication with others, it is noticeable that other protagonists who set great store by a certain kind of honesty actually fail to carry out this principle consistently in interpersonal relations. Françoise has obviously worked hard in the past at being honest with Pierre, but with the advent of Xavière her standards slip somewhat ('il y avait longtemps qu'elle avait cessé d'être d'une sincérité si exigeante'; Inv 291). In any case, neither she nor Pierre has any scruples at all about lying to Elisabeth or Gerbert when it suits their purposes. And Mathieu, like Françoise, can be seen as a victim of the illusion that absolute truthfulness between two people is possible. For seven years he and Marcelle have had an agreement to tell each other 'everything', but it is clearly indicated in the course of *L'Age de raison* that the spirit, or the spirit and the letter, of that agreement has been broken on both sides. These are apparently the strongest examples in all of the books of an important mutual agreement on the value of truthfulness, or any other value, and yet neither is an encouraging illustration of the sharing of moral perspectives. In general, we can say that although there are marked similarities in the situations of individual characters, and close parallels in the discoveries made as a result of these situations, the pre-war stories are marked by the absence of significant agreement on, and communication of, the basic moral principles that constitute the appropriate reactions to these discoveries.

There are, of course, in a number of these books little clusters of characters that we are encouraged to see as groups or sub-groups: the outcasts in *La Nausée* (Roquentin, the Autodidact, M.Achille); Mersault and his neighbours in *La Mort heureuse*, and Mersault and his 'amies' of the 'Maison devant le Monde'; Meursault's Algerian workmates and acquaintances in *L'Etranger*; the trio, possibly plus Elisabeth and Gerbert, in *L'Invitée*; Mathieu and friends in *L'Age de raison*. But it would be possible to take these and other sub-groups one by one and to demonstrate: either that they are grounded simply in similarities of situation (outstandingly in *La Nausée*, where there are visibly no common values between, for instance, Roquentin and the Autodidact); or that on close examination they disintegrate into loose collections of warring individuals (for instance, in *L'Invitée*, *L'Age de raison*, 'Intimité'); or that where there are certain shared moral standards within the group, these are, in one way or another, very rudimentary and circumscribed or of secondary importance in the books.

The sub-groups in *La Mort heureuse* and *L'Etranger* fall into the last and most interesting category. It is plain from the beginning that these groups are powerless, in literary terms, to do much more than reflect characteristics or aspects of the main figures on whom the stories exclusively centre. The actual basis of Mersault's period of harmony with his 'amies' in *La Mort heureuse* is vague, but in any case the period is a temporary one and the values that it embodies insufficient for Mersault, who breaks away of his own volition (155); just as he broke away from his neighbourhood friends and workmates as soon as he had money. And of course Mersault's crime is a barrier in his relations with others to the last, preventing him from sharing his deepest values and thoughts with anyone: he would like to tell Bernard about it but cannot (184), so that the secret of his life dies with him.

As we have already seen, the self-justification that Meursault arrives at also has isolation as its necessary condition. It differs, however, in certain important ways from his perspective while he is living and working as a free man in Algiers. In fact, it is in Part I of *L'Etranger*, when Meursault is in contact with fellow Algerians like Emmanuel, Céleste, Raymond, Masson, Marie and Salamano that we come closest in these stories to an example of a definable sub-group or community that has a shared set of values and norms. As an Algerian himself, Camus clearly had respect for what he considered to be the principles lying behind the conduct of such characters - principles that he categorised as a kind of ethic in 'L'Eté à Alger', one of the essays in *Noces* - but he was also well aware of their limitations. It is significant that Meursault appears to have reached the age beyond which Camus saw young Algerians as burned out, and that his evolution in Part II of *L'Etranger* depends upon precisely the process of reflection that is regarded as inappropriate within the Algerian code. In general terms, Meursault comes to recognise that things are more complicated than he had taken them to be, and to find his justification in a way that would have been inconceivable had he continued living according to his previous pattern. And although the fact that his Algerian way of life is challenged by representatives of another country and another climate (he is condemned 'au nom du peuple français') is undeniably important in the book, the question must arise of how typical Meursault is of the people he mingles with in Algiers. Many - perhaps most - find him rather odd, and it might be a mistake to take the sympathy that wells up for him after his misfortune as tantamount to deeply shared values. In any event, the perspective within which Meursault finds his salvation in the end is not only one that he shares with no one else, but also one that it would probably be *impossible* to share with anyone else. In short, nothing in *L'Etranger* causes us to go back on the view that there is very little genuine communication indeed between moral agents in these books and certainly no systematic or profound sharing of the moral perspectives that follow upon basic metaphysical discoveries about the world.

We now have some idea of the general boundaries that circumscribe the various moral attitudes portrayed in characters in the fictional works of the pre-war period. What marks off these stories is not concentration on the moral life of the individual as such - this could equally well be said about later phases in our authors' work - but the fact that the individual's deepest concern here is shown as relating almost exclusively to his own personal wishes, needs, fears and preoccupations. To such an extent is this the case that the label 'moral' has to be stretched to its utmost limits in one direction if it is to be used to describe that concern. If, in the face of contingency, individuals are desperate to justify their lives, they are not – unless they be in the state of self-deception that each author describes on occasions – concerned to justify themselves to, or through, other people. If they think in terms of responsibility, this has nothing to do with the public acknowledgement of duties, but with responsibility for themselves, and to themselves, alone. Their perspectives are self-centred in all senses of that term, and perhaps even selfish or self-interested. Yet they have ultimately to be considered as moral perspectives, since they constitute the individual's most fundamental reactions to the nature of the world as it is perceived to be, and have the most far-reaching consequences for the conduct of his life as a whole, as well as certain consequences for others.

One of the 'messages' that these works convey is that facing up unequivocally to the fact of solitude and other equally unpalatable metaphysical truths about life constitutes the absolutely minimal basis for any authentic moral position that the individual may adopt. When Camus comments on Meursault that,

> Loin qu'il soit privé de toute sensibilité, une passion profonde, parce que tenace, l'anime, la passion de l'absolu et de la vérité. Il s'agit d'une vérité encore négative, la vérité d'être et de sentir, mais sans laquelle nulle conquête sur soi et sur le monde ne sera jamais possible (1928),

he draws attention to certain features of Meursault in particular, but also touches upon a number of points that apply to many of the major characters that we have discussed. There is a kind of passion for the absolute or for the truth in many of them: they want and need to *know* – and the authors imply that they *should* want to know – what is the case, however uncomfortable that knowledge may be. Characters like Meursault and Françoise need some kind of nudge, since to start with they have life-patterns that insulate them from uncomfortable truths. But this matters considerably less than that they should hold on, should sustain their struggle for lucidity, once the process has begun. At this stage, it seems that the value of their efforts, morally speaking, may lie less in the knowledge or state of mind finally attained than in the struggle itself.

It is also true that such truth as characters do win through to is, at best, 'une vérité encore négative', even though it is a necessary condition of control over oneself, let alone the world. It is 'negative' morally in the sense that it does not of itself permit of any obvious progress. It does not point the way forward, but simply provides the individual with the base from which he must find his own salvation. In the pre-war period it is particularly easy to see that Camus, Sartre and Beauvoir are better at posing and describing moral problems than at solving them. Different individuals - even those armed with roughly the same lucidity - will take different roads, and if it is desirable to judge those directions in some way, the appalling problem is that of finding a common measure. Granted that they are all highly personal 'solutions', how can one assess the relative merits of the directions taken by, say, Mersault, Meursault and Roquentin? It seems that there is little to be said until we have some kind of accepted measure, social norm, or common goal against which we may test them. This is doubtless the root cause of any ambiguity or unease that there may be in the books (or attached to the books) as far as the authors' considered attitudes to their characters are concerned.

In the fiction of this phase, moral considerations lead into an impasse. There is a sense in which even those of the characters' final stances that are not obviously misguided may be regarded as unstable, temporary, transitional, tentative or experimental, although this is perhaps only clear when the problems are looked at with the benefit of hindsight. Nevertheless, it is difficult to see how any significant evolution originating from within those perspectives could possibly have taken place. Now we can easily acknowledge that the whole picture had to be shattered by a massive *external* force, which turned almost everything on its head, brought everything out for revaluation, and obliged the individual radically to re-assess the isolation or solitude that constitutes both the theoretical beginning and end of moral reflection in this period. Such a force came, of course, in the shape of the Second World War.

NOTES

1. See R.Champigny, 'Sens de *La Nausée*'. And on this and other aspects of the end of the novel, see my 'The ending of Sartre's *La Nausée*'.
2. *Albert Camus. Carnets, mai 1936 - février 1942*, p.46.
3. Ibid., p.203.
4. 'A qui les lauriers des Goncourt, Fémina, Renaudot, Inter-allié?, article-interview de Claudine Chonez'.
5. *La Force de l'âge*, II 625.
6. Ibid., II 388.
7. Ibid.
8. *Albert Camus. Essais*, pp. 67-77.

PART TWO

THE 'WARTIME' NOVELS

Chapter Five

COLLECTIVE SITUATIONS AND GROUPS

None of the next group of novels by Sartre, Camus
and Simone de Beauvoir was begun before the outbreak
of the Second World War. These are 'wartime' works
in the sense that they were either conceived and
written during the war, or written shortly after the
war with the war as their setting. Sartre's *Le
Sursis* and Beauvoir's *Le Sang des autres* were both
finished before the end of the war (although not
published until immediately after it). Her *Tous les
hommes sont mortels* was written between September
1943 and the early part of 1946. Sartre's *La Mort
dans l'âme* and those extracts that we have from the
projected fourth volume of *Les Chemins de la
liberté*, due to be called *La Dernière Chance* (the
extracts are entitled 'Drôle d'amitié' and 'La
Dernière Chance'), were written straight after the
war but are set in the war years. Camus's *La Peste*
was conceived and elaborated during the war and is
universally acknowledged to be, in part, an allegory
of the German Occupation of France. More
significantly, provided that the Munich crisis of
September 1938 may be taken as part of the war
experience in a broad sense, then of these six works
(including *La Dernière Chance*), five take the war or
some phase of it as a subject, in one way or
another. While not surprising, this fact is already
worthy of note as a point of contrast with the
earlier books, where the scarcity and relative
insignificance of substantive references to
political circumstances was remarkable.

Yet in the strictest sense these novels are not
'about' the war itself. There is no doubt that it
was the impact of the Second World War upon our
authors that brought about the changes in their
attitudes and preoccupations that we are about to
trace. Indeed, this point has been explicitly made

and developed by each of them in other writings.
From the fiction alone, however, it is fairly clear
that what is of greatest importance for them is not
specifically the war itself, but what it stands for.
It is noticeable, for instance, that descriptions of
the fighting, or systematic accounts of the changing
fortunes and main stages of the conflict are
virtually non-existent in these books. The real
significance of the war here is that it is the point
of intersection of a number of forces that bear
heavily upon the individual. Perhaps it is best to
call these forces, as Sartre and Beauvoir do, the
forces of history. A wholly appropriate and
satisfactory label is rather hard to find, for the
main happenings in the stories are usually not
precisely of a kind that we would find recorded in
history books (though some events in *Tous les hommes
sont mortels* would be so recorded, as are some of
the things related in *Le Sursis*). The fact is that
history has both a subjective and an objective
aspect. That is to say that many of the events
recorded in history books are of a certain
composite, non-personal character, while these same
events as lived through by individuals are likely to
look very different, being much more specific and
less structured. If the novels do not deal with the
happenings of the war in the way that a history book
would, it is because their authors are centrally
concerned with the impact that such fateful events
have upon individuals; with different kinds of
awareness of those events and different reactions to
the pressures that they generate.

In this period, therefore, history stands in
relation to moral matters roughly as metaphysics
stood to moral matters in the earlier period: where
metaphysical discoveries – not to say shocks –
earlier constituted the main stimulus to, and the
framework or base for, reflection on moral issues,
we now find discoveries about the processes and
forces of history fulfilling the same role. And just
as metaphysical discoveries were mediated through
the phenomenon of solitude, so discoveries about
history are crucially mediated through the
phenomenon of the *collective situation*. Here, as
there, the phenomenon itself takes a number of
different forms, and here too, while most characters
have to learn about the phenomenon, certain others
are familiar with it to begin with. It is now the
collective situation instead of solitude that
constitutes the necessary condition, the base-point,
and perhaps ultimately the limit of the moral

perspectives that the stories embody.

Unlike the figures in the earlier books, virtually all of the main characters here find themselves for either most or all of the story in collective situations. Although the concept stands in need of further elucidation and elaboration, it is clear that if there are such situations at all in fiction, then those dominating the whole of *La Peste*, *Le Sursis*, *La Mort dans l'âme* and the extracts from *La Dernière Chance* are among the unmistakable instances. The city cut off by plague, the country or continent under threat of war, the country defeated in war, the forces of a defeated country imprisoned in enemy camps – these constitute veritable paradigms of what one means by a 'collective situation'. Some of these very same situations, too, dominate about half of *Le Sang des autres*, while historical circumstances and political factors are by no means negligible in the other half of that book. And if, as so often, this appears to leave *Tous les hommes sont mortels* out of line, one has only to point out that, although the periods of history involved are far earlier ones, again it is crucial to a good half of Fosca's story that it be set firmly in the context of large-scale historical events. Indeed, much of the interest of this novel, from our present point of view, lies precisely in the fact that the historical circumstances are entirely different from those in the other books (although a few obvious parallels can be drawn: war and conflict prevail here, too, and there is even a case of a city cut off by plague). That is, we are given one chance to assess what is being said about the forces of history on the basis of a set of examples other than the contemporary one of the Second World War.

In these books the Second World War itself constitutes no more than a series of collective situations through which the forces of history operate. Although there is obvious continuity, and although Camus and Beauvoir cover rather longer chronological periods than does Sartre, it is certain moments or phases of the war that form the important units used as settings in the stories. The Munich crisis (*Le Sursis*) clearly yields a different situation from that prevailing at the precise moment of the defeat of France (*La Mort dans l'âme*), or some time after it (*La Dernière Chance*). But even in *Le Sang des autres* and *La Peste* vital differences of situation are registered between the moment when the war (or plague) is about to break out and the

later moments when it is actually raging. And this
serves as a reminder that spatial factors are nearly
as important here as temporal ones, having a
significant bearing on how historical moments are
perceived. The situation some time after the defeat
has a different configuration entirely according to
whether one looks at it from a prison camp in
Germany ('Drôle d'amitié') or as a 'free' man in
Paris or elsewhere in Occupied France (*Le Sang des
autres* and *La Peste*). Similarly, the defeat itself
as portrayed in *La Mort dans l'âme* can look
different according to whether it is seen from the
United States (Gomez), North East France (Mathieu),
Marseilles (Boris), Paris (Daniel), and so on.

In fact, the fragmentation that results from
the adopting of various viewpoints is a vitally
important feature of the presentation of the war in
these books. This point is perfectly clear in the
case of *La Mort dans l'âme* (eight separate
narrative standpoints) and especially *Le Sursis*
(about fifty), but *Le Sang des autres* too shows
almost all of the relevant historical situations
from Hélène's point of view as well as from
Blomart's. And if the narrative of *Tous les hommes
sont mortels* is again a kind of exception, it is no
distortion of the book to say that it looks at human
history as a whole from the viewpoints of two
individuals. In *La Peste*, of course, there is only
one narrator as such, but on five occasions he
quotes at length from another's diary. In any case,
one consequence of Rieux's attempt to speak 'au nom
de tous' is a proliferation and differentiation of
characters which in itself generates the kind of
fragmentation observable in the other novels.
Dominant though the plague situation is, we are made
acutely aware of significant differences in what it
amounts to for the individuals involved: Cottard is
the only character to see it as something that works
to his advantage; Rieux the only one obliged to
fight it actively because of his profession; Rambert
is especially conscious of its injustice because he
is not from Oran in the first place; Paneloux the
only main character who must view it in Christian
terms; and so on.

For our authors, therefore, there is paradox in
the fact that the historical process of the Second
World War breaks down into an indefinite set of
different individual viewpoints and dilemmas.
Mathieu's well-known comments about the elusive
nature of war as a phenomenon, in *Le Sursis*, are of
more than purely theoretical interest, since the

view that lies behind them is part of the very fabric of these novels:

> 'La guerre prend tout, ramasse tout, elle ne laisse rien perdre, pas une pensée, pas un geste et personne ne peut la voir, pas même Hitler. Personne.' Il répéta: 'Personne' – et tout à coup il l'entrevit. C'était un drôle de corps, proprement impensable (1024);
>
> Elle est là, elle est partout, c'est la totalité de toutes mes pensées, de toutes les paroles d'Hitler, de tous les actes de Gomez: mais personne n'est là pour faire le total. Elle n'existe que pour Dieu. Mais Dieu n'existe pas. Et pourtant la guerre existe (1025).

These conclusions are, of course, echoed elsewhere – Fosca discovers that 'il n'y a pas d'Univers' (THM 313), and Blomart insists that '"C'est absurde de vouloir regarder le monde du point de vue de Sirius; nous ne sommes pas dans Sirius"' (SA 201) – and both their paradoxical nature and the actual terms in which they are presented are of the greatest significance to an understanding of the perspectives of this period. We suggested that part of the impact of the metaphysical discoveries made in the books of the pre-war period had to be seen as resulting from their being viewed (by character, author and reader alike) against the conceptual framework and culture of Christianity. Something similar applies in the case of history: the departure of God leaves puzzles and paradoxes at the historical level, as it earlier did at the metaphysical level. But on the whole, although these theoretical issues are built into the very substance and structure of the novels, they constitute a less important centre of interest than what flows from them: that is, the 'practical' problems that the chaotic but compelling circumstances of the war bring for the individual. The focus is still upon the individual, as it was in the pre-war stories, but the context and the main forces in play have changed quite drastically.

Yet history can no more be said to *replace* metaphysics here than collective situations can be said to replace solitude. The problems previously raised by metaphysical discoveries are certainly not resolved by this time, nor is it true to say that they are completely shelved. It is clear, for instance, that characters like Mathieu, Daniel, Boris and Ivich who figure in stories of both the first and second periods are no further advanced in their personal search for self-justification, and that this search taxes them as much as ever. In many crucial respects, moreover, individuals here are as alone as ever *within* the collective situation, since they have always to interpret and react to that situation for themselves. The change is rather that characters in these stories are shown as having new problems and preoccupations *superimposed* upon the old. And, broadly speaking, it is the new superimposed elements that now take a kind of precedence, in that they are shown as giving rise to insistent demands which need to be met at once, and are accorded more emphasis by the authors. At this point the notion of moral perspectives takes on its full significance and value, since one perspective can come to predominate over another without there being the kind of head-on clash between the two that arises between two sets of substantive moral views. Perspectives cannot truly be said to contradict one another, and when a new one comes to prevail without completely replacing the old, rather than confrontation or conflict there is an additional dimension of complexity.

This point can be illustrated if we look upon the collective situation as in some ways a direct extension of the discovery of the Other that we traced in connection with earlier works. It is definitely an *extension* of that discovery, because characters are now not only aware that solipsism is impossible to sustain as a world-view, that they have to live in a world where there are other people: they are also made aware that certain situations they live through as individuals are quite essentially collective ones, ones lived through together with other members of the human race. Thus, for instance, Rieux's belief that he can speak for everyone in Oran is based upon the fact that there has been a situation common to all of its citizens: 'il n'est pas une des angoisses de ses concitoyens qu'il n'ait partagée, aucune situation qui n'ait été aussi la sienne' (LP 1468). This new awareness involves differences of both quantity and quality. In the pre-war stories the impact made upon the lives of individuals by the existence of others almost always arose directly from the presence of others known personally to them, but now it is the fact that there are *many* others, millions of others whom they do not know and never will, that imposes itself in one manner or another. And it is no longer their brute existence or even their latent hostility

that comes as a shock, so much as the point that,
however unknown and however far away others may be,
the individual's own life can never be entirely
separated out from some, or even all, of theirs.
Collective situations make the characters acutely
conscious of interdependence, of the fact that the
lives of sometimes widely dispersed human beings are
closely enmeshed together, in ways that there was no
mention of in the earlier stories.

In this respect *Le Sang des autres* (the
earliest of the wartime novels and the one covering
the longest period of contemporary history) is a
particularly revealing case. It shows more
explicitly than any of the other books the
transition – either the actual transition or a
possible, schematic one – from the discovery of the
Other at the first level to the discovery of
collectives at the second. It shows the extension
outwards from a small number of other known
individuals to innumerable unknown and often unnamed
others. When Blomart's personal relationship with
Hélène, against his better judgement, finally
attains some kind of equilibrium, he sees that this
is at the expense of others like Madeleine and Paul:
'Devant toi, j'étais sans remords. Devant toi. Mais
nous n'étions pas seuls au monde' (139). This is in
fact one of the critical turning-points in the
novel, where Blomart is in the process of
recognising that there are a great many other people
in the world who are, directly or indirectly,
affected by his actions and decisions: 'tout le
reste du monde à l'horizon. Et ils n'avaient pas
choisi' (134). Unlike Françoise and most of the
characters in the earlier stories, Blomart is
becoming aware of the *scale* of the problem of the
Other, of its historical dimension. By the time war
becomes imminent, he has realised that his unwitting
interference in the life of Hélène is no more than
one particular, personalised instance of a general
human ill:

> Pour moi, la guerre n'était pas un scandale
> sans pareil. Ce n'était qu'une des formes du
> conflit où j'avais été jeté malgré moi en
> étant jeté sur la terre. Parce que nous
> existions les uns pour les autres et cependant
> chacun pour soi; parce que j'étais moi et
> cependant pour eux, un autre. Le fils Blomart.
> Le rival de Paul. Un social-traître. Un salaud
> de Français. Un ennemi. Le pain que je mangeais
> avait toujours été le pain des autres. (204)

The solitude and the 'séparation des consciences' emphasised in *L'Invitée* is still recorded as a reality, but superimposed upon it now is an awareness of the inescapable interlocking of the life of any given individual with those of all others.

It is at this point that metaphysical facts merge into historical forces: the individual is, as it were, injected into the stream of history and brought face to face with the general fact of interdependence. This process is copiously illustrated in all of the novels of the period. Even in *Tous les hommes sont mortels*, where the Second World War obviously cannot be shown as the occasion of this sudden awakening, Fosca is seen to become increasingly aware of the existence and importance of people in other countries, and of his own dependence upon them: 'mon destin se décide sans moi' (220). His, of course, is a very curious but fascinating case. His immortality, in a sense, disarms the forces of history, takes him beyond history as a whole. Yet the final message of the story (as the title of the book suggests) is that it is mortality alone - that is, precisely, having a place in history and thereby being subject to its forces - that makes us human. Freed from all the constraints of history, we would have nothing to gain or to lose, therefore no will to live (which is the state that Fosca brings his friend Carlier to; 355). Moral judgements can have no significance at all for an immortal, who sees *everything* done and undone, so that Fosca eventually loses all touch with human morality: 'Savais-je ce que valaient, à leurs yeux, la vie, la mort?' (468). The story of his life (though not necessarily the novel as a whole, which has Régine's problems as a kind of framework) is a strong counterblast to the particular view of interdependence most emphasised in *Le Sang des autres*, which, in spite of its ending, shows the existence of others to be a 'scandal', a 'crime', 'la malédiction originelle'. But if Beauvoir's two wartime novels need to be seen together in that each acts as a corrective to the other, both depend heavily upon the collective situation to teach the individual the basic lessons of human interdependence. One might say without too much over-simplification that whereas earlier the individual was shocked to discover all of the ramifications of the fact that he is really (metaphysically) alone, now he is equally

unpleasantly shocked to realise that in some senses
he can never be (historically) alone at all.

Not that all of the main characters in this
second group of books need to learn this point in
the course of the stories (any more than all in the
earlier group had to learn of their solitude). The
Marxist figures Brunet and Maurice in particular
are naturally shown in *Le Sursis* as having thought
in terms of historical forces well before the war.
Brunet says of the war: 'Elle avait toujours été là,
mais les gens ne le savaient pas encore' (749). And
although Maurice is not certain that war will break
out, he is quite sure what it would represent for
the workers if it did, believing that the
bourgeoisie is afraid of winning a war 'parce que ce
serait la victoire du prolétariat' (743). It is also
true that, in a Humanist as opposed to a Marxist
context, characters in *La Peste* like Rieux, Tarrou
and even Grand are conscious of the interdependence
of human beings before large-scale disaster strikes:
Rieux's profession of doctor and the nature of his
immediate reactions to the first signs of plague
show this; Grand claims early on: '"il faut
s'entr'aider"' (1232); and Tarrou admits, '"je
souffrais déjà de la peste bien avant de connaître
cette ville et cette épidémie"' (1420). Yet all of
the characters who stand in no need of a major
collective catastrophe to bring them to believe in
interdependence are still profoundly affected in the
course of the stories by their experience in
collective situations. The fragments from Tarrou's
diary show that, like Grand, he learns a great deal
during the plague (even if his basic ideas appear to
develop little), while Rieux's attitudes towards men
and their interrelations are obviously elaborated
and refined considerably as a result of the
experience. And although we lose sight of Maurice
too early in *Le Sursis* to say how the war affects
his views, we have a very detailed account of the
evolution of Brunet's attitudes in *La Mort dans
l'âme* and the extracts from *La Dernière Chance*,
where we find that the war situations cause him to
see the whole question of his relations with others
in a radically different light. In short, the
experience of collective situations in these stories
and the consequent exposure to certain extreme forms
of interdependence deeply affect and change even
those characters who are in some measure conscious
of this interdependence from the beginning.

At the other end of the scale, the wartime
novels are characterised by highly memorable

examples of characters drawn into collective
situations with disastrous results, yet neither
having to start with, nor being shown as usefully
acquiring, a clear conception of what is involved,
what forces they are a prey to. Apart from cases
involving children - and one cannot help but think
of the intrinsic and structural significance of the
suffering and death of Judge Othon's son in *La Peste*
- some of the most poignant moments in the books
show naive or inexperienced people caught up in
events not only beyond their control, but also
totally beyond their understanding. One remembers
Marcel's young brother Jacques, killed during a
political demonstration in *Le Sang des autres*; the
young 'typo' shot trying to escape from the Germans
at the end of *La Mort dans l'âme*; the deranged
Charpin's still more chilling death earlier in the
book; the 'postière', loved and brutally abandoned
by Mathieu's friend Pinette; Gros-Louis, the
illiterate shepherd in *Le Sursis*, scarcely able to
believe he is mobilised ('"Quelle guerre?"'), and
failing to see why he should not leave the army the
very moment the crisis is over; the women and
children, the old and sick of Carmona, cast out to
die in *Tous les hommes sont mortels*, because of lack
of food in the city. These are just some of the more
clear-cut examples of innocent victims of
large-scale historical forces, who suffer or die
without any purpose or project of their own being to
blame. The function of such characters is less to
illustrate changes in awareness than to act as a
kind of measure of the strength and extent of the
forces at work in collective situations.

Between these two extremes - of those who know
of human interdependence and the forces of history
to begin with, and those who are bowled along by
those forces without ever being shown as
comprehending them to any important degree - stand
the many characters of this period who are brought
to recognise the extent of interdependence for the
first time; who are forced to acknowledge the
irresistibility of events taking place at the
collective level. These characters reflect in a
particularly clear and direct way the changed moral
perspectives that mark this group of novels as a
whole, although they are not always the central
figures in the books. Indeed, the change of outlook
and awareness involved has different dimensions and
facets and is charted at a number of different
levels as well as through a variety of characters,
major and minor alike. For instance, in the case of

Sarah (who was shown in *L'Age de raison* as the supreme champion of the individual) what we have is one single, striking account of her reactions to finding herself part of a crowd for the first time, namely the stream of refugees fleeing from Paris (MA 1145-54). Charles, the young cripple in *Le Sursis*, is at first convinced that the collective situation of war is strictly the affair of 'les debout' and will in no way affect invalids like himself, but he soon learns that he is to be evacuated from Berck and will be as much caught up in the chain of events as anyone: '"Ils m'auront eu jusqu'au bout"' (762). Charles's realisation is in some respects similar to that of Rambert in *La Peste*:

> 'J'ai toujours pensé que j'étais étranger à cette ville et que je n'avais rien à faire avec vous. Mais maintenant que j'ai vu ce que j'ai vu, je sais que je suis d'ici, que je le veuille ou non. Cette histoire nous concerne tous.' (1389)

It is also similar to that of Paneloux, who, like Charles, begins by thinking that the plague will automatically spare 'les justes' (LP 1297), but by the time of his second sermon is much less prepared to categorise and to think in terms of exceptions: 'Chose curieuse encore, il ne disait plus "vous", mais "nous"' (1401).

La Peste is, of course, a peculiarly fruitful text on which to base study of the change of perspective in question, not least because throughout the book the narrator records the reactions and state of mind of the undifferentiated body of citizens at large ('nos concitoyens'), who are portrayed as shifting their outlook *en masse* in just this way. At first, 'ils oubliaient d'être modestes, voilà tout, et ils pensaient que tout était encore possible pour eux' (1247), but soon 'ils s'aperçurent qu'ils étaient tous, et le narrateur lui-même, pris dans le même sac et qu'il fallait s'en arranger' (1273). Whatever general descriptions of this kind may lack in elaboration and vivacity is more than made up for by the detailed examination not only of Rambert and Paneloux, but also of Blomart and Hélène in *Le Sang des autres*. Hélène, who for a long time seems to refuse to believe that the war has changed anything, finally comes to realise that she too is part of the historical process: '"Je regardais passer l'Histoire! c'était mon histoire. Tout ça m'arrive à

moi"' (301). And Blomart goes some of the way
towards coming to terms with his own personal
scruples when he recognises that he is 'présent à
tous les hommes à travers le monde tout entier, et
séparé d'eux à jamais' (313). There is a revealing
moment in *Le Sursis*, too, when Mathieu's involvement
in the political events of September 1938 is
definitively brought home to him as he reads the
fateful poster announcing his call-up (805).

On the basis of these and numerous other
examples one could go on to give a detailed,
schematised account of different reactions to the
discovery that we are all subject to the forces of
history. It is sufficient here, however, to record
that these novels contain fascinating material
relating not only to crowd psychology and the
reactions of the 'man in the street', but especially
to the ways in which individuals want or resist
absorption into the masses. In the passage near the
beginning of *La Mort dans l'âme* Sarah's horrified
recognition of the nature of crowds is associated
with a fear of losing her individual identity, of
becoming anonymous. The consciousness of this danger
in collective situations is echoed at a number of
points in these novels, perhaps especially by women
characters: Hélène reacts in a similar way at the
end of another fine crowd sequence in *Le Sang des
autres* (268); Régine is constantly preoccupied by
this sort of consideration in *Tous les hommes sont
mortels*; and Odette, in *Le Sursis*, is wary of losing
her identity in a relationship with Mathieu:
'N'importe qui: un homme et une femme qui se
regardaient sur une plage; et la guerre était là,
autour d'eux; elle était descendue en eux et les
rendait semblables aux autres, à tous les autres'
(756). Mathieu himself provides one of the clearest
expressions of the fear of anonymity, as well as of
another common reaction to war, namely the sense
that one's freedom and one's future have suddenly
been taken away:

> il pensait qu'il allait dépouiller ses
> vêtements, sa profession, son identité, partir
> nu pour la plus absurde des guerres, pour une
> guerre perdue d'avance et il se sentait couler
> au fond de l'anonymat; ... plus rien qu'un
> anonyme, sans âge, dont on avait volé l'avenir
> et qui avait devant lui des journées
> imprévisibles. (Surs 832)

(As Rieux remarks in *La Peste*, 'personne ne sera

jamais libre tant qu'il y aura des fléaux'; 1248.)
Indeed, Mathieu's reactions to the Munich crisis and
then to the defeat of France cover many of the whole
range of emotions experienced by different
characters as history erupts into their lives. Above
all, he sees that nothing will ever be the same
again and that a collective situation like war
colours everything in the world.

This all-embracing nature of the forces of
history, together with the earlier point that there
is some fragmentation of general situations in the
stories, yields a further distinctive feature of the
wartime novels. There is a far greater sense of
confusion and puzzlement on the part of characters
now than there was in the pre-war books. As they
become aware of the magnitude of what they are
caught up in, most of the main figures experience a
greater degree of disorientation than did their
earlier counterparts. Mathieu, who is as well
equipped as any to understand what is happening,
looks back on the period covered by *L'Age de raison*
as one when he had a much clearer grasp of events:

> ses difficultés n'étaient jamais qu'avec
> lui-même; il pouvait se dire: 'J'ai eu raison,
> j'ai eu tort'; il pouvait se juger. A présent
> c'était devenu impossible ... Il pensa: 'Je
> pars pour la guerre' et cela ne signifiait
> rien. Quelque chose lui était arrivé qui le
> dépassait. 'Ca n'est pas tant qu'elle me
> dépasse, c'est qu'elle *n'est pas là.*' (Surs
> 1022)

Once more, in his confusion and his very terms he
articulates the feelings of many of the protagonists
in other novels. Rieux, too, notes that 'le fléau
n'est pas à la mesure de l'homme' (LP 1247); and
Blomart's attempt, early on in *Le Sang des autres*,
to restrict himself to work that is 'à une mesure
humaine' is unsuccessful. Even the Marxists, who, as
we have seen, regard the pressures of history as no
novelty and believe that the war is not especially
difficult to understand, find their preconceived
categories and interpretations insufficient to cover
the whole phenomenon, the outstanding example being
that of Brunet.

Generally speaking, then, characters are
overwhelmed, at least for a time, and they have to
struggle to find their bearings in wholly new kinds
of situations, with new terms of reference. And in
the enforced reflections on practical and moral

matters that ensue, they need to consider entities that characters in the pre-war stories gave scarcely any consideration to, namely human *groups* of one kind or another. At the deepest level, the individual stands in the same need of self-justification as ever, but as a result of being subjected, suddenly and inescapably, to the forces of history, he becomes preoccupied with questions about the nature of groups, the interrelations between groups, and his own place in relation to certain groups.

The proliferation of human groups and sub-groups of various sorts in these novels is rather remarkable, and it would be difficult to overestimate their importance to the stories and the moral perspectives that these stories embody. It scarcely needs to be said that in these wartime works nations figure quite prominently, or that the matter of peoples or races is raised through the persecution of the Jews. But we also find that communities within nations sometimes have an important role to play: the city of Oran in *La Peste* is very much an entity in its own right, as is the city of Carmona in *Tous les hommes sont mortels* (its gates, too, are sometimes closed on the world, for reasons of war or plague; 125). A village community is used to some effect by Sartre in *Le Sursis*, and the prisoner-of-war camp is a vitally important type of community later in *Les Chemins de la liberté*. Within or across the boundaries of nation or community, moreover, different kinds of groups are often crucial to the thinking and decisions of the characters: the question of social classes arises whenever Marxists figure in the stories, and trade unions are important in *Le Sang des autres* (56). Inevitably, just as nations must now enter into the moral reckoning, so must the armies within nations. And within the army itself sub-groups cannot be ignored in these novels: officers as opposed to the rank and file, of course, but even different regiments or indeed any other army units. Again, society is occasionally divided up on an entirely different basis, as when Boris sees the war in terms of age-groups: 'ça n'est pas une question de nationalité, c'est une question d'âge' (Surs 1033). Then there are still other groups of great significance that directly owe their existence to specific historical circumstances: any 'Resistance' movements formed in the stories fall into this category, as do smaller and looser groups like the almost random clusters of soldiers to which Mathieu and Brunet belong in Parts I and II of *La Mort dans l'âme* respectively.

In fact, for two main reasons it is useful to stress how these very last groups are formed and maintained. As soon as the defeated French soldiers in Part II of *La Mort dans l'âme* reach what is to be their prison camp at Baccarat, they begin, presumably for their own sense of security, to think in terms of groups, although the basis for these is flimsy in the extreme ('"Nous autres, explique-t-il, on n'est pas dehors"'; 1357). Shortly afterwards the tendency to form groups is seen to be accentuated and the notion of inclusion to be much more restrictive: 'Voici: un groups s'est formé au milieu de cette foule, un groupe de hasard, sans amitié ni vraie solidarité, mais qui se referme déjà contre les autres; Brunet est dedans' (1367). Similarly, the little group of soldiers to which Mathieu belongs in Part I is fortuitously constituted and preserved by no particular bonds: 'Les types se regardaient avec inquiétude: ils n'avaient aucune envie de se séparer, aucune raison de rester ensemble' (1235).

The first important point here is that if the sort of exclusivity that prevails in these cases is generally representative of groups, then we would expect relations between groups to be no more harmonious or successful than the unsatisfactory, competitive relations between individuals that were shown as prevailing in the early novels. Indeed, one of Mathieu's companions, Longin, explicitly makes the comparison: '"Comment veux-tu que les pays s'entendent, si tu les laisses libres? Ils sont comme des personnes, chacun tire de son côté"' (MA 1207). And in doing so he echoes a remark made by an old Frenchman that Gomez meets in New York: '"Les gens et les pays c'est pareil: chacun pour soi"' (1167). It is in fact clear, in general, that one of the main features of these wartime novels is *conflict* between groups of all kinds. *La Peste* is an apparent exception to this pattern, since, unlike any of the other books, it is about just one community. But although Oran is not in conflict with other cities, it faces an external threat, and Camus points out that this brings particular pressures to bear upon pre-existing groups ('soldats, religieux ou prisonniers'; LP 1357). Only when the worst is over do these groups begin re-forming (1442). The second point is that the question of how groups come about in the first place, of whether there is something arbitrary about their formation, is potentially of the greatest relevance to the matter of what attitudes we adopt towards those groups. Although it is no more than one factor, in deciding how much importance to attach to an existing group we are almost certainly influenced by considerations concerning its origins.

These two threads can be drawn together, initially at least, if we pursue for a moment the analogy between the role of metaphysics in the pre-war books and the role of history in these. In Mathieu's first section of *La Mort dans l'âme*, he muses on what it was, and is, to be French:

> c'était tellement naturel d'être français, c'était le moyen le plus simple, le plus économique de se sentir universel. Il n'y avait rien à expliquer: c'était aux autres, aux Allemands, aux Anglais, aux Belges d'expliquer par quelle malchance ou par quelle faute ils n'étaient pas tout à fait des hommes. A présent, la France s'est couchée à la renverse et nous la voyons, nous voyons une grande machine détraquée et nous pensons: 'C'était ça.' Ça: un accident de terrain, un accident de l'histoire. Nous sommes encore français, mais ça n'est plus naturel. Il a suffi d'un accident pour nous faire comprendre que nous étions accidentels. (1178)

One might say that the point here is that history (acting through large-scale collective situations like war) reveals to us the contingency of nations, just as metaphysics shows us the contingency of individual human beings. Furthermore, just as the suggestion was that the (contingent) individual has little meaningful and lasting contact with his fellows and is mostly in a state of conflict with them, so now the implicit view is that, given the existence of arbitrary entities called 'nations', there is nothing surprising about the fact that they are more or less permanently in hostile array. (*Tous les hommes sont mortels* reminds us that this is not merely a mid-twentieth-century phenomenon.) But the close parallel between the roles of metaphysics and history cannot be pressed beyond this point. The basic unit in the wartime period is not the group, but still the individual, so that the issue of the status of nations, for instance, is not treated here in the way that it would be in a work of political theory. The key question is that of how individuals come to regard the nation, how they see themselves

in relation to their own and other nations. To
complicate matters further, there is also the
question of how they see themselves in relation to
non-national groups of different kinds that
international conflict brings into prominence.

In other words, our authors dwell upon the
existence of groups less because these are entities
of intrinsic interest than because they now provide
the terms of reference, and to some extent the
subject-matter, of the moral choices of individuals.
Not that individuals' choices are confined to
pre-existing or randomly-formed groups: they are
free to create for themselves new groups with
specific purposes. Thus much of the interest of Part
II of *La Mort dans l'âme* centres on Brunet's
attempt to form a brand new Communist cell in rather
unfavourable circumstances. Indeed, in a number of
major cases apart from that of Brunet, the forming
of a special group is an integral part of the story,
and is preceded by lively moral discussion of ends
and means. One thinks particularly of the Resistance
movement in *Le Sang des autres* and of Tarrou's
'formations sanitaires' in *La Peste*, but these are
only the most memorable examples. In any case, the
central point at stake is that, whether or not they
need to create groups of their own, individuals are
now almost always obliged to consider with some
degree of urgency to which group or groups they
belong, and perhaps to evaluate the importance of
their membership of one against their membership of
another.

By taking the most obvious example of all, we
can gain a very simple, schematic idea of what these
problems amount to for the moral agent and of the
range of reactions possible. Whether or not the very
existence of France and Germany is contingent, it is
certainly a contingent matter whether one happens to
have been born French or German. Hence in the
context of the defeat of France, a Frenchman may
wish that he had not been born French, or even
deplore his bad luck in not having been born German,
in the way that Schwartz does in *La Mort dans l'âme*
(1178). Interestingly, Schwartz is an Alsatian, and
the Alsatians in the prisoner-of-war camp at
Baccarat are effectively given the choice of
remaining French or deciding that they are 'really'
Germans (1418). In the event, Gartiser and his
companions duly say 'Heil Hitler' and are liberated.
Ivich (unlike Boris, whose status is exactly the
same as hers) adopts a theoretically similar stance,
regardless of the fact that her Russian parents have

had her naturalised: '"Puisqu'ils ne devaient pas le faire, c'est comme s'ils n'avaient rien fait du tout"' (MA 1195). She and the Alsatians, then, 'decide not to be French', while the majority of characters in these novels acknowledge in some way or other (explicitly or implicitly, willingly or unwillingly, and with varying degrees of clear-headedness and firmness) their French nationality, or its equivalent. In *La Peste*, of course, it is to the city of Oran that characters have to decide whether they belong, and the sharpest example is that of Rambert. It is an unfortunate accident that he is present in the city when plague breaks out (just as it is a matter of luck whether one is born in France or Germany) and he regards himself at first as 'étranger à cette ville'. But as we have seen, he later changes his mind and claims: '"je sais que je suis d'ici, que je le veuille ou non"' (1389). His case is the diametrical opposite of those of Ivich and the Alsatians: he could reasonably continue to maintain that he is not Oranais but does not, whereas they have no sound reason for disclaiming French nationality yet do so.

In addition to these two extremes and all the intermediate points on the scale, there is a separate scale for those who are neither French nor German. This is represented, for example, by the conflicting views of Ritchie the American and Gomez the Spaniard in the United States, at the beginning of *La Mort dans l'âme*. Ritchie is relatively detached from the struggle in Europe and does not strongly take sides at all: '"La paix, dit Ritchie, n'est ni démocratique ni nazie: c'est la paix"' (1142). Gomez, on the other hand, utterly refuses to remain detached (1158), even though he has some difficulty in knowing exactly what attitude to strike, in view of France's failure to support intervention in the Spanish Civil War. Their positions raise questions concerning the very possibility of neutrality or abstention, about which there will be more to be said when we examine this sort of dilemma specifically from the individual's viewpoint. It has been sufficient initially to show schematically what issues arise with regard to nations, and to emphasise the central role of the individual's choices and decisions even on this plane.

As soon as one leaves behind this simple national model for understanding the moral perspectives of the period, the very proliferation of groups rapidly becomes a vital factor and complicates matters in a number of different ways. For one thing there is the matter of the *size* of the various groups that enter into the individual's terms of reference. So long as one is thinking of a conflict between groups of more or less the same size (say, between the nations of France and Germany), the individual may be presented with a simple choice in which the alternatives are mutually exclusive. But once there is also awareness of groups of a different dimension and the need to choose between these too, then the permutations and the difficulties are greatly increased. This immediately poses, for instance, the question of the relationship between the two acts of choice, and that of their relative importance.

If this account seems too theoretical and abstract, one has only to think of Fosca's development in Parts I and II of *Tous les hommes sont mortels*. Much of the fascination of the 'early' phases in his life lies in the way in which, as he tries to find where he really belongs, the size of the groups to which he commits himself one after another increases at each turn in the story. At first, of course, his commitment is wholly to the city of Carmona ('Seule sur son rocher, Carmona était un îlot perdu au milieu de la mer'; 133), although Beauvoir already makes it clear that this is a choice of Carmona over any smaller groups like Fosca's own family. But he relatively soon begins to realise that his city is too small a unit either to be entirely viable on its own or to be of any great value in itself ('il y avait en Italie cent autres villes qui se dressaient sur leurs rochers, aussi orgueilleuses, aussi inutiles'; 188). Consequently, in contrast with someone like Antoine, he now looks to Italy as the unit to be worked for and defended ('"La gloire de Carmona compte peu à côté du salut de l'Italie"'; 204), and actually sees his earlier attachment to Carmona as having been an obstacle to the unification of Italy that he now seeks. Predictably, however, Italy too turns out to be too small for Fosca's ambitions and for some time he hopes that throwing all his weight behind Charles the Fifth and his vast empire will provide an arena of the dimensions appropriate to his aims and powers. Yet even when America is included within his scope, Fosca is left dissatisfied, since he is forced to recognise that the kind of unit and unity he has been seeking is a spurious one: 'Carmona était trop petite, l'Italie trop petite, et l'Univers n'existait pas ... "L'Univers était ailleurs, toujours ailleurs! Et il n'est nulle part: il n'y a que des hommes, des hommes à jamais divisés"' (313). There are a number of different 'morals' that might be drawn from this development, especially as one has always to make allowance for the fact that Fosca is immortal. But, for present purposes, what is important is that it registers the existence of certain vital questions concerning the relative size of different groups to which the individual may belong. To a group of what size is it most appropriate that individuals should commit themselves? And what implications does any decision have for their attitude towards groups of different sizes?

These matters are raised just as much by the case of Blomart in *Le Sang des autres* as by that of Fosca. But whereas Fosca's development is, at least in this connection, linear and relatively simple, Blomart's evolution is complex, and thereby richer in moral significance. The emphasis in his case falls rather more upon the way in which commitments to groups of different sizes conflict with one another than upon a general outward extension of terms of reference. There certainly *is* such an extension, but it is a much less clear-cut and smooth one than with Fosca. Unlike Fosca, for instance, Blomart has to make a positive break with his family in order to act out his first real commitment to a group; that is, when he joins the working class and the Communist Party (34). And there is a long period, following the death of Jacques at a political demonstration, when Blomart deliberately *reduces* his sphere of action, working only at the trade-union level (80). The Communist Paul, however, interprets Blomart's new preoccupations as essentially nationalistic ones ('"Comme si la France pouvait séparer son destin de celui du monde!"'; 88), and he is right to the extent that Blomart reacts very unfavourably, for example, to the possibility of French intervention in the Spanish Civil War (148). In fact, it is only when Blomart clearly realises that to think in national terms is inadequate that the way begins to be paved for the final stages in the development of his outlook. He eventually learns his lesson that to pledge and confine oneself to action on one particular scale is invariably to be responsible for injustices on some different scale: 'je regardais sans honte les camarades du syndicat, mais ma bouche se desséchait quand je pensais à nos frères d'Espagne ou d'Autriche' (158). Blomart's story, of course, shades off into all kinds of other moral issues that have nothing specifically to do with groups, but his evolution tells us more than Fosca's about the painful incompatibility between certain commitments and, above all, begins to open up new questions concerning different *types* of group.

From the account of Blomart's development, it is plain that it would not be adequate - and might be quite misleading - to describe the position he arrives at during the war as a choice in favour of France. His is a choice of active anti-Fascism, as opposed to collaboration or pacifism (rather as Rambert's later position in *La Peste*, in spite of talk of 'cette ville', would be better described as a decision to fight against the plague than as a determination to fight for Oran). And it reminds us that the main problems facing many characters in these novels may in fact be seen as cross-cutting the national boundaries that we started from. Indeed, a choice specifically in favour of French nationality here is occasionally to be looked upon with as much suspicion as were the decisions of the Alsatians and Ivich *not* to be French. Thus Monsieur Birnenschatz in *Le Sursis*, who is a Polish Jew, now claims to be French above all else - '"Qu'est-ce que c'est que ça: nous, Juifs? demanda-t-il. Connais pas. Je suis français, moi"' (816) - and refuses all solidarity with Jews in Germany (821). It is in order to save his own skin that he chooses nationality rather than race or religion as the crucial criterion for distinguishing between people. Whatever the rights or wrongs of his attitude, the example shows that we not only make moral choices between different groups of the same type, but also decide which types of groups (and dilemmas) take precedence over others. Just as Birnenschatz decides that national considerations have priority over racial ones, so Zézette has to decide whether, first and foremost, she belongs to the group 'women' or to that of 'socialists' (Surs 1009-13). The crux of the matter again is the very concept of moral perspectives, for what individuals consider the alternatives to be is just as revealing as which of those alternatives they opt for. With these wartime novels, to talk about the conflict between France and Germany is to talk about a general framework of reference forced upon almost all characters, but we need to remember, too, that it is a framework that individuals fill with their own moral content and interpret in the light of the moral elements and conflicts that most preoccupy them.

In this connection, it is important to recognise that if the common view of the Franco-German conflict as a struggle between democracy and Fascism (or even Good and Evil) is a relatively unproblematical one, another view sometimes embodied in these stories is altogether more troublesome. The attempt by Marxist characters to superimpose the categories and structures of the class war upon the groupings and events of the Second World War is anything but a conspicuous success. At a certain static level - for instance, in the identification of army officers with the ruling bourgeoisie - it may work out tolerably well, if only because it tends to be self-verifying. But beyond this, an assimilation of the Second World War to the class war is not shown to be a particularly attractive proposition. Maurice struggles with precisely this problem even before the war proper begins, for after his early optimism ('ce serait la victoire du prolétariat') he begins to realise that the coincidence between the two sorts of war may not be a perfect one:

> La guerre était une longue, longue route, il ne fallait pas trop y penser, sinon on finissait par trouver que rien n'avait de sens, même pas la fin, même pas le retour avec le fusil au poing. Une longue, longue route. Et peut-être qu'il crèverait à moitié chemin, comme s'il n'avait eu d'autre but que de se faire trouer la peau pour défendre les usines Schneider ou le coffre de M. de Wendel. (Surs 832)

And if there is not a match at all points, then the Marxist will be left with awkward questions of priorities to solve. That such questions exist is acknowledged in *Le Sursis* by the fact that we overhear snatches of conversation where they are raised. Gros-Louis hears a man coming out of a bar saying, '"Nous avons la guerre au cul et tu viens nous parler de syndicalisme!"' (768). Then later he is present when some disreputable Marseillais 'discuss' the same matter: '"Moi j'aime mieux la guerre que la grève, dit Daisy ... Pendant la guerre, fini les grèves, dit-elle sévèrement. Tout le monde travaille"' (879). The issues involved, moreover, are ones with which we are already familiar from *Le Sang des autres*.

One thing to be said in favour of Brunet, the main Marxist figure of this period, is that he is not a man to slur over questions of priority of this kind. To begin with, he is completely and utterly committed to the Communist Party. In the way that we have become acquainted with, he attaches importance to it at the expense of all other groups: for the most part, his non-Marxist colleagues in the French army mean little to him (MA 1389), and he admits that his work would leave him no time for any family life (MA 1448). Yet the whole point about Brunet in *Les Chemins de la liberté* as it stands is that his attitude is shown as impossible to sustain in the particular circumstances of the war. His long and acrimonious arguments with Schneider in *La Mort dans l'âme* usually centre on the matter of the Germano-Soviet pact. Schneider has left the Party precisely because of this alliance, and for him it is obviously a major obstacle to any simple identification of the struggle against Fascism with that against capitalism:

> 'Le P.C. n'est pas plus favorable que les nazis aux démocraties capitalistes, quoique pour d'autres raisons. Tant qu'il a été possible d'imaginer une alliance de l'U.R.S.S. et des démocraties de l'Ouest, vous avez choisi pour plate-forme la défense des libertés politiques contre la dictature fasciste. Ces libertés sont illusoires, tu le sais mieux que moi. Aujourd'hui, les démocraties sont à genoux, l'U.R.S.S. s'est rapprochée de l'Allemagne, Pétain a pris le pouvoir, c'est dans une société fasciste ou fascisante que le Parti doit continuer son travail.' (1400)

Brunet can overcome this obstacle only by claiming to know about the future: '"Je sais que l'U.R.S.S. entrera tôt ou tard dans la danse ... les travailleurs russes ne permettront pas que le prolétariat européen reste sous la botte nazie"' (1422). Consequently, his disillusionment with the Party dates from the moment of his discovery, in 'Drôle d'amitié', that the official Party line is now that Russia and Germany have the same fundamental interests and that this fact is the basis of the non-aggression pact (DA 1495). His identification of anti-Fascism and anti-capitalism has proved far too simple to fit the political realities and eventually, deprived of one of his main philosophical bearings, he has only the dying Schneider-Vicarios to turn to in his confusion: '"Le Parti, je m'en fous: tu es mon seul ami"' (DA 1534). In the later extracts from *La Dernière Chance* Brunet is seen to have generalised this reaction, distinguishing between the Party in the abstract sense and its members ('les camarades'): he tells Mathieu that he now finds it impossible to follow the Party line when this involved acting *against* 'les camarades' in any way (DCh 1644).

Brunet, then, is a striking example of a character for whom loyalty to a particular group is of the first importance, yet proves to be considerably more difficult than he had supposed because of the existence of different types of group which bear a somewhat problematic relation to the original one. In certain respects he is unlike many of the main figures of this period, but his eventual dilemma is of a sort very characteristic of the wartime novels in general, where pre-existing and newly-formed groups alike vie for the individual's allegiance; and where conflicts and tensions both between groups of roughly similar kinds and between groups of entirely different kinds bulk large in all moral reflection, as a result of the dominant collective situations.

Chapter Six

PROBLEMS OF RESPONSIBILITY AND ACTION

So far we have recorded the importance of problems
relating to the status of groups, which particular
group and which *kind* of group the individual chooses
to belong to, and the conflicting claims made by
different groups and sub-groups. If we now look a
little more closely into certain aspects of the very
idea of belonging to a group, we shall locate
another range of considerations given prominence in
these novels and forming an essential part of the
moral perspectives of the period.

Deciding which particular group to commit
oneself to, or to regard oneself as belonging to, is
one thing, but actually belonging to that group in
the fullest sense may be another matter. There are
many characters in these stories who commit
themselves to a group, or try to do so, and yet
still cannot bring themselves to believe or feel
that they really belong. And sometimes, regardless
of whether or not they themselves are especially
conscious of the problem, individuals are seen as in
some way alien by other members of the group. Fosca
obviously needs to be mentioned in this connection,
since *Tous les hommes sont mortels* contains some of
the most vivid accounts of a man's estrangement from
his fellows. But the fact is, of course, that Fosca
is not a man at all in the ordinary sense. His
failure to find somewhere where he can feel he
belongs is directly due to his immortality and all
that derives from it. In all other cases, alienation
appears to be bound up with the individuals'
origins, with their status as intellectuals, or with
the business of leadership of the group - or perhaps
most commonly with some inextricable combination of
two or three of these factors.

The matter of origins is probably the one upon
which moral issues proper take the least grip, but

it does have a certain significance in the cases of, for instance, Brunet, Blomart and Tarrou. Brunet and Blomart are both trying to 'belong' to the working classes *despite* their solid bourgeois backgrounds. This is shown as preoccupying Brunet early in *Le Sursis* (748). And there are at least two explicit discussions of the topic in *Le Sang des autres*: Jacques maintains that there will always be an essential difference between Blomart and the workers he is joining ('"Un ouvrier désire *sa* libération; ce n'est jamais que la libération d'autrui que tu désires"'; 24), and Marcel's argument later is virtually the same (37). In this respect, parallels with Tarrou in *La Peste* are not difficult to see. In a long scene with Rieux towards the end of Part IV, Tarrou explains why (like Blomart) he left home at a tender age and made the break with a highly respected bourgeois father. It is true that with Tarrou there does not seem to be any specific commitment to the working classes and that his decision has much less to do with political considerations than with particular views on justice ('"J'ai cru que la société où je vivais était celle qui reposait sur la condamnation à mort"'; 1423). But there is a clear sense in which he, too, opts to join those whose origins are much less privileged than his own. Equally, in spite of his commitment, Tarrou, like Brunet and Blomart, is something of a lonely figure who stands a little apart from the crowd rather than in it: '"J'étais avec eux et j'étais pourtant seul"' (1424).

Nevertheless, the point about all three of these characters is that while their origins may be shown to have marked them psychologically and personally, those origins cannot be seen as ultimately constituting a moral blemish. Just as what is of moral significance regarding nations is not their contingent origins but the ways in which people react to them, so the background that individuals are born into is not to be seen as something that reflects upon them morally: what is important is the attitude that they adopt towards that background. Blomart's answer to Marcel, that, alienated from the workers or not, he will have done his very best, is after all a perfectly fair one.

If characters fail to be fully assimilated into the groups to which they are trying to belong, the main moral issues raised by this phenomenon have much more to do with their being intellectuals and/or leaders of some kind. From early on in *Le Sursis* we find Brunet associating the matter of his origins with that of being an intellectual:

> *Intellectuel. Bourgeois.* Les aimer. Les aimer
> tous et toutes, chacun et chacune, sans
> distinction. Il pensa: 'Je ne devrais même pas
> *vouloir* les aimer, ça devrait se trouver comme
> ça, par nécessité, comme on respire.'
> *Intellectuel. Bourgeois. Séparé pour toujours.*
> J'aurai beau faire, nous n'aurons jamais les
> mêmes souvenirs. (747)

And since he has written regularly for *L'Humanité*
and is invariably looked to for political
interpretations and instructions, we certainly see
him as one of the Communist Party's intellectuals.
It cannot be said, however, that Blomart is quite so
consistently presented as an intellectual. In the
early discussions with Jacques, for example, it is
the latter who is shown as the intellectual, with
Blomart as the practical man of action ('Il
m'agaçait un peu avec ses subtilités
philosophiques'; SA 24). Yet it is to Blomart that
Denise later goes for an opinion on her novel; and,
perhaps most important of all, he does speak at
trade union meetings and in general regard himself
as articulating trade unionists' aims ('c'était pour
eux qu'il parlait ... Par sa bouche, tous chantaient
en choeur'; 87).

In fact, this last point is of particular
substance, in that it provides an explicit
illustration of something quite characteristic of
the heroes in these novels. The question of whether
they are 'intellectuals' or not could easily become
an otiose terminological one, but now we have
located a rather specialised sense of the word –
something like 'spokesman' – which clearly brings
out the link between this question and that of
leadership. A recurring phenomenon in these books is
that of the main figure who believes (or perhaps is
being actively encouraged to believe) that he knows
more than the majority of the members of his group;
or at least is more able than they to spell out what
they all know. This frequently focuses attention
upon the issue of how willing or eager the character
is to employ his special knowledge or talent in the
service of the group. Among those who are willing,
there are significant differences of degree, as the
cases of Brunet and Blomart show: Blomart is modest,
makes only minimal claims to extra knowledge, and
largely confines himself to the role of spokesman,
whereas Brunet claims to know more about even the

desires and needs of his colleagues than they do, and imposes himself upon the group to an extraordinary extent. But the matters being raised are remarkably similar across all of these books and constitute a good measure of how much perspectives have changed since the pre-war period.

In *La Peste* we have two main characters who stand out above the bulk of the citizens of Oran. It is not uncommon for Tarrou to make breathtaking claims about the extent of his knowledge ('"Oui, Rieux, je sais tout de la vie, vous le voyez bien"'; 1425), but in any case he divides people into those who know about the plague and those who do not (1420). By this time the question of origins as the source of estrangement is left far behind, for even Rieux (who was brought up in poverty), although temperamentally more modest than Tarrou, shares his claim to special knowledge: 'Car il savait ce que cette foule en joie ignorait, et qu'on peut lire dans les livres, que le bacille de la peste ne meurt ni ne disparaît jamais' (1474). The final scenes of the book, with Rieux wandering sadly among the joyous crowds, show how lonely knowledge of this kind makes him. Moreover, there is a sense in which both Rieux and Tarrou are acting as spokesmen for the citizens of Oran, namely in recording their story in writing. Tarrou's diary (from which Rieux quotes quite extensively on five occasions) is much more personal, even eccentric, than Rieux's 'objective' record, but it is ultimately the same kind of enterprise, 'une sorte de chronique' (1236). Rieux's account is an explicit endeavour to speak 'au nom de tous' and to suppress his own personal reactions, though paradoxically the very attempt sets him, like Tarrou, rather apart from the community as a kind of witness.

The very last thing that Mathieu sets out to do when he is drawn into collective situations – and he provides us with the most detailed and complex case-study of alienation from the group in any of these novels – is to speak on behalf of others. Yet the little group of soldiers to which he belongs in *La Mort dans l'âme* certainly expect something like this of him. If it is not precisely a question of his being a spokesman, they tend to look up to him because of his education and expect him to pronounce authoritatively on problems that worry them ('A la fin de chaque discussion, ils lui demandaient son arbitrage parce qu'il avait de l'instruction'; 1182). Mathieu strenuously refuses this role and, more generally, he never succeeds in identifying

himself totally with his fellow soldiers. Even in *Le
Sursis*, although he is drawn to those mobilised with
him, he is conscious of a gap or barrier: 'Mathieu
pensait: "Ils ne m'aiment pas, ils me trouvent
fier." Pourtant il se sentait attiré par eux'
(1104). And after the defeat of France in *La Mort
dans l'âme* he is quite unable to resolve the
contradiction in his own attitudes, oscillating ever
more strongly between feeling that he belongs with
the men and feeling cut off from them. There is a
particularly telling sequence where he eventually
reacts to the drunken revelries of his companions by
trying to become as drunk as they are, only to fail
miserably: '"Tu ne fais rien comme tout le monde,
poursuivit Longin. Même quand tu te soûles, c'est
pas comme nous"' (1255).

It is not difficult to see how these
characteristics of so many main figures –
estrangement from other members of the group, an
intellectuality or special knowledge that leads to a
role as spokesman or representative of some sort –
have moral implications. As with the matter of
origins, the crux of the matter is how the
individual *sees* the rather special position he
holds. If we still leave aside for the moment the
non-human Fosca, Brunet is almost certainly the only
example of a major character here who regards his
own separate position as so important that he comes
close to despising more ordinary members of his
group. From the very beginning of Part II of *La Mort
dans l'âme* (when he describes a rather harmless man
whose privacy he has invaded as 'ce gros mollasson
qui s'obstine à vivre, qui vivra sous tous les
régimes, humble, mystifié, coriace, qui vivra pour
rien'; 1346-47), he is shown as viewing even those
with whom (or *on* whom) he will be working as some
kind of substance to be moulded, as 'le matériau'.
Schneider, who, in spite of a far greater
willingness to identify with the soldiers, is
himself by no means fully assimilated into the group
(DA 1470), is quick to notice and comment that
Brunet has little sympathy or respect for the men
(MA 1346; 1379), and even despises them (1424). But,
of course, much of the interest of Brunet's story
lies in the way in which he is forced to soften his
attitude. Before the end of *La Mort dans l'âme*, he
is already castigating his assistants in the very
terms that Schneider used of him:

'Vous méprisez vos camarades. Eh bien, retenez
ça: un type du Parti ne méprise personne ...

Vous ne ferez rien d'eux si vous les méprisez. Tâchez d'abord de les comprendre: ils ont la mort dans l'âme, ces gars-là, ils ne savent plus où donner de la tête; ils seront au premier qui leur fera confiance.' (1432)

Very different from Brunet, Rieux is not only never even tempted to despise his fellows: as we noted, he sees his special position of 'chroniqueur' as involving a moral commitment *in favour of* those less articulate than himself:

Rieux décida alors de rédiger le récit qui s'achève ici, pour ne pas être de ceux qui se taisent, pour témoigner en faveur de ces pestiférés, pour laisser du moins un souvenir de l'injustice et de la violence qui leur avaient été faites, et pour dire simplement ce qu'on apprend au milieu des fléaux, qu'il y a dans les hommes plus de choses à admirer que de choses à mépriser. (LP 1473)

And Mathieu's complicated attitude appears to lie somewhere between these two extremes. He is not always patient with the shortcomings of his fellow soldiers, but explicitly claims not to despise them. Certainly, any disgust he feels is aimed at himself as much as at others: 'Ils ne lui faisaient pas horreur, ces vaincus qui buvaient la défaite jusqu'à la lie. S'il avait horreur de quelqu'un, c'était de lui-même' (MA 1249). Nevertheless, he cannot altogether prevent himself from judging his fellows, or perhaps more importantly, *from seeming* to:

Mais il aurait dû prévoir que la honte et le scandale entreraient avec lui. A cause de lui ces types avaient pris conscience d'eux-mêmes; il ne parlait plus leur langage et pourtant il était devenu sans le vouloir leur juge et leur témoin. (1253)

In the end, however, all of these considerations concerning the way in which characters see themselves and fellow members of their group merge into more agonising moral problems. The protagonists' very particular positions within their groups and their degree of alienation from the ordinary members either render their own personal dilemmas more acute, or open out into general questions concerning leadership.

In both a narrow sense of the term (the person

actually giving orders within the group) and a more
general one (giving a lead to others), leadership is
a vital theme in these novels, a prominent element
in moral perspectives that take the idea of the
group as a crucial term of reference. Fosca (whose
immortality can be forgotten for these precise
purposes), Brunet, Blomart are all leaders in the
narrowest and most specific sense of the word, and,
allowing for the superficial difference of
situation, so too are Rieux and Tarrou in *La Peste*.
Even Mathieu, by *La Dernière Chance*, has become a
kind of leader in his prisoner-of-war camp, although
he tries to deny this fact (1641). Real political
leaders like Daladier, Chamberlain and Hitler come
into *Le Sursis*, just as Charles V figures in *Tous
les hommes sont mortels*. Furthermore, when we take
only a slightly broader view and think of secondary
as well as central characters, it becomes clear that
relatively little can be said about groups in these
novels without reference to the notion of some men
leading others. A significant sequence on the
trivial matter of putting cigarettes into a common
pool, for instance, depicts, in *La Mort dans l'âme*,
the moment at which Brunet emerges as a leader ('Ils
comprennent vaguement qu'ils sont en train de se
donner un chef'; 1383). Neither here nor, it seems,
anywhere else in these novels is the need for
leaders seriously questioned and, remarkably, Brunet
even succeeds in turning this particular situation
into the subject of a *moral* imperative. Indeed, his
continual insistence on discipline among the
soldiers ('Il faudra une discipline de fer'; 1351)
becomes almost an end in itself: he is not quite
sure what exactly he should be doing with his
Communist colleagues, but he is certain that
self-discipline and self-respect must be maintained
at all costs.

Those leading the fight against the plague in
Oran also acknowledge the need for discipline, for
rules and regulations. Judge Othon, for instance,
considers that he must set an example by obeying
them to the letter (LP 1391); and Rieux, very much
against his nature, considers himself obliged to use
force, if necessary, to ensure that regulations are
adhered to:

> Avant la peste, on le recevait comme un
> sauveur. Il allait tout arranger avec trois
> pilules et une seringue, et on lui serrait le
> bras en le conduisant le long des couloirs.
> C'était flatteur, mais dangereux. Maintenant,

> au contraire,il se présentait avec des soldats,
> et il fallait des coups de crosse pour que la
> famille se décidât à ouvrir. (LP 1376)

But then it is quite unmistakably in the interests
of the citizens as a whole that regulations should
be obeyed, and evidently reasonable that the
regulations should be drawn up by those with
greatest knowledge of the situation. In this
respect, as in many others, the position in *La Peste*
is outstandingly clear-cut. Rieux and his immediate
colleagues indisputably have the extra knowledge and
technique to combat the plague and, on certain
conditions that would be difficult to formulate but
are in any case fulfilled here, they have a right in
the eyes of any rational person to go ahead and
combat it in the ways they consider best. In the
second half of *La Mort dans l'âme* the ends are not
nearly so clear and, what is more, whether Brunet
has extra knowledge or not is much more open to
question. He certainly has something over and above
most other members of the group (namely, the
features of character that make him what one might
call a 'natural' leader), yet whether this amounts
to knowledge is precisely the question upon which
the later part of his story turns. Up to the end of
La Mort dans l'âme, it looks as if events may prove
him right: as Brunet alone has predicted, the train
turns out to be taking the defeated French soldiers
to camps in Germany (although already Brunet has
mixed feelings about being proved right; 1442). In
'Drôle d'amitié', on the other hand, his whole
theoretical and moral edifice crumbles when someone
more recently in touch with Party headquarters
(Chalais) appears and convinces Brunet that his
'knowledge' is mistaken.

If there are certain problems concerning the
special knowledge that puts one in the position of
being some kind of leader, there are others in
relation to how one uses or abuses that knowledge.
Hence the traditional question of whether the leader
is justified in lying to the led is raised in these
novels. It is suggested that the principle guiding
Brunet for most of the period covered - expressed in
his claim that the Party and the truth are one and
the same thing - is incompatible with absolute
honesty towards those one leads, for Brunet is first
tempted (on the matter of Schneider's 'guilt') to
set aside questions of truthfulness in the general
interests of 'les camarades', and then comes to
believe, to his confusion, that the Party will

always have to lie to its members (DCh 1645). In *Tous les hommes sont mortels*, moreover, Fosca deceives his own men as well as the enemy on at least one major occasion (164), and he constantly finds it necessary to lie to his subjects or colleagues on the topic of his immortality. Indeed, in spite of the fanciful nature of his story, Fosca, with special knowledge of various kinds that his subjects do not share, is a particularly sharp example of the leader manipulating the masses in the pursuit of aims of which they are not always fully aware. Yet the immortal Fosca is scarcely more unscrupulous in this respect than the real political leaders portrayed by Sartre in *Le Sursis*, who tell the masses only what they want them to know. The very last comment in the book is left to Daladier, who, believing that the crowds awaiting his return from Munich are there to howl at him, discovers that they are cheering: 'Il se tourna vers Léger et dit entre ses dents: "Les cons!"' (1133).

Another way in which leaders may abuse their privileged position is shown in *La Mort dans l'âme*, where the officers flee at dead of night, abandoning their men to the approaching Germans (1233). Yet the officers of the 'chasseurs' who make their last stand in the church tower at the end of Part I are with them almost up to the end, and the men will have nothing said against them. There can be no doubt about the message that leaders should, in appropriate ways, remain with their men, and provided that they do so there is presumably little reason for despising or hating them, as a number of characters in the novels do. Zézette actually exposes the naiveté of Maurice's attitude in this respect in *Le Sursis*: '"Même qu'il serait officemar, dit Zézette, il peut y laisser sa peau comme les copains"' (742). This issue is even taken one stage further in *Le Sang des autres*. The framework for the whole of the book is a dilemma that faces Blomart as a Resistance leader (he is asked for a decision on the first page and gives it on the last), but one lesson that he has just learned is that it can sometimes be positively *wrong* for a leader to be with his men:

> 'Vous voulez que j'envoie les copains risquer leur peau et que je reste à siroter mon café? J'aurais du mal à me supporter.'
> Denise me regarda avec blâme: 'Vous vous occupez trop de vous,' dit-elle.
> Ce mot m'a mordu. Elle a raison. C'est

peut-être parce que je suis un bourgeois, il
faut toujours que je m'occupe de moi.
    'Vos scrupules personnels ne nous intéressent
pas,' reprend-elle durement. 'Nous nous sommes
confiés à vous comme à un chef qui fait passer
le parti avant tout: vous n'avez pas le droit
de nous trahir.' (289)

By this stage the wheel has come full circle on the
issue of leadership: betrayal is seen, in certain
circumstances, as insisting on being with the men
rather than keeping oneself apart. It seems that a
certain measure of alienation from the majority of
members of the group is indispensable to a
successful enactment of the role of leader.
    In any case, it is apparent that one has
difficulty in talking for long about groups and
leaders in the context of the kind of catastrophic
situations described in these novels without
questions of *responsibility* being raised, and these
can take many forms. Since group-conflicts are
involved, it is possible to ask, for instance, which
group is responsible or to blame. But this specific
problem occupies little if any place in the stories
- perhaps another measure of the fact that, however
much the novels are bound up with history, the
preoccupations they mirror are by no means exactly
those of historians. This is not to say that no
answer to the problem can be inferred from the
works: doubtless, the general view of our authors,
at this level, would be that while Germany was
largely responsible for the outbreak of war, France
(with other nations) must bear *some* share of blame
for allowing events in the pre-war years to take the
particular course that they did. This general view
even has a certain importance as the broad framework
within which more specific questions of
responsibility are aired. But it receives in itself
scarcely any explicit treatment in the stories,
which, as already suggested, focus above all on
relations between the individual and the group.
    Accordingly, one major cluster of moral
preoccupations centres on the question of whether
(or to what extent, or how) individuals (and *which*
individuals) are responsible for any disasters
suffered by the group to which they belong. We saw
that in the pre-war fiction the matter of the
individual's responsibility for himself began to
come to the fore as he tried to resolve the question
of self-justification in one way or another. Now,
however, the scale of his major moral problems is

much vaster, for when the individual finds himself in a (disastrous) collective situation, one thing at stake is his responsibility for what has happened to him *and* a large number of others. The complexities of matters like this are so great that it is hardly surprising that no clear answers emerge from this group of novels. While various characters hold strong views on the issue of the individual's responsibility for the fate of the group, it is the very proliferation and confrontation of such views that constitutes one of the main features of the books. It is no accident that moral debates, arguments, disagreements or dialogue in general are so much more prominent here than in the pre-war stories. One reason why these are so memorable is that they offer no facile solutions, but rather display the complex range of possible answers to a complex question.

Firstly, to talk of *any* single individual's responsibility for his group is misleading: much is bound up with who the individual is, or which sub-group he belongs to. A question that immediately arises out of earlier discussions, for instance, is that of the extent to which the *leaders* of a group must bear special responsibility for what it does and what befalls it. At a crucial moment in *Le Sursis* the opposing views of Birnenschatz and Brunet are juxtaposed, with the former claiming that the fate of Europe is in Hitler's hands and the latter suggesting that 'ce qu'il y a dans la tête d'Hitler n'a aucune espèce d'importance' (1000). Other leaders like Daladier naturally hold Hitler responsible, yet later some French soldiers affect to blame Daladier himself rather than Hitler for the war:

> 'Il ne voulait pas nous faire la guerre, dit Moûlu: c'est nous qu'on a été la lui déclarer.' 'Attends un peu: c'est même pas nous; Daladier, il a même pas consulté la Chambre.' (MA 1436)

In any case, it seems rather invidious to single out politicians as such when apportioning blame, and Schneider is not being entirely extravagant when he classes Brunet himself with the political leaders (MA 1425).

However broadly or narrowly the class of leaders may be drawn, because the ordinary soldier or citizen is, by definition, not to be regarded as a leader, he might hope to draw some comfort from

views like these. Indeed, he doubtless succeeds in
doing so, but these novels as a whole show no
tendency whatever to absolve him from all
responsibility. Pinette attempts to see himself and
his colleagues in the ranks as innocent and officers
as responsible for the defeat ('"C'est les officiers
qui ont perdu la guerre"'; MA 1317), claiming that
he and Mathieu would have been efficient soldiers
like the 'chasseurs' had they been properly led
(1321), but these are far from convincing views when
he conspicuously fails to cover himself with glory
in his one bout of action! Yet if it is all too easy
for the soldier from the ranks to shift the blame
onto officers, it is equally facile for the civilian
to see himself as innocent and all soldiers as
guilty. In this respect, Brunet's anger with the man
he breaks in on at the beginning of Part II of *La
Mort dans l'âme* is understandable, for the man
clearly regards himself and his wife as guiltless –
and indeed wronged – simply because they are
civilians: '"Allez-vous-en! Allez-vous-en! Déjà vous
avez perdu la guerre, vous allez pas nous faire tuer
par-dessus le marché"' (1346).

As so often, Mathieu sees more deeply into this
whole question than most, even if his own views come
out as vague and involved. From early on in *La Mort
dans l'âme* he realises that he and his colleagues
will be seen as 'les soldats de la défaite' and will
be blamed for losing the war. He also recognises
that any such charge on the part of civilians will
be unjust, not only because he and his companions,
too, are civilians ('civils en uniforme'), but also
because of the way in which things have come about:

> Ils étaient huit qui avaient perdu la guerre,
> cinq secrétaires, deux observateurs, un météo,
> couchés côte à côte au milieu des poireaux et
> des carottes. Ils avaient perdu la guerre comme
> on perd son temps: sans s'en apercevoir. Huit:
> Schwartz le plombier, Nippert l'employé de
> banque, Longin le percepteur, Lubéron le
> démarcheur, Charlot Wroclaw, ombrelles et
> parapluies, Pinette, contrôleur à la T.C.R.P.
> et les deux professeurs: Mathieu et Pierné. Ils
> s'étaient ennuyés neuf mois, tantôt dans les
> sapins, tantôt dans les vignes; un beau jour,
> une voix de Bordeaux leur avait annoncé leur
> défaite et ils avaient compris qu'ils étaient
> dans leur tort. (1170-71)

But if he is unable to see the soldiers as

completely guilty, he has no wish to argue in favour
of their total innocence either: the stance adopted
by his fellow teacher Pierné, who claims to have
'les mains pures', is unmistakably presented as an
odious one (1205-06). In short, Mathieu arrives at
no simple answer to the question of whether he and
his fellow soldiers are somehow responsible for the
defeat. Yet although he has so much difficulty in
feeling at one with them, he refuses to distinguish
his own case from theirs:

> Innocent et coupable, trop sévère et trop
> indulgent, impuissant et responsable, solidaire
> de tous et rejeté par chacun, parfaitement
> lucide et totalement dupe, esclave et
> souverain: je suis comme tout le monde, quoi.
> (1293)

Leader, officer, soldier of the ranks, whichever
category the individual may find himself in, there
is some reason for blaming him for the defeat of his
nation and some reason for arguing that he is no
more responsible than most.

Nor, as already implied, can the individual
escape all blame if he is merely a civilian. If
soldiers fight (and lose) wars, it is political
leaders and governments who make national decisions
about going to war, and it is all the voting members
of the nation who are responsible for putting
governments in power. There may be a case for
arguing (as one young soldier does explicitly in *La
Mort dans l'âme*) that those in some way
disqualified from voting are not answerable for
disasters in the same way as the rest of the
citizens, but there is no doubt that anyone with the
right to vote - whether he exercises it or not -
bears a certain responsibility for what happens to
his country. Those who actually voted are blamed
when Brunet's group of soldiers argue among
themselves (MA 1362); Mathieu blames Pinette and
himself from having failed to vote (MA 1211-12); and
Denise uses the same point against Marcel in *Le Sang
des autres* (81). This general view, of course,
involves accepting responsibility even if one voted
on the losing side, even if one was opposed all
along to policies adopted by one's government.
Mathieu, once more, is quite clear on this point:

> 'Mais sacrebleu! j'étais interventionniste.'
> Mais ça n'était pas la question. Ce qu'il avait
> souhaité personnellement ne comptait pas. Il

était Français, ça n'aurait servi à rien qu'il
se désolidarisât des autres Français. J'ai
décidé la non-intervention en Espagne, je n'ai
pas envoyé d'armes, j'ai fermé la frontière aux
volontaires. Il fallait se défendre avec tous
ou se laisser condamner avec tous, avec le
maître-d'hôtel et le monsieur dyspeptique qui
buvait de l'eau de Vichy. (Surs 971)

Blomart adopts an identical position on this
particular issue, even if he takes the question of
responsibility to potentially absurd lengths. And,
of course, there are close enough parallels in *La
Peste*. In fact, the plague symbol, with its
associated notions of germs and carriers, offers a
timely reminder of the fact that we cannot possibly
maintain that if someone has not desired catastrophe
he bears no responsibility for it. Yet by this token
it might be difficult to apportion any blame at all:

'*Qui,qui* veut la guerre?' A prendre les gens un
à un, ils n'étaient pas belliqueux, ils ne
songeaient qu'à manger, à gagner de l'argent et
à faire des enfants. Même les Allemands. Et
pourtant la guerre était là, Hitler avait
mobilisé. 'Il ne peut tout de même pas décider
ça tout seul', pensa-t-elle. (Surs 1055)

With the problem of attributing responsibility
and guilt to particular individuals or sub-groups
within nations as complicated as this, it is
inevitable that there should be question of covering
the whole scene with one huge net and talking in
terms of collective guilt and collective punishment.
All three authors show the official representatives
of the Church adopting this line of argument.
Paneloux begins his first sermon in *La Peste* with
the words; '"Mes frères, vous êtes dans le malheur,
mes frères, vous l'avez mérité"' (1296); the priest
in the camp at Baccarat addresses the men in similar
terms, talking of '"cette France pécheresse qui,
depuis un quart de siècle, avait oublié ses devoirs
et son Dieu"' (MA 1393); and the monks who visit
Carmona in the throes of the plague also argue that
the visitation is justified ('"Dieu a envoyé la
peste"'; THM 161). Curiously, although the notions
of sin and mass punishment are entirely unacceptable
to our authors, who are all atheists, in certain
other respects the Church's account of the national
disaster might be seen as unexceptionable. It is
preferable to any view that would see the

catastrophe as entirely the result of pure chance;
and its view of the guilt involved does at least
seem to be of the right dimensions or scale. Perhaps
it is virtually impossible to absolve *anyone* from
blame in situations like these. We have already seen
Mathieu and Blomart - both non-Christians - coming
very close to some idea of collective guilt (indeed,
Blomart frequently thinks in terms of *universal*
human guilt: 'l'absolue pourriture cachée au sein de
tout destin humain'; SA 12-13). And a similar view
is to be found in *La Peste*, particularly through the
character of Tarrou: '"Je sais de science certaine
... que chacun la porte en soi, la peste, parce que
personne, non, personne au monde n'en est indemne"'
(1425). Rieux argues that evil almost always stems
from ignorance, but this is not to deny that the
people of Oran as a whole contribute in some ways to
the spread of the plague. Tarrou's general point
that one has to make a positive and strenuous effort
not to spread the disease goes unchallenged in the
book, even if his own ideals are seen as being
somehow too high.

If this amounts to something very close to the
view that everyone is guilty or responsible in the
case of collective tragedy (the epigraph to *Le Sang
des autres* is from Dostoyevsky: 'Chacun est
responsable de tout devant tous'), it is clear that
something like the contrary view - that *no one* is
guilty or responsible - is also respresented in
these novels. It appears because there are now
visible reasons for doubting whether human freedom
is as great as it was previously assumed to be.
Individuals' 'metaphysical' freedom to decide what
they personally are at the deepest level and to
assume responsibility for that decision remains as
uncontested as ever, but their lack of control over
the historical circumstances in which that choice
has to be made now needs to be reckoned with. In
every one of these books certain characters give in,
if only temporarily, to the temptation of believing
that individuals are powerless to affect the course
of history, are caught in the grip of forces beyond
their control:

Ainsi, à longueur de semaine, les prisonniers
de la peste se débattirent comme ils le purent.
Et quelques-uns d'entre eux, comme Rambert,
arrivaient même à imaginer, on le voit, qu'ils
agissaient encore en hommes libres, qu'ils
pouvaient encore choisir. Mais, en fait, on
pouvait dire à ce moment, au milieu du mois

> d'août, que la peste avait tout recouvert. Il
> n'y avait plus alors de destins individuels,
> mais une histoire collective qui était la peste
> et des sentiments partagés par tous. (LP 1355)

This is Rieux suggesting that belief in freedom is
an illusion in these extreme circumstances, but of
course the general picture in *La Peste* is more
complicated than this. The book cannot possibly be
taken as saying that in times of plague and the like
the individual can do nothing, can exercise no
choice, for the simple reason that all of the
central characters are shown as making vitally
important choices. Yet, equally, it is true that
there are crucial matters in which they have no
choice at all (they cannot choose that there should
be no plague; nor that it should end at a particular
time), and certain respects in which the
alternatives between which they choose are imposed
upon them:

> Cent millions de consciences libres dont
> chacune voyait des murs, un bout de cigare
> rougeoyant, des visages familiers, et
> construisait sa destinée sous sa propre
> responsabilité. Et pourtant, si l'on *était* une
> de ces consciences, on s'apercevait à
> d'imperceptibles effleurements, à d'insensibles
> changements, qu'on était solidaire d'un
> gigantesque et invisible polypier. La guerre:
> chacun est libre et pourtant les jeux sont
> faits. (Surs 1025)

Free to choose oneself one may be, but the choice
never takes place in a vacuum and at least some of
the terms of reference are set out in advance:

> Pages blanches dont l'avenir reposait tout
> entier entre mes mains. Ce n'était qu'un rêve
> puéril d'écolier. Maintenant je savais. Rien
> n'est blanc que l'absence, l'impossible
> absence. Choisir. La paix honteuse ou la guerre
> sanglante? Le meurtre ou l'esclavage? Il aurait
> fallu avoir choisi d'abord les circonstances
> mêmes où le choix s'imposait. (SA 163-64)

Freedom, then, is an equation with two sides,
and although most characters are perhaps aware of
both, it is very difficult to keep them in balance
all of the time. When one is tempted to stress the
restrictions at the expense of the choices (and this

may help to relieve the burden of responsibility and guilt), the result can be a kind of fatalism. Both Mathieu and Schneider have spells when they are fatalistic in *La Mort dans l'âme*; and Paneloux in *La Peste* is even prepared to accept the term 'fatalisme' itself: 'il ne reculerait pas devant le terme si on lui permettait seulement d'y joindre l'adjectif "actif"' (1404). Like Judge Othon, Paneloux is willing to submit himself to Providence, and he does so not only in a general way, but also specifically by refusing the aid of a doctor when he is taken ill (1406). Tarrou accurately predicts his end when, in an especially striking comment, he shows one way in which the issue is bound up with that of guilt and innocence:

> 'Paneloux a raison, dit Tarrou. Quand l'innocence a les yeux crevés, un chrétien doit perdre la foi ou accepter d'avoir les yeux crevés. Paneloux ne veut pas perdre la foi, il ira jusqu'au bout. C'est ce qu'il a voulu dire.' (1406)

Mostly, of course, it is the forces of history rather than of Providence that are seen as arbitrarily controlling our fate and undermining our actions. If only because he has lived longer and seen more history, Fosca in *Tous les hommes sont mortels* is more conscious of this than any other character in these stories. When Régine meets him and 'reawakens' him at the beginning of the book, his attitude is one of complete resignation and passivity. The first blow to his ambition and faith in action had come with the discovery that events on a scale other than the local one have the most profound effects on one's life (222), and this discovery, as we saw, is exactly parallel to that of interdependence made by mortal characters. Fosca's particular tragedy, however, is that he has to go on and on living and making other discoveries of this kind, each one convincing him still more of the futility of any sort of action. He comes to regard history as 'une monstrueuse mécanique' over which individuals have no control: 'il fallait être stupide pour imaginer qu'une volonté humaine pourrait en dérégler le cours' (290). His attitude is only of interest because it is one that can be adopted by mortals who suddenly discover that less is within their direct control than they had believed. They may be tempted to try deliberately to abandon the freedom that remains to them, like

Hélène: 'Pourquoi devrais-je décider?' (SA 270).
Even Blomart, who makes such anguished attempts to
act autonomously and responsibly, finds it something
of a relief to be in the army, where almost all
responsibility seems to be taken from his shoulders:
'Ce n'était pas à moi de parler: quelqu'un parlait
pour moi' (SA 207).

The temptation to regard oneself as innocent
because completely powerless, then, is well recorded
in these novels. There are certain situations here
where individuals have especially good reasons for
regarding themselves as unfortunate and helpless
victims of historical forces. In the Munich crisis,
for example, many individuals, in addition to being
suddenly drawn along by forces they scarcely
acknowledged before, are just as suddenly dropped
again by those forces and left to feel doubly
foolish, doubly manipulated. Thus we have the
unforgettable spectacle of villagers uprooting
themselves to go to war, only to discover that the
army does not want them (Surs 802-03); and of the
'mobilisés' on Mathieu's train mistaking the signs
of peace for those of war:

> Tous ces hommes s'étaient fait violence pour
> partir les yeux secs, tous avaient soudain vu
> la mort en face et tous, après beaucoup
> d'embarras ou modestement, s'étaient déterminés
> à mourir. A présent ils restaient hébétés, les
> bras ballants, empêtrés de cette vie qui avait
> reflué sur eux, qu'on leur laissait encore pour
> un moment, pour un petit moment et dont ils ne
> savaient plus que faire. C'est la journée des
> dupes, pensa-t-il. (Surs 1131)

And the defeat of France in some cases tricks even
those who saw the war coming and adjusted their
expectations accordingly. Thus Boris actually
expected to die, as did his sister Ivich, but was
duped by events. On the other hand, Brunet can claim
that a whole generation of soldiers have been caught
in a different historical trap:

> Ils comptaient sur la guerre pour les faire
> passer à l'âge d'homme, pour leur conférer les
> droits de chef de famille et de l'ancien
> combattant; c'était un rite solennel
> d'initiation, elle devait chasser l'autre, la
> *Grande*, la Mondiale, dont la gloire avait
> étouffé leur enfance; elle devait être encore
> plus grande, encore plus mondiale; en tirant

> sur les Fritz, ils eussent accompli le massacre
> rituel des pères, par quoi chaque génération
> débute dans la vie. Ils n'ont tiré sur
> personne, ils n'ont rien massacré du tout,
> c'est raté. (MA 1428)

Brunet himself, of course, is eventually caught up in - and rejected by - political and historical pressures that even he has not anticipated.

Yet fatalism is seen to be only one of the possible reactions to these large-scale forces that affect the groups to which characters belong, and it is by no means one that the stories recommend. A major strength of the wartime novels is certainly that they graphically record the complexities of calamitous historical events and the *confusion* that these generate. Since some exceedingly difficult and abstract issues are at stake here, it is small wonder that our authors or their fictional figures fail to unravel them, and that the somewhat paradoxical nature of the responsibility that the individual bears for what happens to the group should remain a particular puzzle to leaders and led alike. But not all of the moral reflection in this period centres on what has already occurred. Preoccupation with retrospective questions of guilt can easily become excessive and stultifying, whereas characters are shown as facing continuing problems or dilemmas, some of the most urgent kind. Moral reflection needs to be at least partly forward-looking and questions of past responsibility are rightly seen here as merging into questions of decision and action in the present and the future.

The broad structure of each of Beauvoir's novels illustrates this point especially well. In *Tous les hommes sont mortels* Fosca's account of his own past takes up a great deal (rather more than three quarters) of the book, but he is telling the story to Régine, from whose standpoint the rest of the book is narrated. Régine's life is unsatisfactory and she is seeking a solution to her problems in the present and the future. In the end she draws her own conclusions and 'moral' from Fosca's past - conclusions concerning the inexorable march of history and the futility of individual human effort, which will have the profoundest effects on her subsequent attitude towards life: 'moucheron, écume, fourmi jusqu'à la mort. "Ce n'est que le commencement", pensa-t-elle ... Ce fut quand l'heure commença de sonner au clocher qu'elle poussa le premier cri' (528). The end of *Le Sang des autres* is certainly somewhat less pessimistic, but it too shows us one of the main characters, Blomart, drawing upon all that he has learned in the past from his personal encounters and his experience of the forces of history in order to help him make moral decisions in the present that have the most serious implications for the future.

It would be too much to say that the retrospective matters of responsibility and guilt in these novels are no more than a prelude to more immediate and urgent problems of action, yet these latter necessarily have some kind of priority, in that they *have* to be resolved in one way or another. If we now devote rather less attention to groups as such and more to the question of how the individual treats others in general, together with the sort of dilemmas that this poses when it comes to decisions and deeds, then we shall see other vital aspects of the moral perspectives in the wartime novels.

Characters in the pre-war stories gave little if any thought to the *consequences* of their choices and acts for anyone other than themselves, to such an extent that they sometimes appeared surprised to discover that their acts actually had consequences at all (Pablo, Lulu, Meursault). In fact, in spite of the importance of decisions and acts, there was scarcely a significant concept of continuous action at all in the earlier books. The perspectives and experiences of the wartime characters in this respect are totally different, while visibly built upon those of their predecessors. That is to say that with their sudden injection into the stream of history, these later figures are made to realise that their own actions take effect in a public world shared by others and have repercussions that are just as real for other people as for themselves. In general, this is why the moral problems that have to be faced at this stage are so complex and so agonising. With a few outstanding and corroborative exceptions like Daniel (who, in continuing to see himself and his life more or less in isolation, now stands out like a sore thumb), characters are entirely unable to burke the question of the effect they have upon the lives of others. Awareness of the consequences of their actions is one of the constants in their moral perspectives.

Arising out of, or running parallel to, the point that the (historical) circumstances within which the individual's freedom of choice operates are not themselves chosen by him is the fact that not all of the repercussions of his actions are chosen by him either. It is almost always impossible to foresee or predict these repercussions in detail. Mathieu strives hard for lucidity at the time of the Munich crisis but has to admit that his acts escape him and have consequences he cannot see: 'chacun de mes mouvements allume une ampoule ou déclenche une sonnerie dans un monde que je ne vois pas' (Surs 1023-24). Tarrou started out much more confident about the effects of his actions, but learned his lesson the hard way before coming to Oran:

> 'J'ai compris alors que moi, du moins, je n'avais pas cessé d'être un pestiféré pendant toutes ces longues années où pourtant, de toute mon âme, je croyais lutter justement contre la peste. J'ai appris que j'avais indirectement souscrit à la mort de milliers d'hommes, que j'avais même provoqué cette mort en trouvant bons les actions et les principes qui l'avaient fatalement entra^inée.' (LP 1424)

Fosca similarly learns in *Tous les hommes sont mortels* that he has been doing the opposite of what he intended ('voilà donc l'empire que nous avons détruit, l'empire que je souhaitais établir sur la terre, et que je n'ai pas su construire!'; THM 307), and, like Mathieu, draws the conclusion that no man can foresee the consequences of his acts. When Brunet, in spite of Schneider's warning, goes on working in the dark and is eventually obliged to recognise that he has acted '"sur la base d'informations inexactes"' (DA 1508), his case only illustrates in a particularly extreme way a general dilemma that all of the characters are shown as facing. However, it is perhaps in Blomart above all that awareness of the problem reaches its height. Early on, by unintentionally influencing Jacques, with disastrous results, he comes to see the difficulty and this causes him to be especially cautious in his conduct towards Hélène:

> Et j'ai senti dans mes bras un grand élan pour t'attirer à moi, pour te serrer contre mon coeur; dans mes bras, le geste semblait si facile: facile à faire, et facile à défaire, un geste transparent et tout juste égal à lui-même. Mais j'ai gardé les bras collés à mon corps. Un geste, et Jacques est mort. Un geste, et quelque chose de neuf apparaît dans le monde, quelque chose que j'ai créé et qui se développe hors de moi, sans moi, entraînant

après soi d'imprévisibles avalanches. (SA 99)

Eventually he learns that the same principle applies both to action within the sphere of personal relations and to that within the public or political sphere: 'Je savais à jamais qu'on ne peut pas cerner les limites d'un acte, ce qu'on est en train de faire, on ne peut pas le prévoir' (148-49).

It is not simply that actions have consequences that we are unable to foresee: the real difficulty is that, whether we intend it or not, they usually inflict some harm or damage upon others. This is one aspect of what Tarrou means when he comments on his own youth: '"Quand j'étais jeune, je vivais avec l'idée de mon innocence, c'est-à-dire avec pas d'idée du tout"' (LP 1420). His discovery that he had quite unintentionally been contributing to the death of others was one that he naturally came to regard as having general applicability:

> 'Avec le temps, j'ai simplement aperçu que même ceux qui étaient meilleurs que d'autres ne pouvaient s'empêcher aujourd'hui de tuer ou de laisser tuer parce que c'était dans la logique où ils vivaient, et que nous ne pouvions pas faire un geste en ce monde sans risquer de faire mourir.' (1425)

Even with a resolute determination to do nothing that contributes to anyone's death, the best one can hope for is to become a 'meurtrier innocent' (1426). Tarrou's explanation of these points to Rieux is immediately followed by the sounds of fighting and shooting at the gates of the city (1427), reminding us that even Rieux and Tarrou are representing an attitude and an administration that may have to resort to violence in extreme circumstances. There is also deliberate irony in the fact that, given his terms of reference, Tarrou has seriously to consider the possibility that the man who does nothing but move peas from one bowl to another and the man who spends most of his time spitting at cats are saints!

Again, *Le Sang des autres* expresses still more graphically the point that we can never avoid harming others by our actions. Blomart hurts his mother, Jacques and Hélène (not to speak of the Republicans in Spain and the Jews in Germany) without ever intending to, and this central theme of the book is crystallised in a series of images: the tree trunk across the road just beyond a bend (27), the boulder on the road (313), and so on. Late in the story Blomart reacts to his realisation of this fact in a way diametrically opposed to that of Tarrou, not only throwing bombs that kill Germans, but also thereby indirectly killing some innocent Frenchmen who are the victims of reprisals. (It is interesting that Blomart faces squarely up to the question of reprisals, for while German retaliation is touched upon in *La Mort dans l'âme* (1290-1300), the issue is passed over rapidly or even evaded; and one of the criticisms levelled at Camus, in so far as *La Peste* is meant to be an allegory of the German Occupation and French Resistance, is that the book has nothing to say on the important moral problem of reprisals.) *Tous les hommes sont mortels* also deals explicitly with the question of harming others by our actions. Fosca learns the lesson early on, but he later has to instruct Charles V: 'Imaginez-vous qu'en ce monde vous pourrez jamais faire le bien sans faire du mal? Il est impossible d'être juste pour tous, de faire le bonheur de tous' (249).

By this stage, however, we are approaching another absolutely major preoccupation of individual moral agents in these novels. In spite of Fosca's unequivocal advice to Charles - '"C'est à vous de justifier le mal que vous faites à certains par l'oeuvre que vous accomplissez pour le bien de tous"' (249) - things work out anything but well, and Charles is understandably unconvinced of the legitimacy of deliberately performing evil actions, even with the best of long-term intentions (263). In other words, a standard question of morality, or rather a cluster of such questions, is now in view. Does the end justify the means? Or perhaps better still: Are we ever justified in treating people as means rather than ends? These questions are agitated throughout *Tous les hommes sont mortels*. From the beginning Fosca is ruthless with 'les bouches inutiles' of Carmona (125), and it takes his mortal son Tancrède to ask the crucial question: '"Utile! dit-il. A quoi? A qui?"' (149). Undeterred, Fosca continues to treat some people as means to an end, be they 'les noirs d'Afrique' (248), or 'les Indiens d'Amérique' (287). He even persuades Charles V to regard *himself* as a means to an end ('"Votre santé, votre bonheur ne pèsent rien"'; 239), and justifies the suppression of Luther on the grounds that he is dangerous to the peace of the Empire (256). On all of these counts, as a result of the wide range of his historical experience Fosca is eventually given reason to doubt the validity of the principle involved, although even at the end he hardly seems repentant about any 'unjustifiable' evil he has perpetrated, worrying most about the mouse he has made immortal: '"C'est mon plus grand crime"' (526).

In this respect, once more, the evolution of Blomart in *Le Sang des autres* is of particular interest. At first he is determined to treat people as individuals rather than as part of the masses in the way that the Communists do: '"Les masses sont faites de gens qui existent un à un; ce n'est pas le nombre qui compte"' (91). But he later realises that as far as individuals are concerned, opting for the happiness of one person may be seen as taking another as a means to that end: 'Comment choisir? Les larmes de Madeleine ou les larmes d'Hélène?' (146). And this is a dilemma that he comes to recognise on the political level too:

> Derrière les Pyrénées, les travailleurs d'Espagne tombaient sous les balles fascistes, mais pouvais-je racheter leur sang au prix de vies françaises, au prix d'une seule vie qui ne fût pas la mienne? Les Juifs crevaient comme des mouches dans des camps de concentration, mais avais-je le droit d'échanger leurs cadavres contre les corps innocents des paysans de France? Je pouvais payer avec mon corps, avec mon sang; mais les autres hommes n'étaient ni des pions à manoeuvrer, ni des enjeux, des forces à capter. (157)

Does one have to adopt Fascist methods to defeat Fascism, and if one does, does being anti-Fascist thereby cease to make sense (203)? As the title of the book suggests, these are the main moral issues that tax Blomart throughout. By the end his views on the subject are, as we have seen, greatly changed. He himself *proposes* active Resistance work that will directly involve doing violence to others, not only the enemy and those who have freely chosen to risk their lives, but also the innocent French victims of reprisals. In other words, we have to see Blomart as finally coming around to the view that, at least in extreme circumstances, he is morally justified in treating the lives of some men as means to an end: '"Nous ne devons nous soucier que du but à atteindre et faire tout ce qu'il faut pour l'atteindre"' (249).

Although this sequence of attitudes is by no means generally shared by other characters, the moral problems to which it constitutes a series of responses certainly are. We have already seen Tarrou

coming to disagree with his political colleagues
that some deaths are necessary 'pour amener un monde
où l'on ne tuerait plus personne' (LP 1423), and we
know that he is ever reluctant to use people as
means of any kind, wanting, for example, 'des hommes
libres' for his 'formations sanitaires' (1321).
Rieux, given his rather different role, perhaps
cannot afford such scruples. At least, there are
senses in which he cannot give such consideration to
the individual as Tarrou. He might therefore be said
to treat certain people in ways he considers
undesirable in themselves but has to adopt because
of the end in view. This comes out in the early
contrast between his position and that of Rambert:

> 'Vous n'avez pensé à personne. Vous n'avez
> pas tenu compte de ceux qui étaient séparés.'
> Rieux reconnut que, dans un sens, cela était
> vrai, il n'avait pas voulu en tenir compte.
> 'Ah! je vois, fit Rambert, vous allez parler
> de service public. Mais le bien public est fait
> du bonheur de chacun.'
> 'Allons,' dit le docteur qui semblait sortir
> d'une distraction, 'il y a cela et il y a autre
> chose. Il ne faut pas juger.' (LP 1290)

In fact, every day he has to deal with the sick in a
way that can only be justified by reference to
something like the general good (1291).

Sartre, too, shows himself well aware of this
kind of moral problem, although none of his
characters sees it in quite the same way as those of
Camus and Beauvoir. Someone like Mathieu is
predictably inclined to doubt whether the end
justifies the means (Surs 983). Yet by *La Dernière
Chance* he (like Blomart) is apparently reconciled
to the need to use others without their consent – he
unashamedly manipulates Brunet in order to keep his
own escape network in the camp safe (1651-52) – and
even to the need to commit violence for the sake of
the cause, for he is a party to the murder of the
traitor Moûlu (1647). For the most part, however,
the ends in sight are not particularly clear to the
characters in *Les Chemins de la liberté* and it is
above all the Communist figures who embody this
particular dilemma: Maurice in some measure (Surs
743), but especially Brunet. In *Le Sursis* and for
much of Part II of *La Mort dans l'âme*, Brunet
experiences no such problem. After the defeat of
France he knows at least roughly what he wants to do
and how this will involved moulding the men: 'Il

faudra détruire un à un, patiemment, leurs espoirs, crever leurs illusions, leur faire voir à nu leur condition épouvantable, les dégoûter de tout, de tous et, pour commencer, d'eux-mêmes' (MA 1364). As we saw earlier, he comes very close indeed to despising the men, and he certainly scorns their search for personal happiness ('leur petit bonheur têtu, leur bonheur de pauvres'; MA 1391). But the cracks have already begun to appear in this view before the end of *La Mort dans l'âme*. When Brunet is delirious from lack of food, he thinks of Mathieu and feels obliged to defend himself against the latter's criticisms (MA 1389). And it is not just from Brunet's unconscious that the doubts emerge, for he absorbs Schneider's attacks on his attitude towards the men ('"Tu es un abstrait"'; 1425). In principle, these attacks are very similar indeed to Rambert's early objections to Rieux, and to Rieux's own concern that he is becoming rather like the 'abstraction' that he is fighting against.

Yet it is above all in 'Drôle d'amitié', when the end in sight becomes less clear than ever, that Brunet's attitude towards treating people as means really changes. Unlike Chalais, he is no longer quite sure that the Party is right, or will succeed ('Si le Parti se trompe, tous les hommes sont seuls'; 1517), and at the very end he comes to believe that even if it is and does, the means employed are still not justifiable: 'Cet absolu de souffrance, aucune victoire des hommes ne pourra l'effacer: c'est le Parti qui le fait crever, même si l'U.R.S.S. gagne, les hommes sont seuls' (1534). The point about success is a fascinating one, and it is taken up in *Le Sang des autres* too, where Blomart and some of his Resistance colleagues at least consider the possibility that the end justifies the means only if the end is actually attained (248). In spite of the confidence that Blomart displays publicly, he continues to be haunted by the possibility of having committed 'crimes inutiles': '"Et si tout était inutile? Si je les avais tués pour rien?"' (294). And not only is the very same terminology used in connection with Fosca's treatment of 'les bouches inutiles' of Carmona in *Tous les hommes sont mortels*: the same issue of success arises there too, for Fosca clearly regards different moral considerations as applying according to whether or not he can live on to achieve his ends in the city (142).

In short, all of these books indicate – if only through the extreme unease of characters adopting a definite stance - that the moral problem of ends and means is much too difficult to admit of any simple solution. It constitutes one of the main obstacles or anxieties that the individual characters face when they have to decide how to act in the collective situations they find themselves in. The historical circumstances mean that decisions have serious repercussions upon others, yet those circumstances are precisely what make the need for action so urgent. Indeed, one of the main moral 'discoveries' in these novels is that it is impossible *not* to decide, impossible *not* to act. At least in the extreme situations that the characters are in, what looks like (or is intended to be) an abstention, a deliberate refusal to take sides, *has* to be taken as an action in favour of one particular side; or at least as an action supporting the present situation. We have already noted how the failure to vote may be seen as evidence of responsibility for a disastrous state of affairs; how failure to act on the question of the Spanish Civil War (as opposed to simply calling oneself an interventionist) is construed as siding with Franco; how failure to do anything positive about the persecution of the Jews in the mid-thirties is to allow the spread of Nazism; and so on. In general, the whole of Blomart's story in *Le Sang des autres* is an illustration of the impossibility of abstaining from action, as much on the personal as on the political level: 'Je n'avais pas voulu entrer dans sa vie, j'avais fui, et ma fuite avait bouleversé sa vie. Je refusais d'agir sur son destin et j'avais disposé d'elle aussi brutalement que par un viol (129). He even comes to see that there is no way of entirely opting out through suicide: 'Je serai encore responsable de tous ces actes que mon absence aura rendus possibles' (151).

There is no way of opting out, then, and yet, as we can now recognise, the difficulties in the way of acting deliberately and with a particular end in view are formidable and daunting, almost overwhelming. Nor is there a viable third way in the form of gratuitous action. Philippe hopes to try this way in *Le Sursis*, but finds it impossible to sustain such a position for any length of time (978-79). And Mathieu's case in *La Mort dans l'âme* is of course highly relevant here. His last-ditch stand at the end of Part I is not gratuitous in the sense of arising simply from chance (Philippe literally tosses a coin), and *at a certain level* it presumably has to be seen as an anti-Nazi stance.

But Sartre gives clear indications in advance that Mathieu's 'commitment' at this stage must in other respects be assimilated to gratuitous action:

> Se fendre la main d'un coup de couteau, jeter son anneau de mariage, tirailler sur les Fridolins: et puis après? Casser, détériorer, ça n'est pas une solution; un coup de tête, ce n'est pas la liberté. (MA 1299-1300; cf. 1278)

And the manner of presentation of Mathieu's stand ('je vais mourir pour rien'; 1323; 'Le désir lui vint d'en tuer d'autres: c'était amusant et facile'; 1337) is such that we ought to be in no danger at all of taking gratuitous action as a proposed solution to the problems faced by characters in this sort of collective situation. At bottom, gratuitous action, like abstention, is simply a rather special and undesirable kind of commitment; it obviously offers no coherent answer to the acute problems of action recorded in the stories.

In fact, the wartime novels taken as a whole suggest that there may be no wholly satisfactory answers to these problems. Naturally, characters' situations in the stories are too diverse to allow the possibility of one recommended course of action, or even type of action. But there is more to the matter than this. The 'practical' problem of the unforeseen consequences of one's actions on the one hand, and the theoretical one of whether ends justify means in one's dealings with people on the other hand - these are issues that are essentially *forced* upon characters by large-scale events and need to be reflected upon more carefully than the almost unremitting pressure of history here allows. In the pre-war stories the key question was whether characters faced up to the metaphysical facts of life, but now, for the most part, they have precious little alternative (at least after the actual outbreak of war) but to face up to the extreme pressures that collective situation bring to bear upon them.

It is true that even in extreme circumstances there are ways in which people may deceive themselves, and one certainly would not wish to deny that self-deception is still implicitly attacked in these books, or to assert that the idea of lucidity is jettisoned. Furthermore, the discovery that a great deal of the individual's life is governed, or at least circumscribed, by what happens beyond his reach in no sense undermines the ideal of control over one's own actions and immediate circumstances. The rejection of the ideas of gratuitous action and of abstention or neutrality, among other features that we have noted, confirms this. Nevertheless, it is apparent from our brief examination of wartime dilemmas from the moral agent's viewpoint, as well as from earlier discussion of collective situations and groups, that because of the drastic change of circumstances since the pre-war period, individuals can no longer look to the ideals of lucidity and control alone as their main landmarks. They are now under direct pressure to act in some way, and we need to consider what are the most positive guidelines that they are able to adopt, and what limits the changed circumstances impose upon their moral vision.

Chapter Seven

GUIDELINES AND LIMITS

One common interpretation of the general evolution
of our authors' thought would suggest that, in
contrast with the individualism of the pre-war
period, the war years are characterised by their
'solidarity' with their fellow men. Yet if this is
intended to take us beyond the mere fact of
interdependence to a key *value*, the point is not
entirely easy to establish on the basis of the
wartime novels alone. The major difficulty lies in
saying what precisely the idea of solidarity amounts
to in these stories. Just as Tancrède asked Fosca,
'"Utile! ... A quoi? A qui?"' (THM 149), so we must
try to ask: 'Solidarity with whom exactly? And for
what purpose?'.
        It is clear enough that the radical changes
that come over a number of characters here are
highly relevant to this question. The conversions
undergone by Rambert, Othon, Paneloux, Hélène,
Marcel, Madeleine might all be said to be in the
direction of less self-interest and more
co-operation with their fellow beings. Yet care is
already needed at this point, for even if we ignore
the characters who fail to experience such a change
when they might have been expected to do so, there
is some kind of case for arguing that, say, Fosca
and Brunet actually change in the *opposite*
direction. However, provided it be allowed that *Tous
les hommes sont mortels* is an especially difficult
novel to interpret (should the final emphasis be
placed upon the disillusionment and distress of
Fosca and Régine, or on the clear-sighted optimism
and solidarity of Armand and his colleagues, ·with
whom Fosca becomes involved in the last episode of
his own story?), then there is little doubt that it
is almost entirely the incomplete state of *Les
Chemins de la liberté* that makes for any ambiguity

that there may be. Beauvoir's plot-summary of the unfinished *La Dernière Chance* and Sartre's notes concerning his plans for the volume indicate that the general conclusion of the tetralogy would have been very much in line with the message of *La Peste* and *Le Sang des autres*, with characters like Mathieu, Boris and even Philippe coming around, in the Resistance, to a kind of solidarity quite alien to their thinking in the earlier volumes; and with Brunet swinging back from his extreme position at the moment of Schneider's death to an attitude of co-operation.[1] Something of this movement is already apparent - at least in connection with Mathieu and Brunet - in the extracts from the novel first published in the Pléiade volume of Sartre's fiction (1585-1654). With this evidence in mind, we may say that it would take a rather extravagant sceptic to maintain, on the basis of the fiction alone, that our authors do *not* have in common - doubtless largely as a result of their experience of Occupied France - the idea of collective resistance to oppression. (This is also, precisely, the ideal of Armand and his companions in *Tous les hommes sont mortels* - one which, tragically, the immortal Fosca is unable to share.)

Nevertheless, discussion of the role of groups in the wartime novels may already have suggested that 'solidarity' is a misleading label to apply to this ideal, since to act for the French, for instance, is necessarily to bring oneself into opposition and conflict with the Germans; just as to champion the working classes is to declare hostility towards the bourgeoisie. For this reason, at least in the novels of Sartre and Beauvoir the notion of solidarity with the *whole* of mankind might seem to gain no foothold at all, thus leaving us with what appears to be a major difference between these two authors on the one hand and Camus on the other. For there is no doubt that in *La Peste* the reader is inclined, not to say encouraged, to extrapolate the attitudes of figures like Rieux, Tarrou, Rambert and Grand, and thereby to see the message of the book as a certain kind of humanism of the very widest application. In short, it looks rather as if only Camus generalises the notion of resistance that all three authors share in such a way as to present solidarity as a moral ideal for the human race as a whole.

Yet for two different reasons this neither does full justice to Sartre and Beauvoir, nor takes us to the heart of the question of solidarity. The first

is that while Camus certainly wishes the message of
mutual assistance to extend outwards from
Oran/Occupied France to mankind in general, it is
only the powerfully *symbolic* nature of *La Peste* that
allows him to make such an extension seem plausible
for the duration of the story. For the fact is that
to the extent that the plague does stand for the
German Occupation (or, indeed, for *any* political
tyranny), the solidarity that the book advocates is
no less limited than that in the novels of the other
two authors. It is simply not possible in the end,
as a number of critics have pointed out, to wish
away the incommensurability between fighting the
Nazis and fighting disease or suffering in general.
Camus does not solve, any more than do Sartre and
Beauvoir, the difficult question of whether we can
ever arrive at a state of sympathy with all members
of the human race by a simple and continuous outward
development of our benevolence towards those around
us, or whether no such progressive development is
possible and a separate, qualitative 'leap' is
required if we are to attain solidarity with all
mankind.

The second point is that a *certain* notion of
general solidarity is undoubtedly embodied in
characters like Armand and Blomart, and even in
figures like Brunet. Like Beauvoir's two heroes,
Brunet is actually engaged in bitter conflict with
particular groups of men. But like them also, Brunet
strongly emphasises the need for co-operation among
like-minded people, if their common ends are to be
achieved. One (admittedly restricted) aspect of
solidarity is that involved in the very recognition
of the existence of the sort of groups and groupings
examined earlier, together with an acknowledgement
of the necessity, in collective situations, of
committing oneself to at least one of them. In this
minimal sense at least, all three authors have a
certain concept of solidarity in common: they see
(as they did not see in the pre-war years) the
individual's need to pool his resources with others
in times of threat or catastrophe. If in earlier
books there seemed no way at all out of the
internecine warring that characterised relations
between individuals, now the sinking of personal
differences for the sake of a common goal (Blomart
and the Communists; Brunet and Schneider; Rieux and
Paneloux) marks one step in the direction of
fraternisation and fellow-feeling. There is *some*
sharing of values here, which takes us a little
beyond the extreme individualism of the earlier

stories. It is barely enough, in itself, to merit
the description of a moral ideal, but the concept of
mutual assistance is certainly one of the broad
guidelines that most major characters follow in
these books.

It is true that a whole spectrum of reactions
to catastrophic collective situations is presented
(if we are in no danger of forgetting Rieux, Tarrou
and Blomart, we may need to make a deliberate effort
to remember Daniel, Cottard, Charles, Blomart's
mother, etc), but the lone wolves stand as
conspicuously out of line now as did the conformers
in the pre-war stories. They are not, however,
treated unsympathetically and, in general, our
authors' positions appear to be less hardened and
dogmatic here than in the pre-war fiction. Things do
not turn out well in the stories for those like
Cottard, Daniel and Charles who actively *welcome*
collective disaster because they believe it suits
their own personal ends, but, of course, things very
often turn out badly for the 'solidaires' too. In
any case, the misfortunes of Cottard (because of
Tarrou's resolute attempt to understand him), Daniel
(because he is increasingly aware of his loneliness
and isolation), and Charles (because he is a
helpless invalid) are very much more subjects for
our sympathy or pity than for our rejoicing. And we
find a rather similar picture when we turn to those
who are pacifists and/or unduly eager to make
concessions of one kind or another to preserve their
own lives or interests. Philippe, Pierre and
Birnenschatz in *Le Sursis*, for example, are not
presented as wholly objectionable figures; and
neither Ivich nor the Alsatians mentioned in this
connection earlier are taken seriously enough to
arouse our moral indignation. Only one character,
Jacques Delarue (who is also a target of criticism
in one of the pre-war stories), is now shown in any
detail to be reprehensible and contemptible in his
choice of concession, even cowardice, as a means of
saving his skin (particularly in *La Mort dans
l'âme*; 1301-12). The crucial point is probably that
in these novels even those characters who fail to
live up to those minimal standards of solidarity or
loyalty to some group that are implicitly held up
for our moral approval are still people trapped in
the same broad collective situations as the heroes.
They tend to elicit at least a little of our
sympathy for that reason. The real enemy here, the
real point of contrast in human terms to the
'solidaires' whom we admire, is not the egoist, the

individualist or the solitary, but the (Nazi) oppressor, and he is scarcely portrayed at all in the books.

In certain respects, therefore, even the attenuated ideal of solidarity needs to be seen as a secondary rather than a primary value in the wartime fiction. The stories characteristically commend solidarity as a means to an end: that of combating oppression and injustice. And yet it would not quite be accurate to imply that the primary values of freedom, justice (and perhaps equality) are themselves the dominant moral guidelines in this period. Although some or all of these values come strongly to the fore at particular points in the stories (for instance, in parts of *La Peste* and at the end of *Le Sang des autres*), there is a great deal of material here (and perhaps even whole books, like *Tous les hommes sont mortels* and *Le Sursis*) where they could not be said to be central or very prominent. Moreover, when they do emerge as important enough values to cause men to sink their differences and co-operate in groups, the uniting together against a common foe should not mislead us into supposing that even main figures in the same book, let alone ones in different books, have the same *positive* ideals of justice (Othon and Tarrou), freedom (Brunet and Schneider), or equality (Blomart and his father). The agreement and co-operation between main characters is real enough, but often provisional or temporary. Adverse circumstances dominate the stories to such an extent that it would be highly misleading to imply that protagonists spontaneously unite in order to achieve something constructive: they unite in order to shake off an oppressor. The notion of resistance against oppression understandably shared by all three authors, then, is at the basis of the minimal kind of solidarity picked out above, but is not itself positive or constructive enough to count as a major moral value.

In short, what has frequently been seen as the new and crucial moral principle of the wartime period, that of 'solidarity', proves to be a peculiarly elusive concept in these novels. It seems to depend for its force upon the fact that those working together in a certain group are very roughly agreed on some *other* value (or some evil). And the affirmation of this other principle in turn, as well as the urgency of the need for co-operation in its defence, is brought about by some massive external threat (possibly from a different group); or by some catastrophe that is almost *bound* to bring people together. Yet in spite of all of these qualifications, what is left of solidarity has a definite importance in these stories, in that it still marks something of a shift from the pre-war perspectives and values. Whatever may be the weaknesses and limitations in the positions of Brunet, Blomart, Armand, Rieux, Tarrou, and so on, these characters cannot, in any useful sense, be labelled as selfish, self-centred or self-interested. They are at least *trying* to see the universal implications of their views in a way that the pre-war figures were not, and rightly or wrongly they believe themselves to be acting in some measure in the name of others as well as on their own behalf.

How successful they are in this intention is a different matter again. The view that, in the end, we can do nothing for other individuals in any case is one that enjoys a certain currency in these novels. One thinks of some of Fosca's comments ('"on ne peut rien pour les hommes, leur bien ne dépend que d'eux-mêmes"'; THM 313); of the ending of *La Peste* and *Le Sang des autres*, where lovers and friends are definitively separated by death; of Brunet's disillusionment ('si le Parti a raison, je suis plus seul qu'un fou; s'il a tort, *tous les hommes* sont seuls et le monde est foutu'; DA 1515); of Mathieu, of Daniel, and of many others. Indeed, it would be rather surprising if this were not part of the picture in the books, since the 'séparation des consciences' discovered before the war is acknowledged as a metaphysical reality that it would take more than an historical disaster to change. This fact is, in its way, another kind of restriction upon whatever solidarity the war causes to develop. But in any case the area within which the kind of freedom and control aimed at by the pre-war characters can operate is now seen to be *so* circumscribed that a certain recognition of defeat is built into the perspectives of even the optimistic heroes.

For this reason, it would be over-hasty to dismiss the importance as a moral guideline of the idea of 'doing one's best'. It sounds, and doubtless is, weak as any kind of moral ideal, but it has to be seen against the background of circumstances where the individual feels himself for the most part bewildered and overwhelmed by the large-scale events that now dominate his horizons. Problems of commitment, responsibility and action are so complex that a number of characters, in varying degrees and different ways, give up the struggle to solve them and resort to what might be described as more primitive forms of behaviour. Mathieu notices this in those around him in *La Mort dans l'âme*:

> Tous! Tous! Ils se défilaient: Schwartz muait. Nippert se cramponnait au sommeil, Pinette à la colère, Pierné à l'innocence; terré dans l'instant, Lubéron bouffait, bouchait tous ses trous avec de la bouffe; Longin avait quitté le siècle. Chacun d'eux, hâtivement, s'était composé l'attitude qui lui permettait de vivre. Il se redressa brusquement et dit d'une voix forte:
> 'Vous me dégoûtez.' (1207-08)

But his own final attitude in that book, although admittedly not designed to enable him to *live*, constitutes a similar kind of escape or evasion into a 'magical' world, and probably a much more dangerous one:

> Il tirait, les lois volaient en l'air, tu aimeras ton prochain comme toi-même, pan dans cette gueule de con, tu ne tueras point, pan sur le faux jeton d'en face. Il tirait sur l'homme, sur la Vertu, sur le Monde: la Liberté, c'est la Terreur. (1344)

The incomplete state of *Les Chemins de la liberté* again poses a problem here, but the later extracts from *La Dernière Chance* show quite clearly that Mathieu was to revert to a much more rational, practical and *modest* conduct in his prisoner-of-war camp (1646). They also suggest that, given his personal terms of reference, Brunet's conversion to an extreme form of despairing individualism at the end of 'Drôle d'Amitié' may have been as anomalous a reaction to the complexities of his situation as was Mathieu's gratuitous stand. For in the camp Brunet is shown as being scornful of Mathieu's efforts to help individuals and as likely to seek some new way of continuing to serve the Communist cause. In fact, in all of the novels of this period there is only one character in whom an excessive and defeatist reaction to historical complexities gives us the impression of being absolute and definitive, and significantly this is the immortal Fosca. In almost all other cases (Fosca's companion Régine is a difficult one), human characters eventually appear to draw *some* kind of consolation in their confusion and desperation from the notion of doing their best.

There is clearly a negative, restrictive side to this attitude, since it involves acknowledging that a deliberate limitation of one's aims and expectations in acting is desirable or necessary. This limitation itself has two main aspects. There is, firstly, a recognition that full theoretical understanding of a situation may well be incompatible with the urgent demands of action as such. Thus, for instance, Rieux claims, '"on ne peut pas en même temps guérir et savoir. Alors guérissons le plus vite possible. C'est le plus pressé"' (LP 1389); and that '"le salut de l'homme est un trop grand mot pour moi. Je ne vais pas si loin. C'est sa santé qui m'intéresse, sa santé d'abord"' (1397). Or, again, Blomart eventually decides to act *in spite of* his continuing ignorance of various factors (SA 250). And when someone like Brunet bases his actions upon what he takes to be a full intellectual grasp of the political situation, he comes to grief and is shown to be mistaken. Similar comments would apply to Fosca in the early stages of his life. Even Tarrou, whose moral conduct is entirely admirable in the plague situation, fails to substantiate his claim that it springs from a complete knowledge of life, for as Rieux points out: 'Tarrou avait vécu dans le déchirement et la contradiction' (LP 1459).

As we have seen, the second limitation contained in the idea of doing one's best is a general one concerning the efficacity and scope of individual action. Now aware of the vast historical movements that sweep them along, most characters in these books see that their own efforts count for relatively little in themselves. Mathieu is conscious of this throughout; Rieux acknowledges that the struggle against the plague is 'une interminable défaite' (LP 1324); and in *Tous les hommes sont mortels* Armand has learned a similar lesson, even without Fosca's immortality:

'Si l'on vit assez longtemps, on voit que toute victoire se change un jour en défaite ...'
    Sans doute mon accent l'agaça, car il dit vivement:
    'Oh! j'ai quelque teinture d'histoire; vous ne m'apprenez rien. Tout ce qu'on fait finit par se défaire, je sais. Et dès l'heure où l'on naît on commence à mourir.' (503-04)

This, however, is precisely the point at which key figures make a positive moral response to the restrictions they see imposed upon them. Armand goes on: '"Mais entre la naissance et la mort il y a la vie ... Un avenir limité; une vie limitée; c'est notre lot d'homme, c'est assez, dit-il"' (504). If all human action turns into defeat when we look at it in a sufficiently long-term perspective, this may just as logically be taken to indicate that we should cease looking at our actions in a long-term perspective as that all action is futile. Only the individual himself can choose which stance to adopt and there can be no doubt whatever about which our three authors consider preferable. Even Fosca comes to see in the end that, on the time-scale appropriate to mortals, there can still be genuine victories (THM 520). And although right at the end of his chronicle Rieux emphasises that the plague germ will never die out, there are other senses in which the book ends on a victorious note. Doubtless, if we employ these terms at all, we need to accept that men will be 'ultimately defeated', but the real moral victory consists in recognising this, yet opting to struggle on:

> 'Oui, approuva Tarrou, je peux comprendre. Mais vos victoires seront toujours provisoires, voilà tout.'
> Rieux parut s'assombrir.
> 'Toujours, je le sais. Ce n'est pas une raison pour cesser de lutter.' (LP 1324)

In this kind of context, the idea of 'doing one's best' comes to seem at least a little less vacuous than it might. There are certain things that it may be beyond our power to change, but striving to change them in any case is perhaps the only dignified course of action open to us. Blomart thinks this way about some aspects of his commitment to the working classes:

> 'Il y aura toujours un abîme entre un ouvrier et toi: tu choisis librement une condition qu'il subit.'
> 'C'est vrai, dit Jean, mais du moins j'aurai fait mon possible.' (SA 37)

And not only does Mathieu use the same terminology in his discussion with Pinette on the subject of how they might have behaved differently before the war (MA 1212), he later tells Brunet that he believes

there is nothing to do other than to go on
attempting the impossible (DCh 1653). The principle
involved here applies just as much to cases where
defeat is not the outcome, as Blomart recognises
when Hélène points out that his individual efforts
will make no difference to an eventual *victory*:

Hélène se mordit les lèvres.
    'On gagnera bien la guerre sans toi,
dit-elle.'
    'Sans doute, dit Jean. Mais pour moi ça ne
serait pas du tout la même chose!' (SA 227)

These last cases suggest, as Rieux's
undoubtedly does, that by this stage we have dug
down as deeply into the foundations of moral
positions as it is possible to go. Blomart's comment
has an air of finality about it, like Mathieu's
reactions; and at one point Rieux admits that he
cannot rationally justify his own position as
against Rambert's desire to escape: 'Rieux n'avait
pas d'arguments à lui opposer' (LP 1384). As is
sometimes claimed in works of ethical theory, it
seems that here the only sort of answer that can
ultimately be given to the doubter who persists for
long enough in asking why is simply: 'Because that's
how I see things'. For it has to be admitted that
such attempts as characters make in these novels to
go any further than this towards an explanation or
justification of their fundamental moral stances
raise far more difficulties than they solve. In this
connection, we may remember that the longer Fosca
lives in *Tous les hommes sont mortels*, the more
importance he comes to attach to the idea of acting
according to one's individual conscience: '"Un homme
m'a dit un jour: il n'existe qu'un seul bien, c'est
d'agir selon sa conscience. Je pense qu'il avait
raison"' (405). Yet the weaknesses, and indeed
dangers, in any formula of this kind need no
pointing out. Or again, if we take Rieux's formula,
'"la seule façon de lutter contre la peste, c'est
l'honnêteté"' (LP 1352), we find that he
immediately qualifies this in a fundamental way, and
that the wisdom of doing so is confirmed in the
ensuing exchanges with Rambert:

'Qu'est-ce que l'honnêteté?' dit Rambert, d'un
air soudain sérieux.
    'Je ne sais pas ce qu'elle est en général.
Mais dans mon cas, je sais qu'elle consiste à
faire mon métier.'

'Ah! dit Rambert, avec rage, je ne sais pas
quel est mon métier.' (LP 1352)

The point here is that any moral formulae that
characters dare to, or are obliged to, offer are
recognised as being inadequate. On the theoretical,
and perhaps even on the practical, level they do not
have answers that they regard as fully satisfactory.
When Blomart is asked, in relation to his attitude
towards the Resistance, '"Vous estimez que tous les
moyens sont bons?"', his answer is unequivocal and
crucial: '"Au contraire. Tous les moyens sont
mauvais"' (SA 249). The change that has come over
him is that he has now decided to act rather than to
try to abstain from action, but he still has no hope
of doing something that is morally right through and
through. In other words, there is a certain
tentativeness deliberately built into the 'positive'
moral outlooks of the main characters; not so much
in the carrying out of actions as in the relative
lack of confidence and hope with which they look
upon their own moral judgements. Or, better still,
there is a certain modesty - albeit an enforced one
- in the characters' perspectives. Figures like
Fosca and Brunet (perhaps even, in a different way,
Paneloux), who begin with large-scale ambitions
and/or an apparently unshakable belief in absolutes,
are eventually cut down to size and thereby become
much more 'human' and sympathetic to the reader. The
kind of modesty involved can only be captured in
some such notion as that of 'doing one's best', and
if this, like the idea of solidarity, is a somewhat
vague formula - an arrow pointing in one general
direction rather than anything that could usefully
be called a moral ideal - then this fact is to be
attributed, in large ·part at least, to the
confusing, disorientating nature of the historical
framework posed by these wartime novels.
In short, the impact of history, which
constitutes the most distinctive and important
feature of the moral perspectives of the wartime
period, also places definite limits upon them. It is
to a brief examination of more subtle aspects of
those limits that we may now turn. A point that
needs to be emphasised, for instance, is that the
range of situations covered in these books is a
narrow one. Sartre once advocated a 'littérature des
situations extrêmes', yet even that description
would not be specific enough to define the wartime
fiction. As we have seen, the extreme situations

150

that dominate the stories are, first and foremost, collective ones, and ones associated with catastrophe or the threat of catastrophe. The inevitable result of this is that the prevailing moral outlooks focus almost exclusively on those issues thrust at the individual at a time of collective disaster. One question, therefore, that the moral theorist would wish to ask is how much validity these perspectives would have in entirely different and less extraordinary circumstances. Since the situations depicted here are so exceptional (and even within them characters may, in one way or another, be exceptional cases: in *La Peste*, to take just one sort of example, Othon and Tarrou both catch the plague very late on; Paneloux is a 'cas douteux'; Grand is one of the first to recover from the plague; Tarrou bizarrely displays *two* sets of symptoms), what exactly is the scope of any inferences to be drawn directly from them?

A powerful argument in this connection suggests that only in extreme situations do certain kinds of truth about human beings emerge, and as one would expect, there are traces of this argument in the novels. The coward Pierre, in *Le Sursis*, appears to accept it, even to the extent of lamenting his own bad luck with history:

> Il avait suffi d'un jour pour qu'il découvre son être véritable; sans ces menaces de guerre il n'aurait jamais rien su ... Ça n'est pas juste, pensa-t-il. Il y a des milliers de gens, des millions, peut-être, qui ont vécu à des époques heureuses et qui n'ont jamais connu leurs limites: on leur a laissé le bénéfice du doute. Alfred de Vigny était peut-être un lâche. Et Musset? Et Sainte-Beuve? Et Baudelaire? ils ont eu de la veine. (877)

And one of the last sequences in that book is an expression of Mathieu's determination not to forget the lessons he has learned during the unusual circumstances of the crisis (1132). On the other hand, a major point about the function of 'nos concitoyens' in *La Peste* is the suggestion that after the plague, for the majority at least (and for better or worse), things will go on exactly as before: 'Cottard, Tarrou, ceux et celle que Rieux avait aimés et perdus, tous, morts ou coupables, étaient oubliés. Le vieux avait raison, les hommes étaient toujours les mêmes' (1473). Rieux's reason for writing his chronicle is, precisely, to ensure that there is a lasting record of the injustice and violence perpetrated upon the victims of the plague. Yet the very recognition of the citizens' inclination to forget (which is also implicit in Mathieu's observations) suggests that certain forces in men run counter to the likelihood of their learning whatever lessons the extraordinary circumstances of collective catastrophe may have to offer. What we need to ask, therefore, is whether the stories contain other indications of this kind that the crisis perspectives delineated here have weaknesses or limitations corresponding to their strengths.

This is a good stage at which to remember that the wartime stories have behind them all of the weight of the pre-war moral deliberations already recorded, for having written about individuals seeking their own personal salvation or justification, Sartre, Camus and Beauvoir are unlikely to neglect considerations of this kind completely when it is a matter of examining interdependence and collective situations. In any case, they show themselves to be aware that there is more to life - and perhaps to ethics - than attempting to respond in the most appropriate way, and at the most appropriate level, to collective disasters: '"A la fin, c'est trop bête de ne vivre que dans la peste. Bien entendu, un homme doit se battre pour les victimes. Mais s'il cesse de rien aimer par ailleurs, à quoi sert qu'il se batte?"' (LP 1428). Tarrou's assertion is well illustrated in *La Peste* by the character of Grand, who Rieux suggests should be regarded as the hero of the chronicle (1331). For Grand is one of the few main figures in the book whose life-pattern and state of mind *after* the plague we can picture fairly clearly. He never 'belongs' exclusively to the collective situation to the extent that characters like Rieux, Tarrou and Paneloux do (and, incidentally, to the extent that even those characters who either welcome or strive to evade the crisis do). Furthermore, however ridiculous his writing project seems, it is largely because of it that he shares with Rambert the role of representing the side of Camus's thought that positively affirms the value of life and supports the quest for individual happiness. Rambert himself manifestly portrays a commitment to happiness and love that most of the other characters are unwilling or unable to sustain:

Et justement ce qui reste à retracer avant d'en

> arriver au sommet de la peste ... ce sont les
> longs efforts désespérés et monotones que les
> derniers individus, comme Rambert, faisaient
> pour retrouver leur bonheur et ôter à la peste
> cette part d'eux-mêmes qu'ils défendaient
> contre toute atteinte.(LP 1333)

In general, Camus stresses that it is precisely such
commitments as this that unfortunately have to be
sacrificed in collective situations: 'Il faut bien
le dire, la peste avait enlevé à tous le pouvoir de
l'amour et même de l'amitié' (LP 1367).

Sartre and Beauvoir, too, show some awareness
of this type of limit imposed upon crisis
perspectives, although on the whole they seem rather
less favourably disposed than Camus towards the idea
of trying to hold out *against* collective disasters
and to '"faire quelque chose pour le bonheur"' (LP
1385). Neither Marcel nor Hélène in *Le Sang des
autres*, both of whom are seen to undergo
'conversions' comparable to that of Rambert, is
presented as sympathetically as Camus's journalist.
Whatever positive virtues they may be taken to
represent (and Marcel does have a concern for art,
while Hélène obviously embodies certain qualities of
spontaneity and enthusiasm for life that Blomart
lacks), they are both highly selfish characters to
begin with, and their particular quests for personal
happiness or love have nothing of the dignity of
Rambert's. Nevertheless, one of their functions in
the book is to remind us that there are other sides
to life than those that constantly preoccupy
Blomart. There are similar reminders in *Le Sursis*,
although, interestingly, the 'personal happiness'
perspective is represented almost exclusively by
women. Odette, Ivich, Sarah, Zézette and the women
of Crevilly have all, in their own ways, systems of
values that assign a relatively low place to the
demands of collective crises. They set a
particularly high premium on personal relationships,
private or 'domestic' situations and individual
happiness ('"Nous sommes d'abord des femmes, madame,
des femmes qu'on atteint dans ce qu'elles ont de
plus cher"'; Surs 1011). The treatment of these
characters is such as to suggest that Sartre's own
position may be closer to that of someone like
Boris, who thinks that the good thing about war is
that it is a matter between *men* (Surs 1032), but
here too the call of the world outside the
collective situation, the call of non-crisis values,
is recognised and heard in the novel.

More generally, acknowledgement of the boundaries of the dominant moral perspectives of the period is to be found in these novels in the level of tension between the ideals of loyalty to the individual and loyalty to the group. In times of collective crisis, working for the group to which one has chosen to belong must, when there is a conflict between the two, take precedence over love and friendship, and this may involve making sacrifices in one's personal relationships. When it is clear that Hélène does not accept this view, Blomart breaks with her for preventing him from fighting in the war (he says earlier: '"Je t'aime ... mais il n'y a pas que l'amour"'; SA 228); Rambert, of course, finally gives up his attempts to rejoin his mistress in favour of joining Tarrou's 'formations sanitaires'; Boris enlists in the army in spite of Lola's wishes in *Le Sursis*, and is about to leave to join the Free French Forces in *La Mort dans l'âme*, despite the pain he knows it will cause her; and Fosca takes the immortality potion (in order to be able to further the cause of Carmona) in spite of the instances of his first wife. The point to be emphasised is that the great cost at which such decisions are made marks a kind of limit, in that it is presented as the very highest price that the characters (and authors) would ever be prepared to pay for loyalty to the group. A good contrast is offered by a minor figure like Pinette: to Mathieu's disgust, he is absolutely ruthless and unfeeling in his rejection of a woman friend once the chance to strike at the Germans arises (MA 1293-96). The major characters, on the other hand, are infinitely more sensitive and tormented in comparable circumstances: although their decisions invariably accord with that of Pinette in the end, they are mostly taken with the greatest regret and seen as no more than temporary, even provisional, measures, necessary but unfortunate in the extreme.

A great deal in these books provides general evidence for this last view and we have already touched on some of it in other contexts. But two further and more specific points may be made. Firstly, on only one occasion in these stories is there anything that might be seen (and may have been intended) as a satisfactory resolution of the conflicting claims of individual and group, that is at the end of *Le Sang des autres*. In all other cases, it is evident that the conflict leaves an open wound that continues to fester, visibly and painfully, long after the decision is made in favour of the group. Most commonly, this wound is associated with the way in which the collective crisis actually separates the individual from those to whom he is personally linked by love or friendship, and often the separation is made permanent by premature death. Where death does not curtail these relationships, we are left with the impression that although making sacrifices in one's personal relations is unavoidable at moments of collective disaster, it may well prove impossible later, in less extraordinary circumstances, to make up for lost time. There is a chance that the sacrifice will turn out to be less temporary than it appeared, the possibility of permanent scars.

Even at the end of *Le Sang des autres* death separates Hélène and Blomart, but there is a strong notion of two individuals actually being brought together by their commitment to a group, since the Resistance situation is shown as somehow solving problems that have existed between the lovers. At a certain theoretical level, therefore, it might seem that the basic conflict between personal and political morality that runs through much of the book is fully resolved by Hélène's conversion, which ensures that *all* moral considerations come to point in exactly the same direction at the end. Yet a moment's reflection is sufficient to suggest that this 'solution' is unconvincing and contrived, resting as it does on an extraneous chance element. *As it happens*, Jean and Hélène are able to come together under the same Resistance umbrella, but they might just as easily not have done, for only fortuitous factors bring Hélène to see Blomart again after their break (302). The basic moral issues raised earlier in the book concerning the relative values of a love relationship and a commitment to the group are in fact evaded by something like a stroke of luck. The easiest way of confirming the point is by contrasting the situation here with that in the case of Rambert. Collective disaster *separates* Rambert from his mistress just as surely and just as fortuitously as it brings Blomart and Hélène together. And although Rambert is able to rejoin her in the end, they are seen to be left with a difficult legacy from the crisis (Rieux comments: '"Courage, c'est maintenant qu'il faut avoir raison"'; LP 1467). The ending of *Le Sang des autres*, in fact, goes no way towards showing whether and how the wound perhaps inevitably caused by sacrificing personal relations to the collectivity may be healed.

A second point is that some main characters in these novels are less than absolutely consistent in the matter of giving priority to the collectivity over the individual. Blomart's attitude and conduct are unwavering, but the same cannot be said, for instance, of Fosca, Brunet and Rieux. In the episode of 'les bouches inutiles' in *Tous les hommes sont mortels*, Fosca makes a special, and quite unjustified, exception of his own family (126); and while for the most part Brunet is scrupulously fair and certainly never accepts privileges for himself, he does try to ensure that Schneider receives rather special treatment in 'Drôle d'amitié' (1467-70). It is the conduct of Rieux, however, that is most remarkable in this connection. He defends the rules and regulations in the face of Rambert's arguments (LP 1288-90), as well as on subsequent occasions, yet he himself breaks them at least four times in rapid succession later: to swim with Tarrou (1428); to send a letter to his wife (1431); to treat Grand in his flat (1433); and to treat Tarrou at home (1452). Furthermore, he not only positively encourages Rambert to escape, but is even prepared, astonishingly, to see him go on the very day when he has visited Rieux at the hospital (1388). In comparison with the central issues of the stories these are all undoubtedly trivial exceptions and it is hard to say exactly what their significance is. Nevertheless, it is fair to infer that they betoken some unease on the part of the authors at the whole idea of giving the collectivity precedence over loyalty to loved individuals.

Wartime perspectives are subject to certain limitations, then, because the situations described in the stories are so extraordinary that they involve the temporary witholding of attention from matters that normally predominate in *non*-crisis circumstances. Now, this pattern finally brings us back to a set of considerations mentioned earlier, for our authors' broadly anti-bourgeois stance in the pre-war stories is seen to give way here to a willingness to stand and fight alongside the bourgeoisie, but a willingness of a provisional nature and one that perhaps leaves a residue of unease. As we saw, changes in the official Communist Party line make it all the more difficult for Brunet to reconcile, in the war circumstances, his whole-hearted opposition to Nazism on the one side and to capitalism on the other. There is no means of knowing exactly how he might have resolved this dilemma in *La Dernière Chance* , but it is hard to

see how any solution could be wholly satisfactory.
And once again a suggestion that the 'happy' ending
of *Le Sang des autres* provides a full answer would
be mistaken. As with the reconciliation of Blomart
and Hélène, what we have there is a theoretically
unhelpful alliance between parties whose interests
or views had earlier been shown as implacably
opposed. This is especially noticeable in relation
to the final position of Blomart's father, since the
very starting-point of Jean's evolution had been his
opposition to his father's bourgeois values:"'Nous
rencontrons les sympathies et les appuis les plus
inattendus, dis-je. Imaginerais-tu que je suis
réconcilié avec mon père? La bourgeoisie
nationaliste nous tend la main"' (283). And at the
other end of the political spectrum, the Resistance
movement's alliance with the Communist Party is
explicitly proposed as a matter of expediency:

> 'Tâche de les convaincre de prendre contact
> avec nous et de former comme ici un front
> unique. Plus tard, nous aurons peut-être encore
> à lutter les uns contre les autres. Mais pas
> maintenant.' (210)

The point is not that there is anything in the least
wrong morally with either of these alliances during
the war, but only that their essentially temporary
nature and the way in which they entail a
short-lived suppression of serious differences form
strict limitations to the outlook with which they
are associated.

Because the superficial terms of reference are
so different in *La Peste*, it is not possible to say
exactly the same about Camus's reactions to this
kind of dilemma. However, reading only just beneath
the surface of the book, it is not difficult to find
very close parallels to the unease of Sartre and
Beauvoir. As far as alliances are concerned, much
the same applies here as in *Le Sang des autres*: it
is highly unlikely that Rieux would have been able
to continue making common cause with Paneloux after
the crisis had ended; and what could possibly have
been the future for a temporary association like
that between Othon and Tarrou, given the latter's
views on judges? It is interesting and revealing
that both Paneloux as priest and Othon as judge are
precisely the type of figures that in *L'Etranger*
Camus took to represent the 'official' society that
he wished to attack. It may even be possible to
pursue the argument a little further than this, for

in plague-stricken Oran the nearest equivalent to the bourgeoisie in other books may well be the town administration, and Camus's attitude towards this administration and what it does is a rather ambivalent one. Rieux is something of a rebel at the beginning of the story and through him we feel impatience at the authorities' procrastination and ineffectiveness. But later, while more subtle criticism of bureaucracy is still implicit (for instance, in his account of things that happen to Grand and Rambert), Rieux's detached presentation often suggests that he does not accept the citizens' criticisms of the administration; and he does argue, after all, that the only way to fight the plague is by sound method, systematic attention to detail, regular habits and, above all, good organisation. It looks rather as if Rieux is uneasily accepting an alliance with administrators for the duration of the plague, while keeping his options open for when the crisis has passed. Like Sartre and Beauvoir, Camus appears to be acknowledging that although he is prepared to stifle his opposition to certain 'bourgeois' values for a time, this is strictly only until there is a return to more normal circumstances.

It might be said that all of this amounts to saying that in the wartime stories our authors are temporarily more anti-Fascist than they are anti-capitalist, and that this is an obvious enough point. It does, however, in addition to marking a limitation in the moral outlooks of this phase, tend to confirm what we have already implied, that there is something rather negative about those outlooks, at least in the sense that we are a good deal clearer about what different things our authors stand *against* than what they stand for. It seems that - certainly by force of circumstance - characters are too preoccupied with establishing an appropriate hierarchy among those phenomena to which they are opposed to be able to devote enough time to elaborating an equally strong set of moral desiderata. In the pre-war fiction, too, characters' attempts at constructing their own values produced relatively little that was recognisable as prescriptive morality, but they were at least beginning to gain a toe-hold in their struggle for self-determination. Even if that toe-hold has not entirely been lost in the wartime books, there is relatively little emphasis on its importance for the surmounting of the particular obstacles that individuals are now faced with. And in the struggle to rise above *those*, the moral agent attains only what is, at the very best, an equally precarious perch.

The ideal of lucidity has not been rejected, and is perhaps even assimilated and taken for granted at this stage. But in the earlier books it applied above all to knowledge of oneself and one's metaphysical condition, and this is clearly no longer the only, or even the predominant, issue during the war. Consequently, self-deception, although it claims a few notable victims like Mathieu's brother Jacques, does not figure nearly so prominently here as it previously did. Like so much else, lucidity and self-deception have been rather overtaken by events in the war years. Perhaps more than anything else, in fact, this is the key to the nature of the moral perspectives of the period. By the time most characters make the main discoveries associated with wartime situations, it is already in certain senses too late. Not in all senses, of course, but in enough to ensure that even their most positive reactions have the slightly negative flavour of a defensive, rearguard action. In much the way that some large-scale historical catastrophe was 'needed' to break our authors out of the self-enclosed and rather solipsistic moral world portrayed in their pre-war fiction, so now the only possibility of evolution or development in their outlooks lies in a marked change in the political circumstances, in a prolonged period of peace, with history impinging considerably less, or at least less obviously and painfully, on individual lives. Only in such circumstances could certain questions conceivably be fully answered and the barriers limiting the wartime moral perspectives be lifted.

NOTES

1. Beauvoir's plot-summary is in *La Force des choses* (I, 270-72), and Sartre's notes are to be found in his *Oeuvres romanesques* (2140-44).

PART THREE

POST-WAR STORIES

Chapter Eight

TRANSITION

In her memoirs, Beauvoir records that although by the end of the projected fourth volume of Sartre's *Les Chemins de la liberté* almost all of the main characters were dead, so that 'il n'y avait plus personne pour se poser les problèmes de l'après-guerre', it was precisely these post-war problems that preoccupied Sartre at the time when he was required to finish *La Dernière Chance* .[1] Sartre himself confirmed that the greater complexity of the moral climate after 1945 stood in the way of the completion of his tetralogy, and he suggested that this in turn prevented him from writing other novels.[2] Consequently, we have no fiction at all by Sartre to examine in our search for the moral perspectives that supplanted those associated with the war and the impact of history. There are, however, five books (and twelve stories in all) by Camus and Beauvoir which are, in all senses, post-war products, and which have a much longer chronological span than the first two groups of works. They were conceived and written over some seventeen years; and since the story of *Les Mandarins* begins just before the end of the war, they may be said to cover together the whole of the post-war period up to 1967.

We have seen that the passage from pre-war to wartime outlooks was precipitated by, and accompanied, a shock: the shock of the crisis in Europe and the Second World War. In so far as such a passage ever could be, it was sudden, sharp and marked off by a definable sequence of historical events. This fact is confirmed in the wartime novels, where the transition itself forms part of their subject-matter and is shown as being explainable only as the result of large-scale collective catastrophe. The passage from wartime to

post-war perspectives, on the other hand, was of a
very different nature: it was undoubtedly much more
gradual, and the transition more subtle. This fact
itself, however, shows in only one novel of the
post-war period, *Les Mandarins*, which Beauvoir
started writing in 1949. Her other two works of
fiction - *Les Belles Images* and *La Femme rompue*
(comprising 'L'Age de discrétion', 'Monologue' and
'La Femme rompue') - are both unmistakably products
of the nineteen-sixties. Camus did not begin working
on either of his books - *La Chute* and *L'Exil et le
royaume* (comprising 'La Femme adultère', 'Le
Renégat', 'Les Muets', 'L'Hôte', 'Jonas' and 'La
Pierre qui pousse') - until the early fifties. They
too exhibit distinctive post-war outlooks in their
established form, rather than contributing to our
understanding of how such attitudes were arrived at.
Les Mandarins, therefore, is the only work here to
describe the climate of opinion in the immediate
post-war years and the way in which the perspectives
that were to mark all of the post-war fiction came
gradually into being. Not surprisingly, Sartre has
claimed that it is the real sequel to *Les Chemins de
la liberté* (1880), and it will inevitably occupy a
special place in our preliminary discussion. Apart
from anything else, this will allow us to take the
Second World War as the natural starting-point for
our examination of this group of works, whilst
recognising that by the mid-sixties the war had been
left a very long way behind and a wholly new set of
problems or concerns had replaced its shorter-term
legacy.

     Not that references back to the war are
entirely absent from all of the books except *Les
Mandarins*: there are such references in a number of
cases and they are by no means always trivial. The
significant point is that in these instances the
events and circumstances of the war are seen as
essentially exceptional or extraordinary ones,
confirming that the limits we discerned in the
wartime perspectives came to be openly acknowledged
as such by Camus and Beauvoir. To take a simple
example, the journey into the Algerian hinterland
undertaken by Marcel and Janine in 'La Femme
adultère' is presented as the direct result of the
interruption of normal trading patterns and the
scarcity of cloth during the war (1561-62). We also
learn in 'L'Hôte' that Daru arrived to work as a
schoolteacher up on the Algerian plateaux after the
war and was immediately struck by the silence and
calm that reigns there. In his eyes, even the

circumstances of an incipient Arab uprising are not exceptional enough to justify actions that he might have performed, unwillingly, in wartime, for when the policeman Balducci claims that in times of war we have to do all kinds of things, Daru replies tartly: '"alors, j'attendrai la déclaration de guerre!"' (1614). (There is a rather similar sequence early on in *Les Mandarins*, for when Scriassine suggests that Henri may be guilty of desertion in making a pleasure trip to Portugal, Henri exclaims: '"Une désertion? ... Je ne suis pas soldat"'; I,33.) Again, in *Les Belles Images* it is claimed that Laurence had good reason, in the exceptional circumstances of the end of the war, for being disturbed as a child: 'Les exterminations, Hiroshima: il y avait des raisons, en 45, pour qu'une enfant de onze ans se sente sonnée' (25). This still leaves room, as in the earlier cases, for discussion of just what constitutes a normal reaction in the post-war conditions, or how 'normal' those conditions themselves are, but wartime events are quite clearly being seen as in a category of their own, and being contrasted with peacetime circumstances.

The same is at least partly true of the references to the war in *La Chute*. At one point Clamence expresses some regret at not having been fully involved in the extreme circumstances: 'Mobilisé bien sûr, mais je n'ai jamais vu le feu. Dans un sens, je le regrette. Peut-être cela aurait-il changé beaucoup de choses?' (1538). As usual with Clamence, however, this is not the whole story. His attitude towards the war, as to many other things, is a profoundly ambiguous one. The difficulty is that he wishes at one and the same time to horrify his interlocutor by reminding him of the unspeakable cruelties and inhumanities that took place during the war, and to assure him that, in some sense, such horrors are typical of modern man. It is in this spirit that he tells of the mother who was obliged to choose which of her two sons she would have shot in German reprisals, and of the pacifist whose friendly welcome to all and sundry was responded to by militiamen who disembowelled him (1481). And when he tells his revealing tale about being elected 'Pope' in an internment camp in wartime North Africa, his object is as much to claim that such happenings are representative of the times ('Nous autres, enfants du demi-siècle, n'avons pas besoin de dessin pour imaginer ces sortes d'endroits'; 1539) as to surprise. In fact, *all* of

Clamence's stories and comments have to be seen in the context of his attempt to persuade his interlocutor that human guilt is universal. He cannot afford to allow that we need to discriminate between good and evil and consequently his attitudes have to be ambiguous ones. Early on his comments on Hitler are somewhat equivocal (1481), but his attitude towards the Resistance movement is still more revealing. He was tempted by it, but hesitated, then turned away: 'L'entreprise me paraissait un peu folle et, pour tout dire, romantique ... J'admirais ceux qui se livraient à cet héroïsme des profondeurs, mais ne pouvais les imiter' (1539).

Retrospective attitudes towards the Resistance are, to a very large extent, the crux of the process of evolution from wartime to post-war perspectives, since the Resistance, or at least resistance, was one of the central features of the wartime moral stances that we examined. On this point *Les Mandarins* is particularly useful. The characters at the beginning of the novel, as a result of the Resistance experience and the imminence of the Allied victory, are in a state of high optimism: 'L'air gris-bleu était lourd de promesses, l'avenir s'élargissait à l'infini' (I,23). But the book as a whole is, perhaps above all else, a record of the gradual undermining of this optimism and its replacement by a general, though not unrelieved, state of disillusionment. (There are some minor comments in 'La Femme rompue' that refer back to this shift: 'Maurice a été déçu par l'après-guerre'; 195.) Interestingly, however, from the very first the main figures in *Les Mandarins* are under very few illusions about the direct applicability in the post-war situation of the methods forged during the Resistance; or even about the longer-term significance of alliances formed at that time. Much later in the novel, in the course of making some obvious but vital points about the differences between the Occupation and the Liberation, Robert Dubreuilh suggests that left-wing intellectuals had too readily assumed that there was continuity between the two situations:

> 'La Résistance, parfait, une poignée d'hommes y suffisait; tout ce qu'on voulait, somme toute, c'était créer de l'agitation; agitation, sabotage, résistance, c'est l'affaire d'une minorité. Mais quand on prétend construire, c'est une tout autre histoire. Nous avons cru que nous n'avions qu'à profiter de notre élan:

alors qu'il y avait une coupure radicale entre
la période de l'occupation et celle qui a suivi
la Libération.' (II,337-38)

Yet, in fact, it is far from clear that Henri and
Dubreuilh ever made the mistakes mentioned.
Dubreuilh's wife Anne is portrayed as having a
certain nostalgia for the camaraderie of the
Resistance and its 'sombre douceur' - something that
Henri, too, not infrequently refers to - but from
very early on Dubreuilh is talking in much the same
terms as he does later about the negative side to
their wartime experience (I,62).

Dubreuilh's accusation against the journalists
on Henri's newspaper *L'Espoir*, that they are
pretending there is still a Resistance movement,
scarcely applies to Henri, in any case, for he is
just as scornful as Dubreuilh of the way in which
his faithful assistant editor Luc strives to
preserve the spirit and unity of the Resistance, and
he has already recognised by Christmas 1944 that 'La
Résistance était une chose, la politique une autre'
(I,19). He had appreciated the friendship and
commitment at their true value, and regards the
experience as having been a sufficiently important
and formative one to excuse the later fanaticism of
someone like Lachaume (I,199). But he is much more
sympathetic to Lambert, who buries his wartime
differences with his father, than to Vincent, who
pursues struggles and continues to employ methods
engendered during the Resistance. Henri is
undoubtedly rather horrified that a former leading
figure of the Resistance, Tournelle, might be
suggesting that they should not have resisted at all
(I,250), but his remarks to Vincent - somewhat
reminiscent of Clamence's description of the
Resistance as an 'entreprise romantique' - show a
strong sense of proportion and balance in his
attitude towards the war years: '"Mais bon Dieu! ce
n'était pas l'aventure qui comptait: c'était les
trucs qu'on défendait"' (I,247). One cannot help
thinking, furthermore, that one of Henri's comments
about reactions to his latest novel, the first novel
to appear after the Liberation, may reveal a great
deal of Beauvoir's own later views on the Resistance
and constitute a telling retrospective gloss on *Le
Sang des autres*:

Lambert croyait qu'il avait voulu à travers
l'action collective exalter l'individualisme,
et Lachaume au contraire qu'il prêchait le

sacrifice de l'individu à la collectivité. Tous soulignaient le caractère édifiant du roman. Pourtant, c'était presque un hasard si Henri avait situé cette histoire pendant la Résistance; il avait pensé à un homme, et aussi à une situation; à un certain rapport entre le passé de son personnage et la crise qu'il traversait. (I,192)

The question of Henri's books is of some general interest in this connection, since just as the setting in the novel mentioned encapsulates the whole matter of later attitudes towards the Resistance, so the fact that he considers setting his next novel in 1935 shows that post-war stances have to be adopted in relation to the *pre-war* period as well as to the Resistance. In an early conversation with Anne, Scriassine argues that French intellectuals seem to imagine that after the war they will be able to live exactly as they did before it, and it is quite true that this temptation is to be seen in some of the central figures. It takes Henri himself a while to see why he could not give his new novel a pre-war setting ('il n'avait plus rien à voir avec ce qu'il était en 1935. Son indifférence politique, sa curiosité, son ambition, tout ce parti pris d'individualisme, que c'était court, que c'était niais!'; I,225), and he has to admit that his main aim immediately after the Liberation had been to revert to his pre-war life, with the addition of a few new activities (I,259). Anne, too, has to make a positive effort to remind herself that the pre-war situation will never return. She admits to Paule, a large part of whose problems with Henri arise out of *her* refusal to believe that anything has changed during the war years: '"Moi aussi pendant quelques semaines j'ai eu l'illusion qu'on allait retrouver l'avant-guerre; mais c'était de la sottise"' (I,294).

In other words, we see depicted in *Les Mandarins* a whole range of possible attitudes immediately after the Liberation, all of which have the war as a crucial point of reference. It is true that, if one or two characters would like to go on living as they did during the war, the majority clearly prefer the post-war peace, with the result that, exactly as we might have predicted on the basis of our analysis of wartime perspectives, there is some risk that the great sacrifices made in the war will soon be forgotten. But Anne and Henri are among those who are determined to preserve the memory of the calamitous events. Anne has a personal sense of guilt at having survived when so many people she knew gave up their lives in the struggle, and she is greatly moved by Dubreuilh's claim that the war will not prove to have been in vain (I,340). (In *Les Belles Images*, Laurence remembers how strongly her teacher Mlle Houchet expressed this hope; 25.) And Henri, whatever the implications of his subsequent act of perjury, writes a play which effectively asks the French to remember.

Again, while some main figures like Dubreuilh recognise from the first that adaptations will need to be made in the post-war situation, this leaves room for a spectrum of opinions on *how* things will be different and what precise consequences flow from the facts. It is only after a little time has elapsed in the story that we begin to discern a large measure of agreement among almost all of the main characters on the point that the changes taking place are wholesale ones. Scriassine has claimed prophetically:

'Les progrès de la science et de la technique, les changements économiques vont à tel point bouleverser la terre que nos manières mêmes de penser et de sentir en seront révolutionnées: nous aurons du mal à nous rappeler qui nous avons été.' (I,53)

And the general accuracy of this observation, which is crucial to the perspectives embodied in most of the other books of this period, comes to be confirmed: by Henri, who eventually sees the Resistance as having taken place 'dans un autre monde' (II,294) and regards himself as having lost a whole world without being given anything in return; by Anne, who talks of 'cette paix qui nous rendait à nos vies sans nous rendre nos raisons de vivre' (I,110); and by Dubreuilh, who sees more clearly than ever that everything is now up for questioning: 'Alors quel sens, quelles chances gardaient les vieilles valeurs: la vérité, la liberté, la morale individuelle, la littérature, la pensée? si on voulait les sauver, il fallait les réinventer'(I,278-79).

The particular significance of *Les Mandarins*, then, is that it shows us that it was only when all hope of reverting to a pre-war situation had finally been shattered, and when the exhilaration of the Resistance had been left behind, that the full extent and implications of the break with earlier circumstances could be grasped and outlooks changed accordingly. It also shows that this whole process was rather more gradual than we might suppose from the other post-war books, since there the protagonists experience from the first what characters in *Les Mandarins* come to acknowledge as the story progresses, namely the need to find their own moral direction in historical circumstances very different from those of the war. In the wartime fiction, in so far as individual action retained efficacity at all, it raised fewer problems over ends and objectives than over the right means of achieving them, but now the ends and directions themselves first need to be established, virtually from zero. To a certain extent, therefore, the characters' main concerns here are closer to those of their pre-war counterparts than to those of the wartime figures. There would be no difficulty, for instance, in illustrating extensively from these later works exactly the sort of preoccupation with solitude, even death, that was to be found in the pre-war fiction. Once more, accounts of later perspectives should not be taken to preclude the presence of earlier ones in any way, or even to imply that these are less important: it is simply that, again, broadly superimposed upon the former outlooks are new ones that may be regarded as more specific to, and distinctive of, the post-war phase.

It is noticeable that the standard narrative technique in these stories, rather than having the tone of a chronicle or encompassing a number of different standpoints (only in *Les Mandarins*, with its two 'narrators', is there any variety of viewpoint at all), now approximates to the monologue or diary. That is, interest is less sharply focused on groups as such than in the wartime books. This is not to say that the idea of the collectivity, or society, has no part to play in the post-war works - on the contrary. But society is no longer under severe threat or extreme pressure here in the way that it was during the war. Indeed, as we have already suggested, it is essential that society should now be seen as being in its 'normal' state, however difficult that might be to define. If the same could be said to be true of the pre-war fiction, the crucial difference is that society is by now much more than a mere point of reference for, or contrast with, the individual. The post-war characters, for the most part, no longer live on the very fringes of society, or in conflict with it: they are almost all in very real ways a part of

society. The main focus of interest in these stories
is undoubtedly the individual's problems *within* a
society in its more or less regular state.

Hardly surprisingly, while virtually all of the
main characters in the pre-war stories were young -
scarcely yet 'dans la force de l'âge' - the
principal figures now are invariably older, and
sometimes old. Arising out of this is the equally
obvious but more significant point that they are
almost always established and successful members of
society. Camus suggested that Meursault is condemned
to death 'parce qu'il ne joue pas le jeu. En ce
sens, il étranger à la société où il vit' (1928).
By this token very few of the later characters are
at risk, since up to some point and for some time
they all play the social 'game'. It is true that the
difference between these and earlier figures is
often one of degree rather than of kind (even
Meursault, Mersault and Paul Hilbert worked for
their living within society), but this difference is
none the less a considerable and crucial one. The
post-war characters take their part in the game very
much further and play it with much more success.
They have a far more marked social existence or
dimension than their two groups of predecessors, for
even where the wartime characters enjoyed a regular,
fixed place in society, they were only rarely seen
from this angle, because of the historical crisis.
At their deepest roots, the individual's problems
are doubtless the very same metaphysical ones as in
the earlier phases (how, indeed, could they be
different?), but these are no longer set in a
certain kind of ontological vacuum or dominated and
shaped by historical forces: their distinctive form
now comes from the fact that they are set in the
general context of peacetime society. In an
interview of 1969, Sartre summed up much of this in
saying that he came to realise after the war that
the heroic conditions of the Resistance had been
'une expérience fausse': 'Après la guerre est venue
l'expérience vraie, celle de la société'.[3]

Characters here have to learn about the basis
and workings of society itself in much the way that
their predecessors had to discover metaphysical
truths or facts about the forces of history. They
still stand in need of the quality of lucidity
prized from the first, for their discoveries are no
easier to assimilate than previous ones and the
moral problems they generate no less anguishing. One
might say that while one of the lessons of the
wartime stories was the brute fact of

interdependence, its exact *nature* remained to be understood; or that the historical interdependence discovered there is rather different from the kind of social interdependence that prevails in normal peacetime circumstances.

We need to remember, too, that it is primarily in the stories of this post-war period that interpersonal relations are brought sharply into focus and examined in their own right: for the most part, pre-war characters did not reach the stage of living and co-operating with others on any significant scale, and in the wartime stories larger issues were at stake which severely limited the range of possible relations between individuals. Characters here do not actively wish to stay outside or on the fringes of society, nor are they portrayed as being suddenly thrown, willy nilly, into contact with, and dependence upon, others. They do not see the existence of others simply as an intrusion or encroachment upon their personal liberty: the relationships they have are almost always ones that they have in some sense or other *chosen* to have, associations that they have freely entered into and freely chosen to continue. Human relations are now at last seen as two-way, give-and-take processes based upon the many needs and obligations that arise in the normal course of events in society. It is the full nature, extent and implications of this kind of interdependence that characters are shown as learning about for themselves in the stories, and a typical pattern is for a central figure to participate up to a certain point in the social game before discovering features of it that surprise, trouble or even repel him or her. That such a learning-process takes place at all is partly attributable to the fact that any kind of involvement in society and its normal routines and practices is seen as engendering distinctive problems of its own - problems that the characters in the earlier periods had no occasion to face.

Without being in any way relieved of the metaphysical burden that all have to bear, and perhaps without being able henceforth to ignore completely the forces of history (although these are not so obviously compelling as during the war years), individuals now have to face an additional cluster of problems associated with life in society. The result is that the complexity of their moral dilemmas risks being greater than ever. Often there is a multiplicity of major difficulties, some having to do with particular relationships and others more universal. Beauvoir's women characters are frequently outstanding examples of this and sometimes, like the narrator of 'L'Age de discrétion', they actually draw up a list of their current quandaries: 'Mon corps me lâchait. Je n'étais plus capable d'écrire; Philippe avait trahi tous mes espoirs et ce qui me navrait encore davantage c'est qu'entre André et moi les choses étaient en train de détériorer' (71). But whether or not they list their problems, the heroes and heroines frequently seem to be assailed from all sides at one and the same time. Daru, who at the end of 'L'Hôte', in Algeria, finds himself at variance with European settlers and Arabs alike, presents a very simple example, but Henri's case in *Les Mandarins* (and even that of Anne) is much more complicated:'Maintenant, les problèmes n'arrêtaient pas de se poser, et chacun remettait tout en question' (I,214). Camus's Jonas, too, falls into the same category, even if his problems sometimes seem to be of a more trivial nature:

> 'Le téléphone!', criait l'aîné, et Jonas
> plantait là son tableau pour y revenir, le
> coeur en paix, avec une invitation
> supplémentaire. 'C'est pour le gaz!', hurlait
> un employé dans la porte qu'un enfant lui avait
> ouverte. 'Voilà, voilà!' Quand Jonas quittait
> le téléphone, ou la porte, un ami, un disciple,
> les deux parfois, le suivaient jusqu'à la
> petite pièce pour terminer la conversation
> commencée. (Jon 1642)

The predominant impression at many points in these stories is that of characters caught in a most elaborate network or web of interlocking relations and obligations, the very complexity of which compounds any particular problems they have. This can happen in a single limited area of relations, as it does with Clamence and his women (LC 1527), or it can happen in a number of different areas at the same time, as with Laurence in *Les Belles Images*: 'je m'inquiète pour maman, Catherine me pose des problèmes, Jean-Charles est d'une humeur de chien, j'ai une liaison qui me pèse' (75).

In his own particular circumstances, Henri recognises the sheer complexity of the task of distinguishing one's friends from one's enemies in the post-war situation (LM II,123), and he has clearly registered some earlier remarks made to him by Lambert ('"depuis quelque temps je ne sais plus

distinguer le bien du mal"'; I,220), for he echoes
them on his own behalf after a conversation with
Dubreuilh (II,339). Monique, in 'La Femme rompue',
comes to much the same conclusion by a more domestic
route:

> Je n'ai pas rendu Maurice heureux. Et mes
> filles ne le sont pas non plus. Alors? Je ne
> sais plus rien. Non seulement pas qui je suis
> mais comment il faudrait être. Le noir et le
> blanc se confondent, le monde est un magma et
> je n'ai plus de contours. Comment vivre sans
> croire à rien ni à moi-même? (251)

One can fairly say, without having to stretch the
description too far, that one of the main themes of
these stories is that the complications of life in
post-war society are such as to make it peculiarly,
and perhaps uniquely, difficult to know right from
wrong. The only characters now who confidently claim
to be able to tell good from evil, like Clamence or
the Renégat, are portrayed as deceiving themselves
and/or seeking to deceive others. In his terrible
oscillation from one extreme to the other, the
Renégat may be seen as deceiving only himself, but
in this respect as in others Clamence's reaction to
complexity contrasts directly in its immaturity, its
arrogance and its deep selfishness with the painful
effort of someone like Henri to get things right:
'L'essentiel est que tout devienne simple, comme
pour l'enfant, que chaque acte soit commandé, que le
bien et le mal soient désignés de façon arbitraire,
donc évidente' (LC 1545).
    In discussing characters' attitudes to good and
evil in general, however, one reaches a high level
of abstraction, to which they themselves only fairly
rarely aspire. In order to gain any understanding in
depth of the moral perspectives of this period one
has to examine the detailed ways in which the
individual's problems are seen as arising within
society. However metaphysical, at root, those
problems may be, to try to formulate or state them
without reference to social, institutionalised
situations and relationships would be to risk
impoverishing or distorting the moral content of the
post-war books by losing what is most characteristic
of it. For this reason, special attention needs to
be paid to the intermediate terms between the
individual and society; or, to view the matter
dynamically rather than statically, the points of
insertion at which individuals visibly and

unquestionably take up a place in, and become a part
of, their society. The two most obvious and
important mediations are the family and work.

NOTES

1. *La Forces des choses*, I,272.
2. 'Deux heures avec Sartre, entretien avec
Robert Kanters'.
3. *Situations IX*, p.101.

Chapter Nine

MARRIAGE AND THE FAMILY

If the family may be regarded as a kind of mediation
between the individual and his society, this is
initially because of the social institution of
marriage, which looms very large indeed in the
post-war fiction of our authors. A few of the main
figures marry as the tale unfolds, but many are now
married from the first (indeed, some have been
married for ten, twenty, even thirty years). Their
married state, moreover, far from being incidental,
is often central to the story as a whole. This is
obviously the case with Anne and Robert Dubreuilh
(LM); Laurence and Jean-Charles (BI); André and the
woman narrator of 'L'Age de discrétion'; Murielle
and Tristan (Mon); Monique and Maurice (FR); Janine
and Marcel (FA); Jonas and Louise (Jon); and
arguably the case with Yvars and his wife in 'Les
Muets'. That is to say that in eight instances out
of twelve here the marriage of a main character is a
conspicuous aspect of the story. Furthermore, there
are other marriages in these books which, whilst
receiving less attention than those just mentioned,
could hardly be dispensed with for thematic reasons:
Henri is married to Nadine during the last part of
Les Mandarins; the broken marriage between
Laurence's parents is about to be repaired at the
end of *Les Belles Images*; Murielle's first marriage
(with Albert) is a crucial part of her past as
described in 'Monologue'; and the marriages of the
narrator's son in 'L'Age de discrétion' and elder
daughter in 'La Femme rompue' are essential
components of the plots. The prominence of marriage
in these post-war works is undeniable then, and this
already provides a strong contrast with the fiction
of previous periods.

In most of the first category of cases just
mentioned a particular marriage is analysed in

detail, to a depth never attained in the earlier writings. But the books also contain a few general comments on the institution, including those of two apparently hardened cynics among the characters, neither of whom is married. Monique's younger daughter Lucienne in 'La Femme rompue' is no more than a minor figure, but she does make some telling remarks about marriage near the end of the tale, where they carry considerable weight. Her view is that it is normal for a man to stop loving his wife after fifteen years of marriage, and she is not in the least surprised that her mother should find herself abandoned at the age of forty (245-46). Clamence, in *La Chute*, is just as cynical and sometimes makes explicit attacks on bourgeois marriage (1529). What is more, although the extent of his irony is often difficult to gauge, Clamence's brief but striking anecdotes soon build up a rather appalling picture of the stifling effect of marriage. Thus, for instance, he tells the story of a man whose wife's very perfection drove him to kill her (1485). (This is not unlike the story of Jonas's parents: 'il ne pouvait supporter les bonnes oeuvres de sa femme, véritable sainte laïque'; Jon 1630).

There may be little coherent theory behind Clamence's critique of marriage, but his comments and illustrations do have the invaluable effect of emphasising the great difficulty of formulating any kind of judgement on a particular marriage from the outside, since there may be a considerable gap between appearance and reality. He has a fund of examples to substantiate this, and at one stage suggests two very different ways in which appearances could mislead us about the faithfulness and sincerity of married couples (LC 1493-94). There are also specific instances of this kind of discrepancy in the other stories. Laurence, for instance, sees that when Jean-Charles buys her a necklace to salve his own conscience after an argument, the action would be taken by the outside world as a 'parfaite image du couple qui s'adore après dix ans de mariage' (BI 141); and Monique, in 'La Femme rompue', makes a similar point in much more serious circumstances (217). The great interest of the post-war stories in this respect, in fact, is that by portraying certain imaginary marriages in considerable detail and from the inside they obviate the difficulty of seeing through possibly deceptive appearances to the real quality of the relationship.

We may go on to ask, therefore, how the individual *really* fares within the institution of

marriage in these stories. One immediate - and
predictable - observation is that marriages rarely
run their course smoothly or happily. An acid test,
as Monique eventually realises, is the passage of
time, and we watch her own marriage fall
definitively at this hurdle. Murielle, too, is
separated from her current husband in 'Monologue',
having divorced the first. Janine, on the other
hand, is still with her husband at the end of 'La
Femme adultère', even though she acknowledges that
they should have separated long ago (1572). Her
metaphorical adultery may be less of a threat to the
marriage than the real adultery of Anne Dubreuilh or
that of Laurence, but these extra-marital affairs
come to an end and both marriages, like Janine's,
are still limping along at the end. Jonas's
infidelity is only one of the problems in his
marriage, but he and Louise may perhaps have some
slight hope of a better life together by the end of
the tale (always assuming that Jonas recovers). A
little more positively, however, both Yvars in 'Les
Muets' and the woman narrator of 'L'Age de
discrétion' are shown as eventually drawing
important consolation and strength, in the face of
considerable difficulties and an uncertain future,
from the companionship of their spouse (although the
latter had first to discover that she had rather
over-dramatised what appeared to be a serious rift
between her husband and herself). Finally, the signs
at the end of *Les Mandarins* are that Henri and
Nadine may go on to be at least as happy together as
the troubled times allow (II,482-84), though their
marriage has not had a particularly auspicious
beginning and is, in any case, only a matter of
months old when the story finishes.

Since on this evidence the only marriage that
does not encounter serious trouble at some stage is
that of Yvars, it might be thought that we are
dealing here with a wholesale and rather fundamental
attack on the institution itself. And yet for a
number of reasons it is clear that this is not
exactly what is at stake in the post-war fiction.
For one thing, we cannot simply ignore the traces of
promise in the marriage of Henri and Nadine, or the
evidence of 'Les Muets' and 'L'Age de discrétion'.
Again, it is noticeable that the only two characters
who have anything to say against marriage in general
terms are presented in a rather unattractive light.
Lucienne is hard and cold, and Clamence is still, as
apparently he always was, a hypocrite and an egotist
who makes assertions for his own selfish ends.

Furthermore, whilst we have already seen that these books record the difficulty of judging a marriage from the outside, the fact is that once we have been *inside* a number of marriages in the stories we are not necessarily any nearer to knowing how to form a general assessment of their success or failure. One might, hesitatingly, wish to take the permanent separation of a couple as a major criterion of the failure of their marriage, but in the majority of cases here the union is to continue. Unless, therefore, we arbitrarily adopt what would be a purely external yardstick, we are simply not in a position to talk sensibly or convincingly of failure. Similarly, the fact that a couple manage to patch things up and keep going is not in itself a compelling reason for calling their marriage successful. And if it proves difficult to make judgements on individual marriages, how much *more* difficult it would be to extract a clear and firm judgement on the institution as a whole from these stories! Camus and Beauvoir, in fact, show little inclination to propound any such general view in their fiction.

It is true that more stress is laid on the *problems* that arise within marriage than on any merits or advantages that the practice may have, but apart from the general point that literature always tends to dwell on crises rather than periods of contentment or satisfaction, it needs to be acknowledged that marriage itself does not actually generate those problems: they could, and do, arise in *any* type of long-standing relationship between a man and a woman. Indeed, many are already familiar to us from the earlier fiction, so that in this particular respect we are dealing more with a change of context than one of basic content. In the wartime fiction, the central issues of man-woman relations were either held in abeyance or heavily coloured by the extreme historical circumstances, but the characters in the post-war books face much the same problems in this area as those that taxed the unmarried couples in the pre-war period, like Françoise and Pierre, Meursault and Marie, Mersault and Marthe, Mathieu and Marcelle. Essentially, the problems concerned centre on love and sex, and it is because emphasis is placed squarely upon these in the stories that the institution of marriage as such receives relatively little attention.

It is significant, nevertheless, that while many principal characters in the earlier phases resisted marriage in one way or another, it now

provides the main framework for lasting
relationships. This fact in itself is associated
with changes in our authors' perspective on love and
sex, which is now what we might describe as a
long-term one. At the basis of the cynical views on
marriage expressed by Clamence and Lucienne is the
belief that love does not last as long as it is
frequently thought to, and the general question of
how love is affected by the passage of time - or of
whether there are different types of love at
different stages in a relationship - is one raised
in a great many of these tales. Laurence, the
youngest of Beauvoir's women figures here, has
occasion to wonder whether there can be love without
jealousy (BI 17), but rather more commonly now the
stories concern the relationship between love on the
one hand and, say, tenderness or affection on the
other. What, over a long period, distinguishes love
from kind and considerate conduct towards someone,
'aimer bien' from 'aimer d'amour'? Again the example
of Janine and Marcel in 'La Femme adultère' -
perhaps like that of Jonas's marriage - makes us ask
whether some persisting combination of need and
dependency can amount to love. It does not appear
that Camus and Beauvoir are any nearer than they
ever were to solving basic puzzles of this kind in
inter-sexual relations, but their treatment of the
topic now has a breadth and a resonance that it
lacked as long as love was examined almost
exclusively *outside* marriage.

Similar comments apply to the treatment of
sexuality in the post-war books. Most of the
marriages here are depicted as having enjoyed a
relatively happy start, and the fulfilment
experienced in the early stages is often associated,
either explicitly or implicitly, with intense sexual
activity between the partners. But a character like
Laurence (ten years married) shows us a certain
transitional state where marital sex is acquiring a
somewhat routine aspect: 'l'amour aussi est lisse,
hygiénique, routinier' (BI 27). And the theme of the
deterioration of sexual relations within marriage is
illustrated in a more extreme form in the marriage
of the woman narrator of 'L'Age de discrétion' and
that of Anne Dubreuilh, in both of which cases
sexual activity between spouses has long since
ceased. (If the former case is 'simply' one of age,
the latter certainly is not, as Anne's subsequent
affair with Brogan demonstrates.) The general
suggestion that intense sexual attraction between
two partners cannot be expected to last indefinitely

(which ties in with the attack on the common concept
of romantic love) is part of what lies behind the
surprisingly high incidence here of characters
indulging in sex without particularly wanting to,
although the example of the unmarried Clamence shows
that more is involved than the mere passage of time
('pour certains êtres, au moins, ne pas prendre ce
qu'on ne veut pas est la chose la plus difficile du
monde'; LC 1508).

In any case, this leads on, in the case of
married figures, to the question of adultery, which
also bulks large in these stories. The unremarkable
but realistic impression left on this count is that
much the same problems as those experienced within
marriage also occur in extra-marital situations.
Characters have few scruples about bursting through
the social framework of marriage when it comes to
adultery, but where this does not result in the
break-up of their marriage, it tends only to bring
them eventually back to their starting-point, with
the same difficulties as ever. In *Les Belles Images*,
Laurence comes to find sex with her lover just as
routine as with her husband (63). For Camus and
Beauvoir by this stage sex rarely remains a matter
of simple sensual enjoyment; it always has to be
seen within the context of the individual's whole
life-pattern, and this usually brings complex
factors and powerful forces into play. But at least
these factors can be fully weighed and the whole
topic treated more comprehensively now that marriage
is taken seriously into account.

Yet if the examination of love and sex within
the framework of marriage serves broadly to show
that the basic problems concerned immediately open
out into general issues of personal relationships
that far transcend the framework as such, this in
itself may be seen as *some* kind of comment on the
very institution of marriage. It is striking that in
the post-war fiction individuals accept, or
tolerate, marriage very much on their own terms, and
evaluate its conventions for themselves. We have
already pointed out that characters do not hesitate
to break their commitment by adultery, and more
generally it is clear that they all, without
exception, resist or implicitly deny the official
religious implications of marriage. Furthermore,
more often than not there is something unusual or
strange about the way in which marriage is entered
into here. Robert proposed to Anne for a slightly
odd reason (LM I,71); Nadine almost tricks Henri
into marriage, but in the end he complies because of

his own nonchalant attitude towards it (LM II,481); Monique's premature first pregnancy, too, may not have been wholly accidental (FR 212); Murielle in 'Monologue' convinces herself that she was twice lured into marriage by others, although on the second occasion she probably married for money (117); both Jonas and Laurence apparently entered into matrimony rather passively to say the least (Jon 1632; BI 119); and Janine was partly pushed into it against her better judgement (FA 1560). Now, the implication that people often either marry in a casual, less-than-deliberate way or are actually bullied and tricked into it might point in any one of a number of directions, but, particularly in conjunction with the factors mentioned above, its effect is certainly to undermine the gravity and dignity with which the subject of marriage is normally regarded. (One remembers Meursault: 'Elle a observé alors que le mariage était une chose grave. J'ai répondu: "Non."'; Etr 1156.) In a whole variety of ways, then, and without a frontal attack ever being mounted, marriage is cut down to size or demystified in these books. As a (bourgeois) social institution, it is undoubtedly seen as incorporating traps for the unwary, but the suggestion is that, by and large, it is a great deal less important in every way than is commonly supposed. For clear-headed individuals, it is a 'mediation' through which society impinges surprisingly little on their lives; and the weak or self-deceived are vulnerable in their long-standing relationships whether they are married or not.[1]

What makes marriage such a significant feature of the post-war stories is that it has another major aspect: its influence upon the individual looks very different once our discussion widens out to include children and thereby comes to centre on the family as a whole. If our authors imply that most of the main questions raised with regard to marriage as such may arise just as acutely in *any* established man-woman relationship, the equivalent cannot be said of their view of the family situation, which has to be considered for these purposes as *sui generis*. Of course, it is possible to have and bring up children while remaining unmarried, but there are no major (or minor?) examples of this in the fiction of Camus or Beauvoir (or Sartre). Their characters are only ever shown as having children within the institutionalised framework of marriage and as thereby bringing into being, in an official or legal sense, a new family unit. There is nothing in these

books with which we can sensibly compare and
contrast the family. It is a concept that embraces,
but goes beyond, that of marriage, giving a whole
additional and unique dimension to human relations.
This dimension was scarcely explored at all in their
earlier stories, and is one that yields both
problems of its own and a greater surface of contact
between the individual and society at large, since
parents have more than themselves to think of and
are bound, in some sense or degree, to live
'through' their offspring, as well as leading their
own lives.

The general theme of parenthood could scarcely
be more prominent in Beauvoir's later fiction,
figuring centrally as it does in every one of her
stories from the post-war period (sometimes through
more than one major example). It also has an
importance that we would be unwise to neglect in at
least three of the stories in Camus's *L'Exil et le
royaume*, while in *La Chute* Clamence offers a few
interesting remarks on the subject. For the most
part, however, characters are not shown as entering
into parenthood with any more enthusiasm or
commitment than they entered into wedlock. Sometimes
we are given too little information to be able to
assess how keen the couple were at the time on
having children ('L'Age de discrétion',
'Monologue'), although occasionally the matter is
described in flat, routine terms that do not
encourage us to see them as having exercised much
positive choice ('Les Muets'). In a few instances
the relevant circumstances are actually rather
unedifying: as we have mentioned, the pregnancies
that precipitate the marriages of both Henri and
Monique are somewhat more than 'accidental'; and
Anne says of Nadine: 'Je ne l'ai pas désirée; c'est
Robert qui a souhaité tout de suite un enfant' (LM
I,98). This is not to say that none of the
characters come to find parenthood rewarding:
Maurice and Henri appear to take to fatherhood quite
well, in spite of the initial circumstances; and
Yvars, Jonas, Laurence and the narrator of 'L'Age de
discrétion' are all loving parents. On the other
hand, although we may well wish to discount
Murielle's wild generalisation made on the basis of
her own unfortunate experiences ('On ne devrait pas
avoir d'enfant en un sens Dédé a raison ils ne vous
rapportent que des emmerdements'; Mon 103), it is
true, for instance, that Anne never entirely
recovers from her bad start with Nadine ('je ne
pouvais lui donner ni l'amour ni le bonheur';

LM I,332-33). As with marriage, we would look in vain for a decisive judgement in these books on the general question of whether it is a good thing to have children.

There is certainly little, if anything, here to support the suggestion that having children enhances a marriage or actually brings spouses closer together. Of course, the issue is not made clearer by the fact that there are very few examples of childless marriages to act as a kind of control. Janine and Marcel, in 'La Femme adultère', are the only major case, and Janine frankly admits that she does not know whether children would have improved relations between them or not (1572). Nevertheless, with both Anne and Laurence the very arrival of children is seen to have had a slightly deleterious effect upon the marriage (LM I,98-99; BI 43). In addition, while Monique acknowledges at one point that she may have rather neglected Maurice in favour of their two daughters (FR 129), Jonas's wife is unequivocally presented as relegating him to second place as soon as she has babies (Jon 1633). Similarly, while in 'L'Age de discrétion' the narrator's profound shock at her husband's reaction to her split with her son is of relatively short duration, the children in 'Monologue' have undoubtedly been a constant point of friction between Murielle and her two husbands. If children do keep couples together, this may be in a somewhat degrading way: the suggestion is that Maurice delayed breaking with Monique (just as Dominique delayed breaking with Laurence's father) until the children were grown and independent. Naturally, the difficulty with all of these cases consists in knowing to what extent children are the cause, and to what extent merely the *occasion*, of problems between husband and wife. But what is clear is that having children is seen as a solution to nothing at all: at the very least it provides a new focal-point for pre-existing problems, and in many cases it unquestionably generates certain unique difficulties of its own.

The most important of those in the latter category have to do with the question of upbringing: even Murielle acknowledges that if one does have children, one must bring them up properly (Mon 103). Although in their most direct and obvious form these problems are not dwelt upon in Camus's stories of the period, the unmarried Clamence does, at one or two points, touch upon the fundamental matters of love and authority that are involved (LC 1498;

1545). In Beauvoir's stories, moreover, a
surprisingly wide range of questions about
upbringing are explored in great detail and with
considerable sensitivity. *Les Belles Images*, in
particular, is dominated by such issues, with
Laurence's anxiety about her elder daughter's
growing awareness of suffering in the world forming
one of the main threads of the plot. Laurence is
forced to ask herself what it is appropriate to tell
young children about the evil in the world –
especially since she is trying to 'élever
laïquement des enfants, dans ce monde envahi par la
religion' (76) – and how this affects her attitude
towards the friends they can be encouraged to have.
She has also to bear in mind that her younger
daughter will be influenced by any decisions or
actions taken over Catherine. Again, the book as a
whole asks what precisely the father's role is in
this process and at what point external help, like
that of a psychiatrist, should be sought. Some of
these questions arise in 'Monologue' too, together
with other issues of upbringing. Murielle may be
guilty of using her children for her own ends, but
in any case the story records the effect that
hostility between parents may have upon their
offspring, and the still graver consequences for
young children of the break-up of a marriage.
Furthermore, another delicate matter touched upon
here – that of relations between mother and rapidly
maturing, or even mature, daughter – is investigated
in more depth in both *Les Mandarins* and 'La Femme
rompue'. It is no coincidence that references to the
Oedipus complex proliferate in Beauvoir's post-war
fiction, and especially in *Les Belles Images*, where
Laurence is quite disproportionately shocked at the
end by her father's willingness to take up life with
her mother again.

This last point may also serve to remind us
that there is another level to the question of
upbringing in these works, and one this time where
Camus, too, has some telling examples to offer. The
fact is that we have so far considered the central
figures, like Anne, Laurence and Monique, as
parents, but of course their own status as children
of *their* parents is by no means neglected, even if
the extent to which this side of things is dwelt
upon varies a good deal. We hear of Jean-Charles's
parents, as we do of Clamence's father, and we learn
that Maurice is the child of a broken home, but
these references amount to little. André's mother
actually appears in 'L'Age de discrétion' and has a

certain significance as a point of comparison and contrast, but no more. On the other hand, Laurence's mother and father figure prominently in *Les Belles Images* as full characters in their own right, yet essentially as parents, since the story is told from Laurence's point of view. (With appropriate allowances made for the different nature and scale of the story, the same is true of 'Monologue'.) 'La Femme rompue' is an interesting case which falls between these two extremes, for although Monique's father is dead before the events of the story take place, he may be very important to an understanding of her character and conduct. She admits that the moment of his death was perhaps a vital one for her and her relationship with Maurice (211), and her psychiatrist seems to be of the same mind (239). Moreover, some of her arguments with Maurice over his career have undoubtedly resulted from her wish that he should have much the same place in the medical profession, and the same attitudes to it, as her father did (138).

Some of these examples show Beauvoir's sensitivity to the problem of relating to one's (ageing) parents – something also faced directly by minor characters like Josette and Lambert in *Les Mandarins*. They soon bring us back, however, to the question of upbringing, for the protagonists are usually presented as strongly marked or influenced by their own childhood. The two main cases in *L'Exil et le royaume* (Jonas and the Renégat) are also instances of this, albeit rather indeterminate ones. Jonas's upbringing is alluded to only once, and then with irony, yet it is impossible not to see it as the crucial source of his characteristic detachment and passivity, and hence of all his troubles:

Il nourrissait ainsi une tendre reconnaissance à l'endroit de ses parents, d'abord parce qu'ils l'avaient élevé distraitement, ce qui lui avait fourni le loisir de la rêverie, ensuite parce qu'ils s'étaient séparés, pour raison d'adultère ... Ses parents, ayant lu, ou appris, qu'on pouvait citer plusieurs cas de meurtriers sadiques issus de parents divorcés, rivalisèrent de gâteries pour étouffer dans l'oeuf les germes d'une aussi fâcheuse évolution. Moins apparents étaient les effets du choc subi, selon eux, par la conscience de l'enfant, et plus ils s'en inquiétaient: les ravages invisibles devaient être les plus profonds. Pour peu que Jonas se déclarât

content de lui ou de sa journée, l'inquiétude
ordinaire de ses parents touchait à
l'affolement. Leurs attentions redoublaient et
l'enfant n'avait alors plus rien à désirer.
(Jon 1629-30)

The home background of the Renégat is almost the
polar opposite of this, but again a direct causal
link is suggested between his childhood and his
subsequent development:

Quand j'étais chez moi, dans ce haut plateau du
Massif Central, mon père grossier, ma mère
brute, le vin, la soupe au lard tous les jours,
le vin surtout, aigre et froid, et le long
hiver, la burle glacée, les congères, les
fougères dégoûtantes, oh je voulais partir, les
quitter d'un seul coup et commencer enfin à
vivre, dans le soleil, avec de l'eau claire.
J'ai cru au curé, il me parlait du séminaire,
il s'occupait tous les jours de moi, il avait
le temps dans ce pays protestant. (Ren 1579)

He later thinks a little more tenderly of his
parents and concedes that he may have loved them,
but the emphasis on the harshness of his upbringing
allows Camus to hint that even the shooting of the
missionary can be related back to the Renégat's
attitude towards his father: 'râ râ tuer son père
voilà ce qu'il faudrait' (1580).

If Camus's are contrasting examples, there is a
great deal in common as well as an additional
density in two of Beauvoir's principal cases. While
Murielle claims, 'Mon père m'aimait. Personne
d'autre. Tout est venu de là' (Mon 90), and sees her
mother as the source of most of her problems,
Laurence's view of her parents and her childhood is
almost identical: 'Toute ma vie ainsi: c'est mon
père que j'aimais et ma mère qui m'a faite' (BI 33).
What is of especial interest in connection with
these two characters is the fact that strong views
about their parents' attitudes provide them with
their major points of reference in the upbringing of
their own children. Both are very conscious of the
danger of children becoming exactly like their
parents, and are extremely anxious to avoid the
mistakes that their own mothers made. (Just as in
Les Belles Images, to give another twist to the
spiral, it is suggested that Dominique brought
Laurence up in the way she did precisely to avoid
the horrors of her *own* childhood; 21-22.) But unlike

Murielle. Laurence is just lucid enough to see beyond her own personal case (in Greece her heart bleeds for a charming little girl who risks following in her mother's footsteps; 158), and even to acknowledge the undesirability of basing certain types of generalisation on one's own upbringing: 'Ça m'a bien réussi, ça m'a parfaitement réussi; mais on ne m'obligera pas à élever Catherine de la même façon' (132). In fact, Laurence, perhaps more than any other character in these books, has a very clear perception of the complexities and difficulties of the whole matter of bringing up children, to the point of being more than a little overawed by them:

> C'est effrayant de penser qu'on marque ses enfants rien que par ce qu'on est. Pointe de feu à travers le coeur. Anxiété, remords. Les humeurs quotidiennes, les hasards d'un mot, d'un silence, toutes ces contingences qui devraient s'effacer derrière moi, ça s'inscrit dans cette enfant qui rumine et qui se souviendra, comme je me souviens des inflexions de voix de Dominique. Ça semble injuste. On ne peut pas prendre la responsabilité de tout ce qu'on fait - ne fait pas. 'Qu'est-ce que tu fais pour eux?' Ces comptes exigés soudain dans un monde où rien ne compte tellement. C'est comme un abus. (135-36)

We could say, in broad terms, that at a moment like this the character is recognising and registering one of the pressing ways in which a regular life in society can pose distinctive problems of its own, of a kind unfamiliar to those whose perspectives are dominated by metaphysical or historical factors.

Yet in Laurence's case, as in others, a quite fundamental question - parallel to the one we asked in connection with marriage - sooner or later raises itself: What are the criteria for success and failure in bringing up children? The question needs to be posed in these terms, because by and large the emphasis in the books falls less on different *methods* of upbringing than on the human or moral issues that underlie the whole process. We are occasionally encouraged to consider whether parents are actually doing the right things for their growing children, but more frequently asked to look back and assess the general implications and consequences of certain family situations. And the stories show just how complicated, even unfathomable, this matter is. Part of the difficulty is expressed in Monique's summary of Lucienne's views:

> Selon elle, ce qui compte dans une enfance, c'est la situation psychanalytique, telle qu'elle existe à l'insu des parents, presque malgré eux. L'éducation, dans ce qu'elle a de conscient, de délibéré, ça serait très secondaire. (FR 250)

But the philosophical aspects of the problem are just as far-reaching. Whether or not we accept the evaluations of their own upbringing arrived at by, say, Laurence, Murielle and the Renégat, we are conscious that hindsight is involved and that these are adults implicitly appealing to certain values in making such judgements.

Hence, whatever characters' own attitudes may be, we are invited to ask ourselves, for instance, by what tokens Anne's upbringing of Nadine (or his parents' upbringing of Jonas) could be counted a failure, and by what tokens a success. The open-endedness of such a question is vital in connection with 'La Femme rompue', for, contrary to Monique's own despairing judgement, the text of her diary as a whole does not confirm that her daughters' upbringing has been a clear failure. And similar considerations apply in 'L'Age de discrétion', where the mother has the greatest difficulty in accepting her husband's view that their son has quite simply come to have values very different from those of his parents, let alone the possibility that this very fact might be taken as a measure of the *success* of his upbringing. In both of these stories, as elsewhere, we need deliberately to correct against the temptation to see the woman as exclusively responsible for her offspring. Even when the husband leaves the matter of the children largely to his wife, he still plays a significant role in their formation by his expectations, his presence, and his way of life. If his particular criteria for success in their upbringing are given little prominence in a story beside those of the mother, it does not follow that they are ultimately less influential in the children's development (Jonas, Maurice, André, Jean-Charles).

In the light of these factors, we could hardly expect to extract from these works any precise prescriptions about the upbringing of children. If the task is shown as too frequently falling to, or being seized by, just *one* of the parents, it is by no means certain that this always leads to disaster, at least for the children themselves. If, on the other hand, there is a general suggestion that it is essential that children be left free to develop for themselves, we are given no indication at all of the *extent* of the freedom desirable; nor is this approach invariably seen to work out well (Nadine in *Les Mandarins*). Again, although in the end the problem of differing criteria for success in bringing up children takes us ineluctably back to that of the quality of the relationship between a married couple, no constant correlation is shown between the solidity of relations between husband and wife and 'success' in the rearing of the progeny. Arguments over the children can certainly expose deep underlying differences of values between the parents which are potentially a threat to the marriage itself, but it is not an unequivocal part of the general message of these stories that children will necessarily suffer in the end as a result of such conflicts; nor, for that matter, that they will necessarily become admirable adults where their parents are at one.

The effect of the books as a whole is to stress that in any marriage producing offspring *some* solution has to be adopted to the problems associated with rearing children, but that parents have relatively little idea of the price that has to be paid for any particular solution until it is actually being paid. Such ideas as they have tend to stem from their own experience as children and to incorporate value-judgements that are rarely sufficiently articulated, and which may or may not be shared by both parents. On the value of marriage as such, one felt that Camus and Beauvoir had mixed feelings but at least saw certain disadvantages and advantages with a certain clarity. On the question of how to bring up children, however, one senses a far greater degree of doubt and confusion, a more pressing awareness of the genuine difficulty of knowing what would constitute success. This is not surprising when one considers that children become adults and that the upbringing question thereby merges both logically and chronologically into less specific and more fundamental ones involving general judgements of people or ways of life, as well as inter-personal relations as a whole. Certain aspects of the whole process of having children are unique and pose unique problems, but these cannot be solved - or even tackled at all - in isolation. They are enmeshed with basic questions of values which constantly, though often quiescently, underpin particular issues like that of upbringing and tend to become more and more prominent as children become old enough to have values of their own. Eventually, parents find themselves in the same sort of position with regard to their children as they are with other adults, namely that of having somehow to adjust to individuals with values that are to one degree or another at variance with their own. Except, of course, that these are individuals of whom they have very particular expectations, and with whom they wish to sustain a special and intimate relationship. Both authors recognise, moreover, that the problem has to be seen from the opposite angle too, and that adults can be faced with very specific difficulties in trying to maintain relations with their parents - including, in *Les Belles Images* and 'Monologue', difficulties concerning their own parents' role as grandparents!

Clamence's diatribe against parents and relatives in general - 'ils téléphonent comme on tire à la carabine' (LC 1491) - is typically provocative, but a certain level of conflict and in-fighting does undoubtedly constitute part of the quality of life *en famille* as portrayed in these books. Yet there is love and good will in evidence too, and the balance-sheet on the family would again be a difficult one to draw up (quite apart from the fact that no alternatives are envisaged here). The more one looks at the implications of having children as traced in the stories, the more one is struck by the sheer complexity of the network of relations that is thereby established. Individuals cannot avoid having parents, but the arrival of even a single child of their own creates a whole new series of relationships, as well as bringing about changes in pre-existing ones. On the evidence just examined, this yields potential problems between child and mother, child and father, father and mother, parents and grandparents, grandparents and grandchildren. If we also remember that the number of relationships is greatly multiplied when there is more than one child, and that any problem needs to be seen from at least two points of view, we gain some idea of the richness and intricacy of the patterns generated by the advent of children.

What needs emphasising, perhaps, is the significance of the network of relations itself rather than any one element in it. Our argument earlier was that marriage as such in these books is scarcely more than a somewhat inert framework within which long-standing man-woman relationships are, as a matter of fact, set. By contrast, it is clear that, in having children, characters are seen as bringing something entirely new into being, namely their own family unit, which necessarily overlaps with, and has to relate to, already existing units. In one sense the point is self-evident, but in another less so. It would be a mistake to think that the family is shown here as simply a marriage plus a child: this is a case where the whole is visibly more than the sum total of its parts, since the family produces its own powerful dynamics and constitutes one of the principal dimensions of life in society. We might say that here, most commonly, individuals are placed in relation to the family in much the way that they were placed in relation to their communities or national groups in the wartime works.

NOTES

1. For a rather more detailed examination of this topic, see my own 'Marriage in the later fiction of Camus and Simone de Beauvoir'.

Chapter Ten

WORK, JUDGEMENT AND SELF-SCRUTINY

One tangible way in which a couple's situation is
changed as soon as they have children is that the
matter of financial and material provision for the
family unit acquires greater importance and usually
falls, at least for some time, exclusively upon the
shoulders of the husband. Hence consideration of the
family as such in the post-war stories leads
naturally and directly on to the second major
mediation between the individual and society, namely
work.

This link emerges clearly from a number of
characters' accounts of their early married life,
and perhaps especially from Yvars's:

> Puis les années avaient passé, il y avait eu
> Fernande, la naissance du garçon, et, pour
> vivre, les heures supplémentaires à la
> tonnellerie le samedi, le dimanche chez des
> particuliers où il bricolait. (LMu 1598)

In general, the relationship between work and family
is shown to be a crucial and rather complicated one.
Work may be the means by which the husband provides
for his wife and children, but it develops a
momentum of its own and can easily encroach upon
family life in a number of ways. Yet the pressure
may occasionally operate in the opposite direction
too, with family commitments actually impairing the
man's work. Both possibilities are explored in
'Jonas ou L'Artiste au travail', where the painter,
having been virtually prevented from working at all
by his family circumstances among other things,
swings to the other extreme and neglects his family
by staying up on his curious platform for long
periods, ostensibly in order to work. On the other
hand, the family may also act as a kind of refuge

from the stresses and strains of work: Yvars clearly
views things in this way after his trying day (LMu
1607-08), and both André in 'L'Age de discrétion'
and Jean-Charles in *Les Belles Images* are seen to
pour out some of the troubles associated with their
work to their wives, as a way of relieving the
strain. In these last two cases, moreover, the wives
have professions of their own, which raises
additional questions. Past a certain point in their
children's development wives in these books are
presumed, unlike their husbands, to have the choice
of whether to work or not. If they pursue their own
career, this may double the problems raised by the
husband's job and perhaps change the character of
the marriage and family life significantly, for
better or worse (*Les Mandarins*, *Les Belles Images*).
But if they choose not to have a career, the direct
and indirect consequences of this decision may be
just as far-reaching ('La Femme rompue', 'La Femme
adultère'). In either case, the further matter of a
wife's interest and participation in her husband's
work is frequently seen in these stories as being
one of great importance.

In one sense, then, the issue of work needs to
be considered in relation to the whole network of
relations that we have emphasised as constituting
the family unit. But whilst the family itself is a
social institution, it is one through which (as some
of Beauvoir's stories show particularly well)
certain individuals may actually become more cut off
from society at large rather than drawn into it. In
this respect work is necessarily a very different
kind of mediation, since it usually *forces* contact
between members of a family and non-members. In
short, it is principally work that injects the
family into the stream of society and constitutes
the main channel through which forces flow between
individuals and the community to which they belong.

Hence the occupations of the protagonists here
are almost invariably integral features of the
stories. In 'La Femme adultère' Janine's husband's
job as a cloth salesman is accorded a certain
prominence, and in *all* of Camus's other stories the
particular profession of the central figure is quite
vital: Clamence was a lawyer, the Renégat is a
missionary, Yvars a cooper, Daru a teacher, Jonas an
artist, D'Arrast a civil engineer. If most of these
would be considered 'professional' people, there is
nevertheless already a fair range and variety in the
occupations presented. To it has to be added the
catalogue of jobs performed by Beauvoir's principal

characters. Henri, Dubreuilh and the narrator of 'L'Age de discrétion' are all writers, but the last is a literary critic, while Dubreuilh writes political essays as well as novels, and Henri's main job is actually that of journalist. Of Beauvoir's other central figures, Anne is a psychiatrist and Laurence an advertising agent. And husbands' jobs are by no means ignored, with Jean-Charles being an architect and André and Maurice both scientific researchers.

Of course, characters have to be portrayed as doing something to earn their living, but our authors show positive interest in aspects of the occupations concerned. This interest expresses itself largely through the involvement of the characters themselves, since almost universally their work is work that they have chosen to do and are caught up in to a significant extent. As Laurence says, 'le travail serait terriblement ennuyeux si on ne se piquait pas au jeu' (BI 98). It is true that in the same novel Beauvoir makes some play of the case of certain young women engaged in highly repetitive and dull work (79), and that Camus, too, shows an awareness that for many people work is either mindless routine or physical exhaustion, for Yvars comments: 'ceux qui faisaient des discours sur le travail manuel ne savaient pas de quoi ils parlaient' (LMu 1606). But Beauvoir never takes up the matter in detail, and even Yvars's desire to escape from work is rather different in nature from that of, say, Mersault or Meursault, since he has a certain commitment to his job and takes a definite pride in his own skill. In 'Les Muets', furthermore, Camus's own interest in skilled manual work is reflected in the detailed descriptions of the cooper's job and the workshop atmosphere, as well as in the general theme of the story. From one angle or another, the chosen occupations of the main figures in almost all of these stories are examined with considerable curiosity.

Our authors' general preoccupation, however, is with particular jobs as pieces in the whole social jigsaw puzzle; or, more accurately, with the dilemmas faced by individuals as they situate themselves in relation to the expectations associated with their own occupation. Works entails involvement with employers, colleagues, and possibly 'consumers', producing a broad area of contact between the individual and society. As a result, difficulties concerning occupations arise especially acutely at a time when society is changing. Thus in *Les Mandarins* - the only story to cover the rather special, troubled period immediately following the war - we find that all three main figures at some time entertain the gravest doubts about their professions (at different points both Henri and Dubreuilh abandon writing; Henri gives up the editorship of his newspaper; and Anne becomes less and less convinced of the value of psychiatry), and these doubts are clearly attributable in large measure to the changing political and social climate. In 'Les Muets', too, we see Camus asking a question that directly relates the matter of an individual's occupation to large-scale developments in society: 'Que peuvent faire des tonneliers quand la tonnellerie disparaît?' (1599). Or again, to take a different kind of example, Daru's problems in 'L'Hôte' are manifestly bound up with the political state of Algeria as a whole, in that he is put under pressure because the Arab population is close to the point of rebellion. Admittedly, there are also many cases here where characters' doubts about their work bear very little relation to factors of this kind. It is for reasons of a more personal sort that Clamence gives up his legal practice; that the Renégat betrays his mission and shoots his successor; that Jonas stops painting; that Laurence has worries about the advertising profession; and that the narrator of 'L'Age de discrétion' undergoes a minor crisis over her role as an academic critic. Yet we may still say that individuals' problems with their work are associated with its social aspects in the broadest sense, for, whether changes are taking place or not, the crux of the matter in every case lies in increasing awareness of, and insight into, the precise nature and implications of that work and its status in society.

To have a specific job, even one that has been freely chosen, is to have a more or less defined role, a particular place in society, a particular function to fulfil, a particular set of relationships with others. Even the Renégat, Daru and D'Arrast - all of whom are portrayed outside their own societies - are where they are precisely as a result of their jobs and the functions assigned to them by their society. The initial questions, therefore, are how thoroughly individuals understand the role and the pressures associated with their occupations, and how far they are prepared to accept them. In these books, circumstances are constantly forcing characters to face up to the expectations

that society at large has of members of their
profession, and the precise value placed upon that
profession. This in turn frequently leads
individuals to try to spell out more clearly to
themselves how they personally think their work
should be carried out and what value they themselves
attach to it. Their own view of their occupation may
differ considerably from the generally accepted one,
but they have always, in some sense, to start from,
and situate themselves in relation to, society's
expectations and demands. Because of the weight of
society bearing down upon them and the web it has
spun around them, the critical matter will often be
that of how viable any individual's personal
conception of his or her work is, and whether it can
be put into practice without damaging compromises or
concessions.

Some of the sharpest illustrations of these
points are to be found in Camus's short stories. It
is clear enough, for example, what society expects
of coopers, but 'Les Muets' shows that they may have
their own idea of what working involves, and that
when this conflicts with what society presses upon
them, they may be prepared to dig in their heels,
even at some cost to themselves and their families.
Yvars believes his son is right to want to be a
teacher (LMu 1606), yet there is irony in this
reflection, since in the very next story, 'L'Hôte',
Daru is seen facing a dilemma over his role as an
instituteur in the Algerian hinterland. He willingly
takes on the extra task, assigned to him by
'l'administration', of distributing wheat to the
poor indigenous Arab families (1612), but is
horrified at being asked by the local policeman to
escort an Arab criminal to the nearest gaol (1614).
Like Yvars and his colleagues, he has his own view
of what doing his job involves and draws a line
beyond which he will not go (although while they are
concerned with their dignity as workers, for him it
is a question of 'l'honneur'; 1621). Something very
similar can be said about D'Arrast in 'La Pierre qui
pousse', who does not altogether conform to the
conception that the pompous officials of Iguape have
of him as a civil engineer sent by 'la Société
française de Rio' and goes his own way in certain
respects, insisting for instance on actually
visiting one of the huts in the poor quarters of the
town and fraternising with the occupants.

These characters all stand at the same end of
the spectrum as far as their reaction to their
publicly assigned function is concerned. They are

reasonable men whose conceptions of their jobs are justifiable and perhaps admirable ones, even - or especially - where they diverge from those of their paymasters. But in cases like 'Le Renégat' and *La Chute* a highly personal, not to say eccentric, element enters into the picture. The Renégat is trained as a missionary, but, significantly, goes off on his own initiative (and with money from the treasurer's office!) to convert the wildest and most dangerous tribe known (Ren 1582). Far from being under pressure from society to accept unpalatable features of his role, he takes on the job of missionary precisely in order to satisfy his own deep psychological needs ('je rêvais du pouvoir absolu'; 1581). From the fact that he does not simply fail in his mission, but goes out of his way to prevent subsequent success by shooting his replacement, we can see that, unlike the earlier characters mentioned, he does not wish to qualify, restrain or refuse society's expectations of the missionary, but is perverting the very ends for which his official role exists. If the Renégat is unique in these stories in his fanaticism, the case of Clamence in *La Chute* runs parallel to his in certain respects. Clamence, too, has to be seen as having carried out the functions of a lawyer in a very particular way and essentially for his own ends. His needs are so specific, in fact, that he has gone on to invent his own occupation, that of 'juge-pénitent'.

In the major examples in Beauvoir's stories, the very nature of the main functions associated with the occupations concerned, or the central content of the work, is intrinsically more contentious. At one level, what is expected of Laurence as an advertising agent, in *Les Belles Images*, is fairly simple: '"Il faut que je persuade les gens de recouvrir leurs murs avec des panneaux de bois"' (8). Yet she recognises that much more than this is at stake, that there is necessarily an element of deception in the selling process, and that her professional activities rest upon a lie. In *Les Mandarins*, Anne's profession of psychiatrist is a more reputable one, but one in which she loses faith during the post-war period, when 'curing' patients consists in enabling them to forget the war and neutralising their past. Her own conception of psychiatry involves making people whole, so that she deplores the way in which Paule's whole reason for living, her love for Henri, had to be destroyed in order for a cure to be effected (II,353). Anne's

earlier assumption that everyone's life can be given
some meaning is increasingly called into question by
both what is happening in the world at large and the
course being followed by her own personal life.
Indeed, much of the fascination of her case, as with
Laurence, is that it displays the intricacy of the
interaction between individual and society in the
matter of work.

Like Anne, Henri emerges from the war with a
relatively simple faith in his profession of
journalist: his role is to make his paper speak for
those who cannot speak for themselves (LM I,147). He
is soon forced to acknowledge, however, that sordid
financial considerations may undermine his ambitions
for *L'Espoir*, and that various pressures make it
almost impossible for him to continue writing
honestly while still giving the kind of lead
required (I,215). The tangible results of certain
early painful acts of integrity are only much
misunderstanding and the odium of some of those he
respects, then later Henri resigns the editorship of
his paper as soon as his personal conduct threatens
its good name (II,333). And in spite of his earlier
renunciation of literature he goes on to devote
himself entirely to his other profession of creative
writer. Yet by the end of the novel, having
recognised that escaping to Italy in order to write
his books would be something of an evasion, he
decides to stay in France and maintain some degree
of involvement in journalism and politics. In other
words, fluctuations in Henri's attitude towards both
journalism and writing eventually moderate: unlike
Anne, who becomes more and more of a solitary figure
as the story progresses, he is in a number of ways
settling into his own rather special dual role
within society.

Some of the discoveries made by Jonas are
virtually identical with those of Henri.[1] Once he
has been adopted by the artistic world, Jonas finds
that the obligations placed upon him extend far
beyond that which is beneficial to his own art: he
is expected to praise and encourage his disciples,
pestered to support all kinds of political causes,
and so on. By the time his reputation has faded and
his admirers are falling off, the source of his
inspiration has dried up altogether: 'Il pensait à
la peinture, à sa vocation, au lieu de peindre' (Jon
1647). Even when he emerges from a period of
self-indulgence and dissipation, he is still unable
to paint; and he produces no pictures at all while
sequestered in his elevated closet, the suggestion

being that he will never work again (1653). In spite
of some ambiguity in the ending, the general message
of 'Jonas' is clear enough, and might in some
measure serve as a motto for Henri, too: 'Il était
difficile de peindre le monde et les hommes et, en
même temps, de vivre avec eux' (1642).

The narrator of 'L'Age de discrétion', who
writes scholarly works on thinkers like Rousseau and
Montesquieu, has to learn the rather different
lesson that there are those (including her beloved
son) who do not share her deep belief in the supreme
value of books and culture. And like Jonas and
Henri, she discovers that once a work has been
brought into being, it can take on, in the eyes of
the consumer, quite different characteristics from
those intended by its creator. She comes to believe
that her powers of original comment are waning as a
result of age, and needs to be encouraged by her
husband, but André himself has problems over his
work, being quite convinced that at his age he can
no longer do original scientific research. 'Jonas'
and 'L'Age de discrétion' counterbalance *Les
Mandarins* quite well, with little emphasis falling
on political pressures as such and the treatment of
the theme of work concentrating heavily on personal
and social factors.

In general in these stories there is a movement
from the simple to the more complex in characters'
attitudes towards their jobs. Most frequently
(D'Arrast and Laurence probably being exceptions),
they set out with a relatively elementary and more
or less idealistic notion of their work, only to
discover that things are much more complicated and
difficult than they suspected. This is obviously the
case with Henri, Anne and Jonas, but it applies even
in the case of a fairly straightforward figure like
Yvars, whose awareness of the complexities of
boss-worker relations is considerably increased by
his day's experience at the factory. Characters
learn the hard way that their own view of their
occupation is not necessarily the one that is shared
by those with whom they have to deal, but, as we
have seen, another major difficulty is that although
an 'official' version of the nature and range of
their functions exists, there is often more to the
job than meets the eye, since this version ignores
other, somewhat less reputable factors that tend to
come to light in particular circumstances. The few
characters like D'Arrast and Laurence who do not
need to be under pressure to understand the true
nature of their jobs see from the first that there

is a gap between appearance and reality: Laurence knows that she is selling security rather than wood-panelling, and D'Arrast pays less attention to the officials of Iguape than to the poor whom his dam will actually help. Yet all have to situate themselves in one way or another in relation to the account of their functions sanctioned by society. It is this that most characters come to understand clearly only when the events of the stories have forced the realisation upon them. They eventually acknowledge that they cannot go their own way to the extent of completely ignoring what others expect of them in their work, but have to take cognisance of, and adopt a definite attitude towards, these expectations. The gradual discovery that they enjoy rather less independence than they thought, and of the ways in which they are enmeshed in the web of relations that constitutes a society, is broadly parallel to the characters' sudden awareness of their 'historicity' in the wartime books.

In fact, having a job and thereby an assigned role is merely one especially important example of the general way in which living in society is shown here to involve, necessarily, incurring the judgement of one's fellow men. We saw individuals already discovering in the pre-war books that others judge them quite independently of their own will or wishes, but with the normal processes of social intercourse interrupted by the war, it is only in the post-war stories that this point is explored in great detail. Naturally, artists and writers experience the process of judgement in a heightened form through the reception accorded to their works, and we watch Henri, Jonas and the narrator of 'L'Age de discrétion' grow increasingly sensitive to the various pressures that this generates. But in any case, individuals are constantly providing those around them with material on the basis of which they may be judged, since all words and all actions constitute such material. Hence Henri's reactions to the way in which his writings are received are no more than one facet of his growing awareness, as the post-war period proceeds, that large numbers of people (including, in the shape of his readers, many who do not know him personally) are expecting very specific things of him, and are more than ready to judge and criticise him if he falls short of their expectations:

> 'Vous me faites marrer! dit Henri. Vous êtes
> tous là à attendre des choses de moi: que

> j'entre au P.C., que je le combatte, que je
> sois moins sérieux, que je le sois davantage,
> que je renonce à la politique, que je m'y
> consacre corps et âme. Et tous vous êtes
> déçus, vous hochez la tête avec blâme.'
>   'Tu voudrais qu'on s'interdise de te juger?'
>   'Je voudrais qu'on me juge sur ce que je
> fais, et non sur ce que je ne fais pas.' (LM
> II,125)

At this point Henri has reached a stage that Daru
reaches only right at the end of 'L'Hôte', that of
being misjudged on all sides: Daru resists the moral
pressure brought to bear upon him by his peers and
encourages the Arab criminal placed in his charge to
regain his freedom, only to find that his conduct
has been wholly misinterpreted: '"Tu as livré notre
frère. Tu paieras"' (1623).

    If Henri eventually passes through his
subsequent phase of taking a certain perverse
delight in being in the wrong ('Il avait tort,
radicalement tort, sans réserve, sans excuse: quel
repos!'; LM II,171), Clamence deliberately persists
in, and develops, a stance similar to this for his
own personal ends. Of course, he regards the
propensity to pass judgement as a distinctive
characteristic of modern man, and the mainspring of
La Chute is his concern to escape the judgement of
his fellows, which he so obsessively fears. It is to
this end that he creates the role of
'juge-pénitent': 'Puisque tout juge finit un jour
pénitent, il fallait prendre la route en sens
inverse et faire métier de pénitent pour pouvoir
finir en juge' (1546). This role is something of a
parody of the legal profession to which he so
successfully belonged for some time in Paris, for it
is apparent that from the stage when Clamence
recognised that there was a judge just beneath the
surface in his own character (1504), he lost any
respect he may have had for the law, being happy to
bend or ignore it for his own purposes. In stories
like 'L'Hôte' and 'La Pierre qui pousse' we also
find traces of Camus's characteristic hostility
towards judges and legal judgement.

    Something of the kind is to be found in
Beauvoir's stories from this period, too. Both
Murielle (Mon 93) and Monique (FR 166) make adverse
comments on aspects of the law, although in both
cases they are interested parties. In any event, the
law is held in little respect in Beauvoir's tales.
Architects talking together in *Les Belles Images*

have few scruples about breaking the law in land
deals (149), and Laurence gives no sign of being in
the least disturbed by this. And the characters in
Les Mandarins have no regard at all for the law:
acts of violence, even murder, are committed without
the main figures expressing any anxiety about
considerations of illegality as such. They are all
more concerned to work out the *moral* rights and
wrongs of their positions, as Henri does when it
comes to his act of perjury (II,319-20). The
significant point about the law for our authors is
that its processes constitute the most formal and
definitive expression of the phenomenon of
judgement, which is a general feature of life in
society. Courts and their procedures simply
exemplify in an extreme form what is happening all
of the time in normal social intercourse. Thus, for
instance, it is the analogy with the law that occurs
to Henri as he awaits reactions to his play: 'Il ne
s'agissait pas d'une apothéose: un procès ... Il se
sentait aussi seul que dans le box des Assises
l'homme qui écoute en silence son avocat' (LM
II,118).

Judgement is such an all-pervasive phenomenon
in these books, however, that it can even be found
in the bosom of the family. It is true that in this
context the boundaries of the concept become a
little obscure, and also that there are some major
cases of forbearance and tolerance, where harsh
judgement might well have been justified (Laurence
and her mother; Louise and Jonas; Henri and Nadine).
But although we may not be altogether disposed to
believe the paranoid Murielle in 'Monologue' - 'Ils
me jugent ils me condamnent et pas un ne m'écoute'
(99) - it is clear, for example, that the mother
comes to judge her beloved son extremely harshly in
'L'Age de discrétion', and that neither Janine nor
Laurence fails to recognise serious faults in her
husband or to express criticism where appropriate.
Clamence, as usual, makes the general point
forcefully and colourfully:

> observez votre propre famille, vous serez
> édifié. Mon cher ami, ne leur donnons pas de
> prétexte à nous juger, si peu que ce soit! Ou
> sinon, vous voilà en pièces. Nous sommes
> obligés aux mêmes prudences que le dompteur.
> S'il a le malheur, avant d'entrer dans la cage,
> de se couper avec son rasoir, quel gueuleton
> pour les fauves! (LC 1515)

Exaggerated or not, his comments do at least evoke the horror of the discovery that our nearest and dearest are judging us from the outside, as non-members of the family might. Monique, in 'La Femme rompue', illustrates this graphically: 'Maurice ne me jugeait jamais, il était ma sécurité: et me voilà devant lui, plaidant coupable, quelle détresse!' (180). In her case, the struggle to see herself as others, including her husband, see her eventually brings on a severe identity crisis.

One of the distinguishing features of the post-war perspectives is that, as a result of having more extended and more prominent social roles than their predecessors, the central figures here almost all become strongly aware, sooner or later, of how they look (and how they 'ought' to look) from points of view external to their own. They become far more conscious than were characters in previous periods of the 'public' side to their existence. Anne expresses astonishment at Claudie's views on work and success ('Elle croyait que le travail n'était pour nous qu'un moyen d'arriver au succès et à la fortune'; LM I,307), and in this she could doubtless be taken to be speaking for most of the main characters. Yet we cannot afford to forget that they are, for the most part, highly successful people. Indeed, for Clamence, Henri, Jonas, Dubreuilh and the narrator of 'L'Age de discrétion' success itself brings its problems. Part of the son's difficulty in the last case is that his parents have been so successful (29), while in *Les Mandarins* Henri eventually agrees with Josette that '"la célébrité aussi est une humiliation"' (II,130), and discovers, just as Jonas and Clamence both do, that being successful and busy means neglecting certain people and thereby unwittingly making enemies.

The success of characters like Anne, Laurence, Daru and D'Arrast is of a less spectacular kind and does not bring them so much into the public eye, yet even in these cases we are very conscious of some sort of distinction between their public and private lives, even their public and private selves. Such a division inevitably leads to conflict in certain cases. Thus at some points Henri faces the same basic dilemma as Rambert in *La Peste*, namely whether to sacrifice precious aspects of his private life, things he especially prizes as an individual, for the greater good of the collectivity as a whole. But in general now individuals no longer have the threat of large-scale catastrophe hanging over them. Already holding their place (through the family, work, and so on) in a relatively stable society, they are not exactly called upon to decide whether or not to belong to a group, but *how far* to belong. And to take this decision they have to assess both what they themselves are and stand for, and what the society around them represents.

As far as self-scrutiny is concerned, its importance in each of these works of fiction is quite self-evident and would be difficult to over-state. Its links with the general phenomenon of judgement in society, however, do give it certain features here that distinguish it from the kind of self-scrutiny that characterised the pre-war and wartime books. It is not simply that on the practical level, because of their assigned roles, protagonists can no longer just ignore or deplore the way in which others see them. Their own judgement of themselves, or what we may call for convenience their 'self-image', is now deeply coloured by the social experience. The recognition that being judged is an inescapable feature of life in society means that individuals can no longer rest content with any original, ingenuous view they may have had of themselves. To a greater or lesser extent they are obliged to try forming the sort of picture or judgement of themselves that another *might* have formed with access to the privileged information that only the individual concerned has. But this can give rise to a particular kind of inner struggle - between original self-image and mediated self-image - and the outcome may be stress or confusion of a serious nature.

The case of Clamence in *La Chute* is an exceptional one, in that he has come to believe that others' judgement of him was too favourable! As a successful Parisian lawyer, he was thrown into confusion by his discovery that the image he had been presenting for others was a total fabrication, a systematic falsehood, and he describes very persuasively a number of minor incidents that led him to this discovery. But it is, of course, Clamence's self-image and not others' view of him that is shattered by incidents of this kind. When at a later stage he deliberately sets out to destroy the image he has hitherto been projecting (LC 1523), he does so precisely because he himself can no longer give credence to it. We emphasised earlier that the whole story revolves around his attempt to avoid the judgement of others, but what needs equal stress is the fact that it is because Clamence comes to see *himself* in a harsh light that he is so anxious to control and manipulate the way in which others see him. He is afraid of what others would think of him if they knew what he knows about himself, and this fear motivates his every action. Clamence's case brings out especially well both the importance of *changes* in one's self-image and the complexity of the interaction between that image and the judgement of others. It thus has considerable significance as a point of reference, even if Clamence is a rather unrepresentative figure by virtue of the all-absorbing quality of his preoccupation with his own image.

It is revealing to compare and contrast him, for instance, with the main figures in *L'Exil et le royaume*. There are strong characters like Yvars, Daru and D'Arrast who, whatever their problems and limitations, are not exactly afflicted with great self-doubt. But then neither do they have a particularly refined image of themselves, for these are eminently practical men in whom self-scrutiny - important though it is - is almost entirely confined to what is required for the answering of questions directly raised by their job or other aspects of their daily lives. They may lack a dimension or intensity of self-awareness that Clamence has, but their implicit scorn for elaborate introspection is based on a position of strength and stability. On the other hand, there are also some cautionary tales in this collection. It is unquestionably the Renégat's lack of self-knowledge (as his seminary teachers point out; Ren 1581) that leads him to disaster. Even after his first terrible volte-face, there is a suggestion at the end of the tale that he may again have come to see himself differently and may be changing direction once more. Both Janine and Jonas, too, in their separate ways, seem inadequate to the task of finding, let alone holding steady, their image of themselves. The ending of 'La Femme adultère' actually leaves Janine more fragmented as a personality than ever, with no clear picture at all of what she really is; and Jonas visibly fails to make any progress towards self-knowledge, his final 'illumination' being at worst a pure illusion and at best a potentially self-destructive insight.

Beauvoir's stories present the same mixed picture with regard to the struggle that characters are conducting with, or towards, their self-image. Although his development runs parallel to that of Clamence for a moment, Henri is basically much more like Yvars, Daru and D'Arrast: his period of intense and debilitating introspection is in a sense forced upon him, running counter to his deeper nature. The ending of *Les Mandarins* shows that he is never entirely happy when turned in upon himself, but has a need to transcend himself through work. Anne has perhaps previously enjoyed too successful a relationship with Robert and too successful a life generally to be very concerned with her self-image, but in the course of the story her awareness of ageing and the particular pressures of the post-war years lead her into disorientating affairs with other men and eventually to near-suicidal doubts about her real identity. Somewhat similarly, both Monique and Murielle undergo severe identity-crises brought on by a certain kind of over-reliance on their husbands; and the narrator's possibly more short-lived crisis in 'L'Age de discrétion' arises out of an over-dependent relationship with her only son. Finally, one of the references in the title of *Les Belles Images* is to the way in which Laurence's mother shaped her during her childhood, making her into 'une belle image' (21-22). The whole story is about Laurence's consequent difficulty in finding herself, and such optimism as there is in the ending relates to Catherine's future rather than to Laurence's, for the latter's grip on her self-image is still very far from strong: 'Qu'a-t-on fait de moi? Cette femme qui n'aime personne, insensible aux beautés du monde, incapable même de pleurer, cette femme que je vomis' (181).

Since knowing what one is is necessarily bound up with knowing what one has done and been in the past, the activity of retrospection plays a notable part in every one of these stories. And what is most frequently at stake is, disturbingly, an inquiry that involves some kind of *revaluation* of the past: when characters compare their present view of things with their view in the past (and indeed with their view *of* the past), mistakes or puzzles are exposed and serious adjustments often need to be made to long-cherished beliefs. Some come to believe that they were badly wrong earlier in their lives (Clamence, the Renégat), others look back rather ruefully, or with a mixture of anger and nostalgia (Janine, Yvars), and Beauvoir's heroines are often forced into the position of considering the possibility that their whole view of their past may be mistaken (André's wife, Monique, Anne). All of this, in turn, reinforces characters' awareness of the worrying gap that can exist between appearance and reality in the case of human action. Monique's rather pathetic cry, 'Comme tout devient compliqué dès qu'on commence à avoir des arrière-pensées!' (FR 181) - which strongly recalls Clamence's nostalgia for the primates ('Ils n'ont pas, eux, d'arrière-pensées'; LC 1478) - could almost serve as a motto for this group of stories. There is a far stronger sense here than in earlier periods that people are rarely quite what they seem.

In addition to these disconcerting features of self-scrutiny, characters seeking to arrive at a reasonable judgement or an accurate picture of themselves have always to contend with the old enemy of self-deception. Some fall heavily at this hurdle: Murielle's descriptions of herself in 'Monologue' are visibly belied by both the content and the manner of her diatribe as a whole; and Monique's self-deception in her diary in 'La Femme rompue' is none the less real for being different and more subtle, and for being periodically illuminated by flashes of lucidity. In stories like 'L'Age de discrétion', 'La Femme adultère', 'Jonas' and *Les Mandarins*, matters are much less clear-cut. Characters may be partly self-deluded rather than shot through with self-deception; or they may deceive themselves at one moment but achieve lucidity at another. Delicate and controversial issues of interpretation are involved in many cases, and there can be no question of suggesting that hard-and-fast criteria exist for identifying self-delusion in the characters. Indeed, it is again a strength in these books that they illustrate the inadequacy of such general criteria and show how intricate and personal the subject of self-deception is. All of this, furthermore, turns our attention to the fact that self-scrutiny is not to be seen as an end in itself: we can, and should, always ask what *results* it produces, and what a character *does* with the results it yields.

This is another important respect in which Clamence is an unrepresentative but crucial figure. Being judged by others leads characters in these books to set out to judge or revalue themselves, but we leave many of them at a point where it is not clear how they will subsequently react to the discoveries they have made (Anne, André's wife, Monique, Laurence, Janine, Jonas, D'Arrast). In fact, the risk that the process may lead to a paralysing kind of confusion is one that is quite extensively recorded in the stories. Clamence, however, passes through such a state of confusion, and the simple fact is that we must disapprove of, even deplore, the particular form that his concern with his self-image subsequently takes. He eventually reacts to the discovery of his own duplicity by claiming that no serious distinction can be drawn between good and evil, and is so dispirited morally that he cynically sets out, in his role of 'juge-pénitent', to manipulate others by deliberately falsifying the impression that they gain of him. In this respect he stands in contrast to most of the other main characters, who are, in varying degrees, at least *trying* to achieve lucidity about themselves and some measure of honesty in their relations with others. The result of Clamence's self-scrutiny is that he becomes a traitor to his fellow men: he rightly belongs in the last circle of Dante's *Inferno* (LC 1483).

As we have seen, Henri, too, at one particular stage grows tired of the exhausting struggle to continue distinguishing between right and wrong. He half persuades himself (like Mathieu in *La Mort dans l'âme*) that real freedom consists in doing what is wrong, and for a while, like Clamence, he takes refuge in drink and debauchery, suffering a great deal from not being able to live up to his reputation as a paragon of virtue (LM II.171). But unlike Clamence, Henri eventually comes through this phase with a continuing determination to do what he sees as right, however difficult this may be. There is a particularly significant moment when, having just committed perjury and received in reward the dossier incriminating his young mistress Josette, he refuses to see his own misdeed as a reason for not finishing an article denouncing an injustice:

> Il reprit son stylo. Il allait parler de justice, de vérité, protester contre les meurtres et les tortures. 'Il faut', se dit-il avec force. S'il renonçait à faire ce qu'il avait à faire, il devenait doublement coupable; quoi qu'il pensât de lui-même, il y avait ces hommes, là-bas, qu'il fallait essayer de sauver. (LM II.327)

He is unable, in the long run, to renounce his moral responsibilities altogether in the way that Clamence does, just as he is unable, ultimately, to live happily in a world over which he is not exerting at least as much control as he can. When he tells Nadine at the end of the book that "la vérité c'est qu'il ne faut pas s'occuper de ce qu'on est. Sur ce plan-là, on ne peut pas s'en tirer"' (II.48), he is exposing the principal weakness of Clamence's stance

and registering the existence of limits to the value
of self-scrutiny that are implicitly recognised in
all of the stories of this period. For, on the
whole, the emphasis in these books falls not on the
advantages, but on the *dangers* inherent in those
processes of self-scrutiny generated (or at least
intensified) by judgement in society. It is no
coincidence that Henri has so much in common,
morally speaking, with characters like Daru and
D'Arrast, who obviously carry a great deal of
Camus's sympathy: all are men who believe that
self-absorption is no substitute for action in the
external world.

It is significant, too, that Henri's part of
Les Mandarins should end with his decision not to go
to live in Italy, for in a number of cases here some
kind of involvement with the community is held up as
one of the main points of contrast with an
excessive, self-defeating kind of self-scrutiny.
There is a pendulum movement, with life in society
driving characters to look at themselves, and the
dynamics of that process eventually leading them
back towards society. The point is that the
characters whose self-scrutiny is carried too far
and visibly does them no good at all are precisely
those who indulge in it at the expense of direct
involvement in the affairs of the outside world. In
Les Mandarins, Anne, who with some justification is
accused by her daughter of living her life with kid
gloves on, of avoiding involvement, is in a far more
parlous state by the end of the book than either
Henri or Dubreuilh, both of whom eventually
recognise the definitive need to concern themselves
with what is happening in the world at large. This
is, admittedly, to touch on one distinctive feature
of the woman's situation in particular (especially
as portrayed by Beauvoir), namely the fact that
those women who in large measure devote themselves
to their husbands and families commonly deprive
themselves thereby of the direct contact with the
world and the 'transcendence' usually enjoyed by
men. In this respect, it is interesting that when
things begin to go wrong at home for them, both
Laurence and Monique make desultory attempts to
catch up on current affairs, implicitly
acknowledging that they have been rather too turned
in upon themselves and that part of the remedy lies
in their own hands. It is arguable that Janine is in
much the same position in 'La Femme adultère', but
from Camus's stories it is clearer that the matter
goes beyond a specific comment on women's condition.

The men characters who, like Clamence, the Renégat and Jonas, come to grief largely as a result of their own attitudes are also characterised by their failure to reach outwards and engage with the social reality beyond themselves: Clamence (who admits that 'Moi, moi, moi' has been the constant refrain of his life; LC 1500) is ultimately a pathetic figure in his failure to make meaningful contact with others and to belong somewhere; the Renégat is so totally obsessed with himself and his personal drives that disaster is inevitable when he comes into contact with a refractory outside world; and Jonas, who from the first has others act as a screen between himself and the world (his wife even does his reading for him!), gradually withdraws more and more into himself, to the point of living in complete isolation on his perch.

Looking at these stories as a whole, it is clear that there is no simple message to the effect that one has to be politically or socially involved to a high degree in order to preserve one's sanity and equilibrium (Yvars, Daru, D'Arrast and Henri are all, in their different ways, anxious to *contain* the extent of their commitment). But there is undoubtedly a broad suggestion that, for their own sake, individuals have to find some stable point between extreme individualism on the one side and blind loyalty to the collectivity on the other. Work (like the family) automatically casts a net of expectations and obligations around the individual and these embody some of the myriad ways in which living in society involves being judged by others, as well as thereby being forced to judge oneself. There is no question at all of individuals simply and docilely accepting, in all of its facets, whatever role or combination of roles society thrusts upon them, or whatever judgements may be pronounced upon them by others. Yet the implication is that we all badly need to be aware that there are limits of various kinds to our independence; limits, for example, to how far our own scrutiny of our values and our worth can be carried out without weakening our ability to cope with the world, and even to live with ourselves.

NOTES

1. I have pursued such parallels and some others touched on in these chapters in 'Heroes of our time in three of the stories of Camus and Simone de Beauvoir'.

Chapter Eleven

SOCIETY AND THE INDIVIDUAL CONSCIENCE

There is one main line along which characters'
reflections develop in these books that we have not
yet pursued. Having their established position in
society, and being called upon to decide how far
they should embrace, and how far resist, the various
implications of that position, individuals are bound
to scrutinise the society around them at the same
time as their own values. In fact, as we have seen,
there are obvious dangers in following one line of
inquiry at the expense of the other, and the
post-war books as a whole keep the two in balance.
      At the most general level (that of the basic
contents of the stories), this point manifests
itself in a characteristic mixture or blend of the
personal and the social, the individual and the
universal. Clamence says accurately of his
monologue, 'Je mêle ce qui me concerne et ce qui
regarde les autres' (LC 1547); and *Les Mandarins*,
with a struggle between private life and public life
at its core, and with a considerable proportion of
the text devoted to Anne's personal adventure in
America, is also an obvious example of such a
mixture. So is *L'Exil et le royaume*, for while the
balance is definitely tipped one way rather than the
other in certain stories, in others the personally
and the socially significant are inextricably
intertwined, so that the collection as a whole fuses
the two elements very satisfactorily. Like *La Chute*,
Les Belles Images has its own unique tone and terms
of reference, but it too blends the particular and
the general with marked success: Laurence's crisis
at the end is brought on by a combination of factors
in which her concern with the state of society is
ultimately indistinguishable from her personal
worries. Even *La Femme rompue*, though evidently much
more restricted in range as a collection than

212

Camus's, unmistakably broaches social as well as personal matters. Mostly these have to do with the situation of women in society, but in 'L'Age de discrétion' ageing and retirement also figure as themes. What is more, the narrator in 'Monologue' mingles references to her own life and relationships with comments on modern society in a way fundamentally similar to that of Clamence. In short, while not all characters assume the role of commentator on society as openly as Clamence and Murielle, all have experiences which, however personal, tell us as much about society itself as about the individuals involved.

Indeed, the perspective within which society is viewed in these works is one of their most distinctive features. The account of society here is an immeasurably more detailed and informed one than in earlier periods, and although it is a highly critical account, the criticism, unlike the early anti-bourgeois attitude, comes *from within* and is based upon characters' first-hand experience of the phenomena under attack. At the same time, there is also a much more marked recognition than in the pre-war and wartime works that industrialised, urbanised European society is quite distinct from other types of society. This is something that Camus, with his Algerian background, was doubtless always conscious of and, as we saw, different types of society were already in conflict in *L'Etranger*. But there, as in *La Mort heureuse* and *La Peste*, European society is a rather shadowy concept. In his post-war stories, Camus's emphasis is different. 'Jonas', like *La Chute*, depends heavily upon its European setting, while the presence of Western society or Western-type society (which by this time would probably take in life in the city of Algiers itself) hangs ominously over his other stories. Janine and Daru, in their different ways, are both in some measure fleeing from city life, while the Renégat (who actually refers to 'la sale Europe'; Ren 1580) and D'Arrast (who claims that 'là-bas, en Europe, c'était la honte et la colère'; PP 1678) are also escaping, to the Algerian desert and the Brazilian forests respectively. In all of these latter cases the whole culture of the indigenous population is radically distinct from Western European culture and this draws the main characters into conflicts of values. Furthermore, the broad technical developments that are affecting Yvars's job and life in 'Les Muets' ('la construction des bateaux et des camions-citernes'; 1598) clearly have their origins in industrial society rather than in Algeria itself.

In Beauvoir's stories, too, what she wishes to say about life in Europe since the war is thrown into relief by contrasts with different societies or cultures that are either built into the very structure of the tales or form minor themes within them. For part of *Les Belles Images*, for example, Laurence accepts her father's view that things are considerably better in less advanced countries:

> Socialistes ou capitalistes, dans tous les pays l'homme est écrasé par la technique, aliéné à son travail, enchaîné, abêti. Tout le mal vient de ce qu'il a multiplié ses besoins alors qu'il aurait dû les contenir; au lieu de viser une abondance qui n'existe pas et n'existera peut-être jamais, il lui aurait fallu se contenter d'un minimum vital, comme le font encore certaines communautés très pauvres - en Sardaigne, en Grèce, par exemple - où les techniques n'ont pas pénétré, que l'argent n'a pas corrompues. Là les gens connaissent un austère bonheur parce que certaines valeurs sont préservées, des valeurs vraiment humaines, de dignité, de fraternité, de générosité, qui donnent à la vie un goût unique. (84)

Interestingly, this is a rather similar view to that expressed by Clamence in a revealing aside about Greece (LC 1525), but it is rudely shattered later in *Les Belles Images*, when Laurence discovers that the Greeks are simply *poor* (162). At the other end of the spectrum, we are reminded in *Les Mandarins* of the opposite kind of contrast that Western Europe was seen to form, just after the war, with America, the land of promise and plenty. When Anne returns from her first trip to America, it is the austerity of life in France that strikes her, yet the story spans a period of great change and by the time Anne goes on her third visit America represents something quite different for her: 'Maintenant l'Amérique, ça signifiait bombe atomique, menace de guerre, fascisme naissant' (II,388). Monique, too, visits America in 'La Femme rompue' and in so far as her daughter Lucienne represents its 'new' values, finds it as alien as Anne eventually does. 'L'Age de discrétion', in a series of minor references, takes this process of contrast perhaps a little further, with the suggestion that the French have become rather isolationist and that it is the highly mysterious Chinese who may hold the key to the future (77).

In short, the comparing and contrasting of life in post-war Western Europe with that in different societies and cultures is, as the importance of travel in these works suggests, a characteristic ingredient of the stories. Camus and Beauvoir are never so exclusively preoccupied with the question of the individual's place in society that they lose sight of that of Western society's place in the world. Understandably, the wartime books concentrated largely on Western Europe and on the immediate and relatively short-term aspects of the pressure of historical forces. Here, where the perspective is a longer-term one - as much geographical, social and political in the widest sense of those terms as historical - we see an awareness of the structures and developments of the world as a whole.

In particular, the existence and problems of underdeveloped countries or of what we may very loosely call the Third World are emphasised in a way that is distinctively modern and casts a rather different light on the interdependence discovered and stressed during the war. The first major post-war journey recorded in *Les Mandarins* is Henri's trip to Portugal, when both he and Nadine are horrified by the poverty that they find in certain quarters of Lisbon and elsewhere (I,143). As we have seen, this kind of discovery is made in Greece by Laurence near the end of *Les Belles Images*, and both novels also refer to other parts of the globe where there is famine and extreme poverty. Henri is later preoccupied with India and China for a while ('Beaucoup de choses devenaient futiles quand on pensait à ces centaines de milliers d'affamés'; LM I,372), while the unease of Laurence's daughter Catherine initially centres on the idea of 'les gens malheureux' and specifically on the poster proclaiming that two thirds of the world's population are hungry (BI 29). Again, in 'L'Hôte' Daru is acutely aware of the poverty of the Arabs whose children he is teaching; and in 'La Pierre qui pousse' a great deal is made of the conditions of the natives living in the huts in the 'bas quartiers' of Iguape.

For our authors, however, poverty is invariably a form of oppression, and their concern with the Third World covers political factors as much as economic ones. It is the cruel gap between the lives of the rich and the poor that strikes characters so forcefully in Greece and Portugal: what Henri promises to write about in the French press when he returns from Portugal is 'la tyrannie politique, l'exploitation économique, la terreur policière, l'abêtissement systématique des masses, la honteuse complicité du clergé' (LM I,145-46). Similarly, the events of 'L'Hôte', which begins with the policeman Balducci on horseback leading a walking Arab prisoner up the hill by a rope, depend crucially upon some such contrast and 'oppression'. And the feature of life in Iguape that D'Arrast takes exception to is the division of its inhabitants into well-off local dignitaries (including police and judges) and impoverished workers. Much of this, of course, is bound up with a growing consciousness of the evils of colonialism. It is significant that the problems of Madagascar come forcibly to the attention of the main characters in the course of *Les Mandarins* and although, largely for chronological reasons, there is little direct trace of the upheavals of the Algerian War in these books (it is referred to in 'L'Age de discrétion' as 'cette guerre qui nous avait ravagés et qui semblait maintenant n'avoir jamais eu lieu'; 33), the issues involved clearly underlie a number of the stories of *L'Exil et le royaume*. Perhaps by the mid-sixties major preoccupations had changed somewhat, but in 'L'Age de discrétion' André, ever willing to combat oppression, is still particularly sensitive to suffering and injustice all over the world: 'Prisonniers politiques espagnols, détenus portugais, Iraniens persécutés, rebelles congolais, angolais, camerounais, maquisards vénézuéliens, péruviens, colombiens, il est toujours prêt à les aider dans la mesure de ses forces' (16). The phenomena of poverty and oppression, then, are seen as ultimately inseparable and there is general sympathy here towards victims of all kinds. When characters like Murielle and Clamence attack humanism or praise servitude they are presented in a thoroughly objectionable light.

Comparisons and contrasts with other cultures, including an increasing awareness of the difficulties of the Third World, also indicate the main thrust of the criticism of Western society itself in these books. In the context of the world at large, Western society is the home of the over-privileged, but as Nadine suggests, a similar polarisation can be discerned within countries like France itself, with the working classes constituting the poor and oppressed: '"c'est toujours ceux qui

travaillent le plus qui bouffent le moins"' (LM
I,26). And seen from Brazil the European scene looks
much the same:

>   'Il n'y a ni seigneurs ni peuple.'
>   L'autre réfléchissait, puis il se décida:
>   'Personne ne travaille, personne ne souffre?'
>   'Oui, des millions d'hommes.'
>   'Alors, c'est le peuple.' (PP 1669)

Yet relatively few of these stories as a whole
express very directly the strong solidarity with the
working classes of Europe that is so characteristic
of the main figures in *Les Mandarins*. The
implications of some of Camus's stories, including
those set outside Europe, undoubtedly run in that
direction and Clamence's views, as we have just
mentioned, are visibly held up for our disapproval.
But this is a little too indirect to count as sharp
criticism of the class sytem of Western societies as
such, and Camus's only other story set in Europe,
'Jonas', has nothing to say on the topic of social
class. After *Les Mandarins*, what is more, Beauvoir's
sympathy for the working classes becomes less
visible. It is true that some of Catherine's concern
for the oppressed in *Les Belles Images* centres on
young working women in France, but Laurence herself
is actually contrasted as a character with her
colleague Mona, whom she sees as having what
Jean-Charles calls 'la mystique du prolétariat'
(71). Laurence is also anxious to point out that
nowadays most workers have a washing machine, a
television and even a car (73). Similarly, although
the elderly married couple in 'L'Age de discrétion'
remain committed left-wingers, they are obliged to
admit that their position is an uneasy one: '"aucune
cause n'est tout à fait la nôtre"' (78). The fact
is that while the poorer classes tend on the whole
to be seen in these books as a more or less
undifferentiated mass, sympathy for them is
expressed less through detailed portrayals of their
plight than through an emphasis on the culpability
of the various more privileged groups in Western
society where wealth, power or influence is
concentrated.
    Thus, for instance, both authors are especially
hard in their stories on groups formed by those who
have enough money and leisure to pursue artistic and
intellectual activities but do so less for the sake
of those activities than for reasons of personal or
social prestige, or gain. In *Les Mandarins* there are

a number of memorable scenes where Anne and Henri attend the unspeakable 'salons' of Claudie Belzunce and Lucie Belhomme. Much as they are in demand, they never feel in the least part of the proceedings, if only because they see through the behaviour of the participants so easily. Anne is particularly struck by the insincerity and pretentiousness of such gatherings and eventually discovers that literary circles are much the same in New York and Chicago. And when he writes a play, Henri also discovers the malice and hypocrisy of the theatre-going public of Paris (LM II,128-29). Camus, no doubt drawing heavily, like Beauvoir, upon his own personal experience as an author, records similar phenomena in 'Jonas', where the artist's 'friends' and 'admirers' frequent his flat – to his great inconvenience – as long as his reputation is high, but desert him as soon as it falls and indeed hurry to spread word of his eclipse (1644). Beauvoir also has characters attack the art world and the world of letters in *Les Belles Images*, hinting at corruption or at least charlatanism (94).

The important notion, however, is that the very existence of such closed circles of people is ultimately dependent upon privilege and wealth. Members of the circles concerned need to dispose of at least a certain amount of money and leisure (although their object may well be to gain more of both), and the groups described are usually associated with a degree of ostentation, opulence, frivolity and waste. This aspect of society is consistently stressed in *Les Belles Images*. The members of the jet-set portrayed there are not altogether the idle rich, but some have country houses; they discuss the relative merits of Bermuda and Tahiti for holidays; they talk of smart Parisian receptions; and they are entirely obsessed with expensive gimmicks, gadgets and possessions. Not only is all of this obscene in contrast with the extreme poverty in other parts of the world and the relative poverty in some sections of French society: the scramble for money and possessions is also shown in many of the stories as intrinsically foolish and corrupting. In some respects this is best brought out in the rather less well-off bourgeois figures like Janine's husband in 'La Femme rompue' and Irène in 'L'Age de discrétion', whose concern with money shows them to be just as thoroughly unattractive and small-minded as characters like Jean-Charles. In fact, almost everything in these books points either directly or indirectly to the conclusion that money and possessions constitute a millstone around the neck and alienate us from true human values.

The gap between rich and poor within a society, exploitation and 'servitude', the preoccupation with material possessions - all of these targets of criticism show that our authors are effectively engaged in a fundamental attack on the capitalist system that prevails in the Western world, at least if one takes the concept of capitalism rather broadly. The stance of Henri and Dubreuilh and, to a lesser extent, of André and the narrator of 'L'Age de discrétion' is firm and unambiguous in this respect, while in many other cases the deleterious consequences and implications of capitalism are displayed in particular incidents and situations. Most clearly of all, we see Yvars's boss in 'Les Muets' struggling, in the face of changing conditions, to save his business

> Les patrons voyaient leurs affaires compromises, c'était vrai, mais ils voulaient quand même préserver une marge de bénéfices; le plus simple leur paraissait encore de freiner les salaires malgré la montée des prix.
> (1598-99)

His enlightened (or calculating) promise that he will rectify matters when things pick up again is insufficient to restore the good relations that obtained before the sad but inevitable events of the strike. But this story expresses a rare sympathy for the bosses, and more commonly characters find themselves victims of those operating the system. Thus Jonas (who entirely lacks the business acumen of his slightly unscrupulous father) suffers financially at the hands of property-owners as well as art dealers:

> Mais les nécessités de l'entassement urbain et de la rente immobilière avaient contraint les propriétaires successifs à couper par des cloisons ces pièces trop vastes, et à multiplier par ce moyen les stalles qu'ils louaient au prix fort à leur troupeau de locataires. Ils n'en faisaient pas moins valoir ce qu'ils appelaient 'l'important cubage d'air'. Cet avantage n'était pas niable. Il fallait seulement l'attribuer à l'impossibilité où s'étaient trouvés les propriétaires de cloisonner aussi les pièces dans leur hauteur.
> (Jon 1633-34)

More seriously, Henri discovers to his cost that running a newspaper is ultimately a financial rather than an ideological matter (LM I,211), and is obliged to make arrangements for backing that eventually cause him to give up the editorship.

Clamence's general position, as usual, is an ambiguous one. As we have seen, he is certainly in favour of some system of 'servitude' and hierarchy, but his lack of interest in money is one of his more attractive features. D'Arrast in 'La Pierre qui pousse' evidently shares this characteristic: when 'le coq' describes the whole business of buying and selling in the Western world as a 'saleté' (1669), D'Arrast seems to agree and claims that he is not altogether a part of it. Yet there is some slight ambiguity in his position too, for he does represent 'la Société française de Rio' and later acknowledges 'l'avantage pour sa société d'avoir obtenu l'adjudication de ces longs travaux' (1672). Clearly, much depends upon the humanity and the good will of those bound up with the capitalist system: while neither Camus nor Beauvoir holds any brief for that system as a whole, and while they would surely repudiate the standard sorts of justification offered by Jean-Charles and those like him (BI 148-49), they do not wish to suggest that everything built upon capitalist foundations (for instance, aid to underdeveloped countries, or medical advances) is necessarily evil.

At bottom, they are probably less concerned with the underlying economic structure of the Western world as such than with the whole pattern and movement of society; that is the general lifestyle and the values that have emerged since the war. Like so many of Clamence's comments, one that he makes about the nature of modern urban life in Europe is especially evocative:

> Sur le Damrak, le premier tramway fait tinter son timbre dans l'air humide et sonne l'éveil de la vie à l'extrémité de cette Europe où, au même moment, des centaines de millions d'hommes, mes sujets, se tirent péniblement du lit, la bouche amère, pour aller vers un travail sans joie. (LC 1549)

His observation is not so much an economic as a social, or even a moral one, and like his reference to 'la créature solitaire, errant dans les grandes villes' (1536), it is one that awakens echoes in anyone who has lived in an industrial city. *La Femme rompue* also draws attention to the harshness of life in cities like Paris (FR 125) and to the way in which they grow and spread physically (AD 11). And *Les Belles Images* catches the flavour of certain aspects of urban life outstandingly well, emphasising all of the environmental pressures as well as the less tangible strains that drive people in cities to flight, tranquillisers and sleeping-tablets, even suicide. The odd references to overpopulation and Murielle's (admittedly, obsessive) concern with pollution and contamination (Mon 95) are developments of this kind of perspective that give Beauvoir's later stories a very modern ring, although *La Femme rompue* at least lacks the enlivening touch of irony about contemporary life that we find in Camus's *La Chute* and 'Jonas'. There is a similar pattern in the expressions of the horror that both authors share over the recent history of the Western world. While some of that history figures directly in *Les Mandarins* and forms the background to Laurence's troubles in *Les Belles Images*, Camus holds it slightly at a distance in *La Chute*, where Clamence's comments on Hitler and his accounts of the terrible events and trends in twentieth-century Europe are, again, usually tinged with mockery or paradox. And whereas the constant threat of nuclear holocaust hanging over the head of modern man figures as an oppressive theme in Beauvoir's stories, Camus has Clamence remark on it in a different tone, almost as if it is simply one more of the monstrosities of the modern world to be put up with (LC 1519-20).

More interestingly perhaps, while both writers are in some measure contrasting these public horrors with, or at least setting them alongside, intense private (particularly sexual) relationships, Beauvoir does so with the utmost seriousness and as if with a heavy heart – one thinks of the thoroughly unsuccessful affairs of Anne and Laurence, of Murielle's disastrous relationships, and of the tragic effects of Maurice's affairs – whereas Camus, at least in *La Chute* and 'Jonas', does so with a certain lightness of touch. His remark that Jonas's father ended up publishing only sex books because of the perennial popularity of the subject echoes a well-known comment on modern man by Clamence, who himself has a long series of casual, and very amusingly described, affairs. The comment, curiously, constitutes a remarkably apposite summary of the contents of *Les Mandarins*:

> Il m'a toujours semblé que nos concitoyens
> avaient deux fureurs: les idées et la
> fornication. A tort et à travers, pour ainsi
> dire. Gardons-nous, d'ailleurs, de les
> condamner: ils ne sont pas les seuls, toute
> l'Europe en est là. Je rêve parfois de ce que
> diront de nous les historiens futurs. Une
> phrase leur suffira pour l'homme moderne: il
> forniquait et lisait des journaux. Après cette
> forte définition, le sujet sera, si j'ose dire,
> épuisé. (LC 1479)

One might also compare this observation with some
opinions expressed by the paraphrenic Murielle in
'Monologue'. Although we have general reasons for
doubting the judgement of these two characters, and
although Murielle's comments lack the wit and irony
of Clamence's, certain insights by both into modern
society register with some force. The point is not,
then, that Camus's treatment of these topics is
intrinsically superior to that of Beauvoir, but that
he aims at the same targets with slightly different
weapons and that his more ironical approach does not
denote a lack of concern. The differences of tone
and emphasis cannot conceal the fact that both
authors are anxious about much the same features of
modern life in the Western world.

In the light of the sort of criticisms of
Western society just outlined, it is obvious that we
cannot take the fact that most characters in the
post-war books have a regular place within that
society to amount to general assent to its values on
our authors' part. Indeed, a figure like
Jean-Charles in *Les Belles Images*, who is well
pleased with the way in which society works and
optimistic about man's future, is presented as being
either in the worst kind of self-deceived state or a
man of crass insensitivity and some stupidity. The
way in which he explains away the unsavoury aspects
of modern life that are upsetting his daughter rings
quite hollow, and his account is steeped in
self-satisfaction and complacency:

> Jean-Charles est devenu lyrique, comme chaque
> fois qu'il évoque l'avenir: les déserts se sont
> couverts de blé, de légumes, de fruits, toute
> la terre est devenue la terre promise; gavés de
> lait, de riz, de tomates et d'oranges, tous les
> enfants souriaient. (30-31)

And he doubtless agrees with Gilbert's tendency to

dismiss all victims of society as 'des faux frais' (BI 58). He is, of course, strongly contrasted with his wife Laurence, who at least recognises and acknowledges the evils in society and has a bad conscience about them. Just as in the pre-war and wartime books there was a certain cluster of facts (metaphysical and historical respectively) that *had* to be seen and admitted, had to be faced with lucidity, so here the suggestion is that to turn one's back on, or pass over in silence, certain features of peacetime Western society is to indulge in self-deception of the most serious and reprehensible kind. It is in this respect that the two strands of self-scrutiny and scrutiny of society that we have been following come together: a degree of self-awareness, honesty and integrity is indispensable to a critical evaluation of society. Laurence's father, like some of the hangers-on in 'Jonas' (1637), is eventually shown to be lacking in some of these qualities, with the result that his particular attack on modern society is thereby undermined. Yet although one or two characters here are shown outside an urban context, few if any could be said to have broken away completely from what they deplore in European society: most (including *all* of Beauvoir's protagonists) either fail to recognise its general flaws or feel that they have no option but to maintain their social position in spite of all that is wrong around them.

In fact, both Camus and Beauvoir in their different ways record the temptation to give up altogether any struggle that persistent moral disapproval of particular features of society may involve:

> La mauvaise conscience - sur ce point, pour une fois, papa et Jean-Charles sont d'accord - à quoi ça sert? Cette affaire de tortures, il y a trois ans, je m'en suis rendue malade, ou presque; pour quoi faire? Les horreurs du monde, on est forcé de s'y habituer. (BI 29-30)

If only the reprehensible characters like Clamence, Murielle and the Renégat give in completely to this temptation, most of the others vacillate and weaken from time to time in accordance with the flaws in their own particular character. Often they find themselves progressively less and less wholeheartedly engaged in the things they do ('nous ne sommes qu'à peu près en toutes choses'; LC 1480). In any case, the strain is considerable and there is some talk in these books of the difficulty of merely *continuing*:

> Oui, on peut faire la guerre en ce monde, singer l'amour, torturer son semblable, parader dans les journaux, ou simplement dire du mal de son voisin en tricotant. Mais, dans certains cas, continuer, seulement continuer, voilà ce qui est surhumain. (LC 1533-34)

Monique's plight at the end of 'La Femme rompue' is how to go on without Maurice, but as Gilbert says when Laurence claims that her mother will not be able to tolerate being alone: '"On supporte, on supporte"' (BI 47). And although Janine thinks at the end of 'La Femme adultère' that she has found something to make her forget the long anguish of living and dying, there are signs that her relief will be short-lived. It is significant that many of these cases concern the general plight of women, for of course the strong suggestion in Beauvoir's stories at least is that the (married) woman's lot in modern society is a peculiarly harsh one.

Both authors, in any case, are acutely conscious of how the problem of continuing is compounded by the loss of powers associated with ageing, and these last two points are brought together in characters like Janine, Monique, the narrator of 'L'Age de discrétion' and even Anne (who is 39!): '"Il est trop tard même pour les regrets; il n'y a qu'à continuer"' (LM I,127). More generally, there is often a strong sense in these books that the characters are already fully developed ('hommes faits' or 'femmes faites') and cannot change themselves in any significant way, however much they might like to do so. Clamence recognises this impossibility ('Que faire pour être un autre? Impossible'; LC 1550), and Scriassine claims that there is only one illness of any importance, that of being oneself (LM I,114) - a point that Anne later acknowledges. There is, of course, the possibility of suicide, and Anne herself comes very close indeed to taking this way out at the end of *Les Mandarins*. Laurence also reflects on this recourse on more than one occasion in *Les Belles Images*, while Clamence characteristically rejects it on the grounds that he would not be there to see its effects (LC 1513). Murielle's daughter Sylvie in 'Monologue' has actually committed suicide (113).

Between the alternatives of simply going

painfully on and ending it all there is an
intermediate process that figures with notable
prominence in these stories, that of breakdown. The
difficulties of defining 'breakdown' are real
enough, as are those of distinguishing between
mental and physical disorder (there are at least
three cases of what may uncontroversially be called
psychosomatic illness here: Monique's bleeding in
'La Femme rompue', Laurence's anorexia in *Les Belles
Images*, and the similar state that Murielle recalls
in 'Monologue'). Nevertheless, it is hardly
disputable that under the strain of living with
themselves and in a society they disapprove of, a
formidable number of characters here break down,
either temporarily in a way that is somehow
self-rectifying, or seriously enough to require
medical assistance. Murielle, Laurence, Monique and
Jonas are all actually seen receiving the attentions
of a psychiatrist or doctor, and the Renégat - whose
obsessions, after all, arose long before he left
France - is unmistakably deranged. While her husband
is away the narrator of 'L'Age de discrétion'
undergoes a dreadful period of depression verging on
a breakdown; and Anne's state of mind is at least
one stage worse when she contemplates suicide near
the end of *Les Mandarins*. Clamence gives way at one
point too ('Un jour vint où je n'y tins plus'; LC
1522), passing through a sequence of states that he
describes largely in terms of sickness and cure.
Moreover, the minor characters in the books
sometimes provide cases of severe stress or mental
illness. For a time this is true of Dominique in *Les
Belles Images*, while *Les Mandarins* offers many
examples: Paule, as we have seen, has a mental
breakdown in the very fullest sense of the term; a
friend of Brogan's comes to visit him when she
breaks out of a mental hospital; and, of course, we
see Anne dealing with those disturbed in various
ways by the events of the war. In the face of this
catalogue of breakdowns and psychiatric troubles, we
can see that another of Clamence's provocative
remarks is not entirely without foundation:

> Savez-vous ce qu'est devenue, dans cette ville,
> l'une des maisons qui abrita Descartes? Un
> asile d'aliénés. Oui, c'est le délire général,
> et la persécution. Nous aussi, naturellement,
> nous sommes forcés de nous y mettre. (LC 1535)

Of the instances of breakdown among main
characters that of Laurence is probably the most

revealing and certainly the best documented. She has had at least one major crisis before (five years earlier), as well as a number of minor ones; and they were all, in large measure, what Jean-Charles calls 'crises de mauvaise conscience', thereby linking Laurence's personal state of mind directly with the state of the world. Fascinatingly, now in the course of the events of *Les Belles Images* the question arises of what she should do about her own daughter Catherine, who is coming to be disturbed by the suffering of others, which her mother can no longer conceal from her. For some time Laurence gives way to the pressures, from her husband in particular, to try to 'cure' Catherine of this sensitivity, outstandingly by referring her to a child psychiatrist. But in combination with other family factors, the fact that she is going against her better judgement in this respect brings Laurence to crisis-point at the end of the book, where she is unable to eat and is 'terrassée par une galopade d'images et de mots qui défilaient dans sa tête' (179). In a close parallel with *La Chute*, the last pages of the novel see the central figure on her sick bed claiming, among other things, that her chance in life has passed. As we have seen, this is only one of a number of cases where increasing personal, domestic and social pressures bearing upon a central figure eventually build up to a serious crisis.

What is quite certain is that the stories as a whole contain remarkably few detailed, constructive suggestions for improving Western society. Yet they do not all end on a note of unrelieved pessimism, and we need to ask what positive moral pointers – over and above those implicit in the very criticisms of society themselves – emerge from the post-war fiction. Laurence, for instance, does not simply lament her own lot at the end of *Les Belles Images*: she pulls herself around sufficiently to insist that Catherine see the psychiatrist no more and be allowed to make and keep whatever friends she chooses. In spite of anything that Jean-Charles may say, Laurence will not have Catherine brought up in a state of ignorance and indifference: 'Pour moi les jeux sont faits, pense-t-elle en regardant son image – un peu pâle, les traits tirés. Mais les enfants auront leur chance. Quelle chance? Elle ne le sait même pas' (183). It is obvious enough, however, that neither of the two aspects of this final stand by Laurence is of very considerable moral significance. The resolution (which, after all, has

still to be carried out) to open Catherine's eyes
and the hope that 'un rayon de lumière filtrera
jusqu'à elle' (181) are very vague and amount, at
best, to another statement of the ideal of lucidity
that is embodied in our authors' books from the
pre-war fiction onwards and can by now be taken for
granted. Besides, there is something inherently weak
about a moral stance that lays exclusive emphasis
upon children and the future.

The other positive side to Laurence's
rebellion, that is her stress on the value of
friendship (172), is possibly of less moral
importance in itself than lucidity, although the
topic does have a certain place in the post-war
stories. Particularly touching is the bond between
the artist and Rateau in 'Jonas'; and although the
friendship between Henri and Dubreuilh has its very
obvious ups and downs, it is a striking feature of
Les Mandarins and outlasts more transient phenomena.
But it would not be easy to draw any firm or useful
conclusions about friendship from the books as a
whole, for the 'friends' that Beauvoir's women
characters have tend to be the sort that obviate the
need for enemies, while some of Clamence's acerbic
comments on friendship cannot entirely fail to
strike home. The fact is that to make very much of
this theme one has to extend it to cover, say, the
sort of companionship experienced by man and wife in
'L'Age de discrétion'; the relationship between
workmates in 'Les Muets'; and the
less-well-developed links that spring up between,
for instance, D'Arrast and 'le coq' in 'La Pierre
qui pousse'. And by this stage one is not talking
about friendship specifically but, equally, about
concepts like fraternity, solidarity and humanity.

Now, there is no doubt that these notions lie
near the very heart of the moral content of the
post-war stories: the only difficulty is, once more,
to give some definite substance and shape to our
authors' fictional treatment of such ideas. As with
the wartime books, we can surely say with a certain
confidence that the thrust of the stories as a whole
is towards solidarity rather than away from it.
Clamence's extreme egotism and selfishness ('pour
être heureux, il ne faut pas trop s'occuper des
autres'; LC 1516), like Murielle's, has the clear
effect of alienating us morally, thereby stating the
case for some kind of solidarity indirectly.
Something similar could be said about the Renégat,
who actually weakens at the end and appeals to
'hommes autrefois fraternels, seuls recours'

(Ren 1593); and even, to take a less complex case, about 'Les Muets', where the workers allow pride and stubbornness to stifle the expression of their basic humanitarian feelings towards their boss. The case of Jonas is scarcely more difficult to accommodate either, for the fact that on discovering the single word on his canvas 'on ne savait s'il fallait lire *solitaire* ou *solidaire*' (Jon 1654) should not lead us to suppose that Camus himself could not make up his mind which direction to take: he is pointing out, rather, that an artist needs a certain solitude as well as solidarity if he is to continue to reflect and create. Some other stories (particularly those centring largely on women's problems: 'La Femme adultère', 'L'Age de discrétion', 'La Femme rompue') can scarcely be read as making a plea for solidarity in any broad sense of the term, but neither do they run counter to the general hypothesis that there is such a plea in the books as a whole.

The real problem, then, is again that of the exact nature and scope of the solidarity (or fraternity, or humanity) that the stories hold out as an ideal. What it is important to recognise is that this issue, like virtually all other moral matters in the post-war books, has to be seen in the light of the critical attitude towards Western society at large that we have latterly been outlining. Part of the message of these works is undoubtedly that of solidarity with the poor and the oppressed, be they in Europe or in the Third World, but as in the wartime fiction this immediately raises the question of what attitude should be adopted towards those who are not poor and oppressed, and not particularly concerned about those who are. It is clear that *some* degree of hostility is the only appropriate stance, but this is now a very much more complicated business than previously. Solidarity in wartime was in certain respects an easy matter of uniting against a common enemy, but it risked obscuring important distinctions and differences. Now that there is no obvious common foe, it is to a large extent those distinctions and differences that create difficulties for the individual. (While Jean Blomart and his father could make common cause against the Nazis during the Occupation, in the post-war situation Blomart would presumably have to *oppose* his father again on behalf of the poor.) Social relations of one kind or another now bring individuals into constant and close contact with those with whom they are in serious disagreement. They are called upon to cooperate with such people, and there is no single, ready-made issue, no external threat that naturally results in open conflict or in a complete polarisation of opinions: individuals themselves must *choose* the ground on which they wish to make a moral stand and thereby alienate some of those around them. This sort of problem taxes Henri throughout *Les Mandarins*, and is experienced, in a different context, by both Daru (who offends his friend Balducci in standing up for his principles) and D'Arrast (who slights the dignitaries of Iguape in his determination to see the conditions of the poor and to help 'le coq'). Laurence, too, has to take her stand over Catherine in opposition to the members of her own family and others.

All of this makes the ideal of 'solidarity' a still more elusive one theoretically than it was in the wartime books. Since individuals are no longer obviously pinning their faith in some readily identifiable group, there is no question of duty to the collectivity overriding all else, and it is often not clear how far they are acting in the name of abstract ideals and how far out of loyalty to particular persons. Laurence's rebellion may be indirectly connected with the plight of the starving, but it crystallises around the distress of her own daughter. There is something restrictive as well as something expansive in her final stance. Early on in *Les Belles Images* Laurence has pointed out that it is all very well trying to live 'planétairement' in the way that Jean-Charles advocates, but in the meantime she does not even know the people who live on the floor above her (26), and although this exposes the hollowness of Jean-Charles's attitude, it also suggests certain limitations in her own. The narrator of 'L'Age de discrétion' claims to have no time for talk of non-communication, but she too acknowledges that actual communication does not stretch very far: 'Si on tient à communiquer on y réussit tant bien que mal. Pas avec tout le monde bien sûr, mais avec deux ou trois personnes' (9). As with Laurence, her final position – and indeed her story as a whole – may be seen as begging some important questions as far as solidarity is concerned. Is communicaton with one or two people ever likely to lead to communication with the whole of mankind? And what should we think of it, if it is not? Is the companionship of two ageing members of the

privileged classes in an industrial society any kind
of guide at all to what can and ought to be done
about the starving millions outside Europe, or is it
something entirely separate? In the wartime books,
all three authors may have drawn *some* consolation
from the belief that friendship and intimacy were
being snatched away by irresistible historical
forces (Tarrou, Hélène, Schneider), but now
individuals themselves are fully and unmistakably
responsible - often in a direct and immediate way -
for any particular failure of communication, any
breakdown in personal relationships. They must also
take full responsibility for any success, in the
sense that it may be possible to achieve this only
at the expense of commitment to humanity at large.
Fundamentally, we are back with Blomart in the
period before the outbreak of war, when he was
hopelessly trying to weigh the tears of those he
knew against the blood of unidentified victims of
oppression.

For some kind of balanced reaction to this sort
of dilemma, and for such constructive suggestions as
the post-war books contain on solidarity and
fraternity, we need to go back to the stories of the
mid-fifties, and particularly to the group of
genuine heroes mentioned earlier: Henri, Yvars, Daru
and D'Arrast. These are characters who hold onto
some ideal of solidarity and/or fraternity, however
vague, in spite of everything. Unlike Laurence -
who, for all her criticism of capitalist society,
shows no sign of giving up a profession that feeds
upon and reinforces the very worst within it - Henri
will actively work on to improve the world in his
own way, though without much hope of success. His
final position is similar to that of a moral hero of
the wartime books, Rieux: he cannot do more than his
best, and although this will not be enough, it is
certainly better than doing nothing at all.
Disillusioned Henri may be in the end, but he is
admirably clear-headed and stable. His personal life
is in order and in no way undermined by his
'abstract' ideals. When appropriate, he can
subordinate personal feelings to rational beliefs
and aims: he acknowledges that although friendship
with Lachaume is impossible after all that has
happened, nothing prevents them from working
together (LM II,446). Similar points could be made
about a character like Yvars, who is in an entirely
different situation. His experience at the factory
is saddening, but he will not allow it to undermine
the pride he takes in his work, or his solidarity

with his workmates; nor will he permit it to disturb his successful family-life. Daru, of course, is in a much better position to help others, but he is not unlike Yvars in his very solidity and sense of perspective. He shows the greatest humanity towards his Arab prisoner in spite of the fact that he has no wish to accept a 'fraternité' with him that circumstances could easily impose (Ho 1620). If he is finally misunderstood by all, that is his tragedy and the tragedy of many good men the world over. D'Arrast, on the other hand, who shares much of the deep humanity of Daru and Henri, is eventually accepted into a community that has earlier rejected him. What is perhaps most significant in his case, however, is that although he helps 'le coq' fulfil his rather absurd promise, he has no idea whatever why he is doing so (PP 1683; 1684). It may be the very instinctive nature of his reactions that makes him acceptable to a different society, and if there is a measure of optimism at the end of *L'Exil et le royaume* (as well as something aesthetically satisfying in the fact that, finally, the helper is himself helped), this is based upon something *other than* a fully rational appraisal of the merits and implications of solidarity and fraternity.

In any case, the picture painted by the post-war books as a whole is a very gloomy one, and constructive suggestions for rectifying the deplorable features of Western society so memorably recorded in the stories are seriously lacking in substance and detail. Exile, as Camus suggests in his *prière d'insérer* to *L'Exil et le royaume*, can point the way to the kingdom, 'à la seule condition que nous sachions y refuser en même temps la servitude et la possession' (2039), and in this *negative* sense these books undoubtedly have moral force. (It is interesting to note the parallel with the 'vérité encore négative' that Camus saw in Meursault and with the strong negative aspect detected in the wartime perspectives.) Yet the post-war books might equally well be seen as a monument to the difficulty of fulfilling Camus's condition. It would be wrong to suggest that here the individual's experience of society in peacetime is *always* such that we are left deeply uncertain whether it is ever possible for one person to communicate with, and help, another. But the odd pockets of optimism are invariably associated with particular personal relationships and gestures, or with extremely modest and still vague hopes for the future: they offer no more than the faintest glimmers of hope for an improvement in the levels of collaboration and justice among men at large. As in the wartime stories, the only type of solidarity that can ultimately be said to be advocated across all of the stories is an absolutely minimal one that amounts to recognising that unles we go on trying to cooperate and to help one another, the very *possibility* of improvement can be ruled out.

Indeed, the key to the post-war perspectives in general is probably the fact that, seen from the inside, society is evidently not the large-scale cooperative enterprise that in theory it might be expected to be. Through mediations like the family and work, individuals here are fully integrated into society, but this broad feature of their situation not only marks off the post-war period from earlier ones, it also, in the end, constitutes the major factor limiting individuals' outlooks and their actions. When characters have the highly critical view of Western society already traced, it is difficult not to see most of the dilemmas they face as falling under the general description of moral problems provided by Dubreuilh when he is reconciled with Henri and learns of the latter's perjury:

'Vous savez ce que ça prouve, cette histoire? dit Dubreuilh avec une soudaine animation. C'est que la morale privée, ça n'existe pas. Encore un de ces trucs auxquels nous avons cru et qui n'ont aucun sens ... Dans un espace courbe, on ne peut pas tirer de ligne droite, dit Dubreuilh. On ne peut pas mener une vie correcte dans une société qui ne l'est pas. On est toujours repincé, d'un côté ou d'un autre. Encore une illusion dont il faut nous débarrasser, conclut-il. Pas de salut personnel possible.' (LM II,343)

Like Henri, we may hesitate to accept the demise of personal morality, but the fact remains that the wheel has virtually come full circle since the pre-war period, when the *central* preoccupation was personal salvation: now all of the post-war books encourage us to see ethical questions strictly within a social context. Given the benefit of the doubt, a few figures (like Clamence, Murielle, and just possibly the Renégat) might be said to have some notion of what is wrong with society but nonetheless to be proposing, on a purely personal basis, solutions that are clearly false. But our heart goes out to those characters who retain enough lucidity not to go astray, not to betray their insights, and yet are somehow bound in the end - as the stories so graphically show - to be 'repincé, d'un côté ou d'un autre'. One thinks immediately of Henri, Anne, Jonas, Laurence and (outside Europe) Yvars and Daru. However good their intentions, they find that their room for manoeuvre is severely circumscribed and sometimes scarcely know where to turn.

Clamence probably has more ordinary cases in mind when he explains why he finds criminals more moral than those running bourgeois society, but he also registers an important limit beyond which such an argument may not be pursued:

> je les trouve plus moraux que les autres, ceux qui tuent en famille, à l'usure. N'avez-vous pas remarqué que notre société s'est organisée pour ce genre de liquidation? Vous avez entendu parler, naturellement, de ces minuscules poissons des rivières brésiliennes qui s'attaquent par milliers au nageur imprudent, le nettoient, en quelques instants, à petites bouchées rapides, et n'en laissent qu'un squelette immaculé? Eh bien, c'est ça, leur organisation. 'Voulez-vous d'une vie propre? Comme tout le monde?' Vous dites oui, naturellement. Comment dire non? 'D'accord. On va vous nettoyer. Voilà un métier, une famille, des loisirs organisés.' Et les petites dents s'attaquent à la chair, jusqu'aux os. Mais je suis injuste. Ce n'est pas leur organisation qu'il faut dire. Elle est la nôtre, après tout: c'est à qui nettoiera l'autre. (LC 1479)

(In another context, Henri at one point uses some of the very same terms and probably has the same analogy with piranha fish in mind: 'Mangé, dévoré, nettoyé jusqu'à l'os. Il ne serait plus question d'écrire'; LM I,235.) Clamence, like Dubreuilh, is describing very well the way in which the particular place occupied by individuals within society, far from automatically guaranteeing that they take the right direction morally, necessarily puts them under pressures of various kinds that are more likely to pull them off course. But Clamence is also pointing out that he himself, the critic of society, is part of, and helps to run, that society; and for once the ambiguous position that he is in is one shared by virtually all of the main figures.

Most other characters are less selfish than

Clamence. In fact, in opposing poverty and oppression they are expressing a greater altruism than their wartime counterparts had the opportunity to show, for the latter were fighting at least partly for their own survival. But unlike the pre-war characters, they are anything but outsiders to the society they castigate, and they must therefore bear their share of responsibility for the sort of community to which they belong. However much they may be inclined to blame the nature and structure of society for particular evils, firm limits are set to the plausibility and legitimacy of such blame by the fact that society is composed, precisely, of individuals like themselves, whose complicity in the system varies only in extent or degree. We have already noted the rather equivocal positions that many characters occupy in relation to the working classes and to various privileged groups within society, and similar ambiguities could be traced at other levels and in other cases. In an interesting comment on the origins of *Les Belles Images* Beauvoir herself has described her intention as to 'évoquer cette société technocratique dont je me tiens le plus possible à distance mais dans laquelle néanmoins je vis; à travers les journaux, les magazines, la publicité, la radio, elle m'investit', and categorised Laurence as 'une jeune femme assez complice de son entourage pour ne pas le juger, assez honnête pour vivre cette connivence dans le malaise'.[1]

All of the emphasis in the post-war books falls on the individual conscience. Moral agents are prodded neither by the opposition of society nor by historical forces and have to decide entirely on their own initiative which features of life in Western society are acceptable and which unacceptable. They doubtless recognise that the individual influences and affects society, just as society influences and affects the individual. They probably see that the formulation of criticisms is a precondition of the first of these processes, but find the social system such a complex web and so weighty a burden that they cannot easily overcome their feeling of powerlessness. In general terms, the only hope is that individuals will go on trying to improve things on a scale appropriate to their powers rather than give up the struggle. If it is not clear - as it was, at least in retrospect, in earlier periods - how this somewhat depressing picture could ever change drastically, then one can only say that it would be surprising if it were

clear, since this is still the broad situation that
Western man finds himself in. For those with roughly
the same metaphysical views and the same political
or humanistic leanings as our authors, the
perspectives embodied in the post-war stories are
familiar and perhaps insuperable.

NOTES

    1. *Tout compte fait,* p.172.

CONCLUSION

The pattern of shifting moral perspectives that we
have traced in the fiction of Sartre, Camus and
Simone de Beauvoir is one that stands on its own and
has intrinsic interest. The three phases described
reflect very clearly the outline shape of the lives
of most people of their generation and will
therefore be meaningful to many. These phases
present, moreover, three distinct types of broad
moral framework within which individuals may find
themselves.

At another level, however, it is clear that the
full significance of our results in relation to the
writings of the three authors as a whole could only
be measured against the background of other patterns
that it has been no part of our purpose to examine,
and which it would be entirely inappropriate to try
to sketch in here. The question of the precise
extent to which the phases that we have postulated
and the changes of perspective that we have detected
are confirmed, or undermined, by the content of our
authors' *non*-fictional works is obviously one that
deserves an answer elsewhere. Furthermore, at least
two other areas would need to be charted before the
present analysis could be set in its proper context.
Since our central concern has been perspectives
common to the fiction of these writers, a detailed
and systematic account of the major *differences* in
their outlooks would be of the greatest relevance to
what we have found. And since much of our emphasis
has been placed on changes of perspective that
correspond to large-scale changes in circumstances,
a great deal more remains to be said about such
continuity of views as underlies those changes.

Yet if all of this underlines the narrowness of
the preceding review, it does not run counter to any
of its conclusions, always provided that no

incautious claims are made on their behalf. The aim
was always primarily to make a *contribution* to an
understanding of the authors' outlooks. More
positively, it can undoubtedly be said that there
are certain features of the broad configuration of
results set out in the earlier sections and certain
details in the findings that merit particular
attention, irrespective of what might be produced by
inquiries with different terms of reference.

Firstly, the similarities in the perspectives
of the three writers have proved to be sufficiently
extensive and profound to show that the linking of
their names, whether under the label
'existentialist' or not, is perfectly justifiable
for certain purposes. It emerged from the 'pre-war'
stories that they share certain fundamental
metaphysical views, which form the basis of all
their subsequent reactions to the world; the
revelations brought by the Second World War were
seen to be fundamentally the same in all three
cases; and Camus and Beauvoir were shown to have a
very great deal in common in their outlook on
post-war Western society. Within this broad
structure, moreover, there are exceedingly close
parallels in the specific moral preoccupations of
the authors; in both the angle from which they
approach issues that concern them and their
attitudes towards the types of solution that offer
themselves. At the same time, the general diversity
in the subject-matter of their stories is such that
only in the wartime period could they be said to be
adopting substantive moral positions that come close
to being identical. As well as being more accurate,
it does more justice to their individuality as
novelists and thinkers to see them as sharing
certain perspectives rather than a particular moral
code or even particular moral opinions. Differences
and contrasts in their judgements at the most
detailed level are actually best understood and
appreciated in the context of common perspectives.

It is also noteworthy that the range of topics
and considerations embraced in such perspectives is
wider than might have been anticipated. There is a
tendency - perhaps stemming from popular
understanding of what 'existentialism' is - to
identify Sartre, Camus and Beauvoir with the sort of
'anti-society' stance that they are taken to have
struck before, and during the early years of, the
war. Close scrutiny of the books we have classified
as their wartime novels already corrects this
impression to a marked degree, but, equally, their

moral reflections as a whole are not entirely dominated by the standard problems of action, commitment, responsibility, ends and means that characterise the wartime stories. When the post-war books are also taken into account, it becomes apparent that Camus and Beauvoir, at least, have been concerned with moral and social issues that have a more distinctively modern ring than is now usually associated with existentialism. In general, morality for all three authors can be seen to be less a matter of individuals doing exactly as they wish than is commonly supposed, and rather more a question of individuals situating themselves in relation to certain groups *as well as* formulating and expressing their own beliefs honestly and independently.

In fact, one of the main lines of force running through all of the material we have examined is that along which individual and group are pulled together or pushed apart. Society figured in the pre-war stories almost exclusively as a centre of opposition, which sometimes threatened the individual but could often be largely ignored. When in the war period, on the other hand, society itself was under threat, individuals had little choice but to adopt a position in relation to a variety of groups that necessarily dominated their horizons. And after the war they somehow found themselves well and truly part of just the kind of society that pre-war protagonists were alienated from. The struggle against oppression, which before the war was seen as one that individuals had to wage on their own behalf against society itself, could only be conducted at all during the war if they committed themselves quite strongly to a group or groups. Yet in the post-war years, by their very membership of an advanced industrial society (whose faults, in any case, they openly acknowledge), individuals risk being charged with complicity in the oppression of the under-privileged in their own country as well as elsewhere in the world. In short, there is constant tension in the stories between individual and group, which pulls characters first one way then the other and remains, at the general level, one of the most important factors in the changing moral perspectives that the stories embody.

The fictional heroes and heroines in these books have a certain appeal (perhaps especially for young people) which results from their determination not to be wholly swallowed up by the collectivity. What careful analysis of the stories shows, however,

is that ambiguities or fundamental and persisting
difficulties arise from their failure to accept that
their way of life and, paradoxically, their very
autonomy depend to a great extent upon the society
with which they are linked. After the war, the
obviously parasitic relationship in which the
pre-war figures stood to society is surpassed, but
it is replaced by an equally ambivalent association.
The problems of responsibility for and within the
group raised so acutely during the war remain
painfully unresolved. Individuals can no longer take
consolation in the belief that historical forces
beyond their control are carrying them along; nor is
what they discover in the post-war period
metaphysical in nature and therefore immutable. They
cannot bring themselves to take full blame for the
deplorable features of post-war Western society, yet
their own complicity in those evils is by no means
negligible. In short, the individual's uneasiness in
face of the group is as great as ever, and one feels
that this is because Sartre, Camus and Beauvoir
never entirely stabilise their own attitudes towards
the society to which they belong. One of the
consequences of this is that the ideal of solidarity
that is sometimes taken to be their main positive
guideline is itself a particularly imprecise and
precarious one. A key question implicitly raised by
the wartime novels - that of whether love for the
individual or for a small group like the family
naturally extends outwards into love for all
humanity, or whether the two are quite different in
kind, even in some measure opposed to each other -
is by no means entirely answered in the later
fiction, with the result that the reader may be left
in some doubt about the exact nature, scope and
implications of the writers' 'solidarity'.

In the end, any deficiencies of this kind
probably stem from the general nature of our
authors' perspectives, or the particular angle from
which they approach ethical matters. It has always
been stressed that the type of morality envisaged by
thinkers like Sartre, Camus and Beauvoir is the very
opposite of the standard Christian type, according
to which there are certain *a priori* values that do
not depend in any way upon contingent events,
situations and choices on earth. What has perhaps
not been sufficiently appreciated, however, is that
the views of such thinkers may be marked in subtle
ways by the very fact that they begin by explicitly
rejecting one specific framework for morality. The
novels show outstandingly well that since these

three writers cast aside from the very first any idea of having abstract and eternal values handed down to them, their moral perspectives are necessarily bound up inextricably with the process of *discovery*. Individuals have to create their own values, but they do so in the light of particular things that they learn about the world. We have seen just how crucial their metaphysical, historical and social discoveries are to the moral positions they adopt. Indeed, it is difficult to avoid the impression that their morality consists principally of reactions to those facts and circumstances that happen to *force* themselves upon their attention. If the proponent of *a priori* values always seems to being running ahead of facts and events with his pre-established views, the characters in these stories appear to be perpetually just a little *behind* those facts and events and, in their moral stances, to be adjusting in a rather belated fashion to what they discover.

Even this may be to put too favourable a gloss upon their perspectives, for as often as not characters come very close to being overwhelmed by what comes to light. It is almost as if they have a permanent backlog in their moral reflections, consequently having to spend time and energy taking a grip upon things and never quite reaching the point of thinking out the implications of their reactions and decisions in a systematic way. In this sense, we might wish to think of our three authors as having over-reacted against *a priori* morality, or perhaps simply as finding themselves to be seriously disorientated, in the specific circumstances of their times, as a result of their wholesale rejection of such morality. In contrast with their theoretical writings, which tend to be confident and assertive, their fiction is particularly revealing in this respect, betraying the rather fragmentary nature of their moral stances and pointing up the lack of a stable basis for their perspectives. It may be, for instance, that thinkers rejecting *a priori* values have no real alternative but to begin by considering whether morality is not of its very essence a *social* phenomenon, yet the extreme individualism of our authors' pre-war stories clearly shows that they failed to do this. Characteristically, by the time certain lessons about society have been learned, in the post-war period, protagonists are overwhelmed by social forces of one kind or another and can scarcely see the wood for the trees.

Certainly, we have noted at each stage of our inquiry that the facts or discoveries that form the foundations of the moral perspectives of a particular period also constitute the principal limitations imposed upon those perspectives. The very nature of the discoveries made somehow prevents progress. What is not clear is to what extent this is an inevitable concomitant of a morality of discovery, and to what extent a function of the troubled history of the twentieth century. But, interestingly enough, this observation does go some way towards explaining why (despite the ending of *Le Sang des autres* and despite the general title of Sartre's tetralogy) there is less emphasis on the idea of freedom in these stories than might have been expected. Any theoretical account of our writers' moral views that stresses freedom as both their basis and the supreme goal of morality really needs to be seen in the light of the evidence of their fiction. The reader does not come away from these stories strongly impressed by the degree of freedom enjoyed and exercised by individuals. On the contrary, as we have just suggested, he is rather more likely to be struck by the ways in which their choices are visibly limited by the circumstances in which they find themselves. This is not at all to contradict the metaphysical assertion that man is free (as opposed to determined), but it does bring out the vital importance of the *contexts* within which that freedom operates — something not always stressed in the early philosophical writings in particular. The exact implications of all of this for our authors' ethical theory proper and its relevance to the general development of their thought would have to be traced separately. All that needs to be indicated here is that these general points emerge with some force from their fiction, while they may well be less clear in their essays.

It is now possible to see, in fact, that while the difficulties of taking just works of fiction as the source for an author's moral preoccupations and views are very real ones, the procedure also offers significant advantages or benefits. The main problem is that aesthetic factors proper invariably have the most crucial bearing upon the moral impact of a novel, and that in trying to decipher and describe the writer's own outlook one is frequently obliged to build upon particular interpretations of a text that are of a contentious nature. Such interpretations ought ideally to be justified in the usual, approved way, for the risk is that they will

241

appear somewhat arbitrary when much of the supporting critical evidence has to be omitted. But the contentiousness and apparent arbitrariness constitute a fair price to pay for a richness and nicety in the presentation of moral stances that is perhaps necessarily absent from any ethical treatise. For in addition to giving us a clearer idea than an ethical essay might of how an individual's moral views come to *change*, there is no doubt that the novels we have examined also bring out the ambiguities, irreducible complexities, and even perplexities in our authors' moral attitudes. It is easy enough (and probably right) to see some of these as representing deficiencies in the moral theory behind the stories, yet the potential *exploratory* force of the novel in moral matters is one that should not be under-rated. There is little tendency in these works of fiction to simplify ethics in any way, or to offer tidy solutions that the writers themselves find unsatisfactory or facile. Quite often we sense that they are using the genre to explore outlooks that they are in some sense uncertain about, or do not wish to pronounce upon. If properly handled, this is a distinct virtue in a novel, giving to its content just the kind of open quality that averts didacticism or moralising. Even in the case of an issue like that of solidarity, the very ambiguities are a mark of penetration and an indication of the authors' persistence in pursuing difficult and central moral questions rather than evading them. Only if we measure against over-precise expectations or by standards appropriate to the philosophical essay do these features of the books constitute a weakness. Only if we are seeking a prescribed moral code rather than moral perspectives do they leave us disappointed. In one way or another almost all of the stories manage to embody more than a single viewpoint on any given moral question, and the very nature of the novel genre is allowed to militate against dogmatism, giving us some impression of the background of hesitations and doubts against which the writers arrived at, or are continuing to try to arrive at, their own positions.

The substantive or prescriptive moral content of these books is undoubtedly thin, and, unless this is *always* the case with good fiction, it may be a manifestation of the notorious general difficulty of deductively deriving an ethic from the sort of metaphysical premisses that our authors accept. But however that may be, the great quality of these stories, in the area that we have been investigating, is that they enable readers to see as if through the eyes of at least one other moral agent; to adopt for a time perspectives that might have remained totally alien to them. At one point in *Les Mandarins* Henri acknowledges that this is something that a universalised account of morality cannot achieve:

> 'Une morale de l'universel, on peut tâcher de l'imposer. Mais le sens qu'on donne à sa vie, c'est une autre affaire. Impossible de s'en expliquer en quatre phrases: il faudrait amener Lambert à voir le monde avec mes yeux.' Henri soupira. C'est à ça que ça sert la littérature: montrer aux autres le monde comme on le voit.(I,425)

It can plausibly be argued that the main contribution made to ethics by thinkers of an existentialist persuasion lies not in a proposed moral code or any normative judgements they may proffer, but in insights into the fundamental nature of morality, into the experience of being in situations where one has to make vital judgements and take vital decisions.[1] In any case, the stories that we have examined give us a far greater grasp than we might otherwise have of the different ways in which a moral problem may be looked at; of different views of what does and does not constitute a moral problem; and of the range of complexities associated with being a moral agent at all. They succeed in doing what Camus implies all good novels do, that is in making us more sensitive to the perspectives of others and helping us to understand our own more fully:

> Nos plus grands moralistes ne sont pas des faiseurs de maximes, ce sont des romanciers ... Nos vrais moralistes n'ont pas fait de phrases, ils ont regardé et se sont regardés. Ils n'ont pas légiféré, ils ont peint. Et par là ils ont plus fait pour éclairer la conduite des hommes que s'ils avaient poli patiemment, pour quelques beaux esprits, une centaine de formules définitives, vouées aux dissertations des bacheliers. C'est que le roman seul est fidèle au particulier. Son objet n'est pas les conclusions de la vie mais son déroulement même.[2]

NOTES

    1. A thesis of this kind is cogently argued by F.Olafson in *Principles and Persons. An ethical interpretation of Existentialism*. I am indebted to this work for some of my own emphases.

    2. 'Introduction aux *Maximes* de Chamfort', *Essais*, pp.1099-1100.

BIBLIOGRAPHY

(a)   Works of Fiction Studied

SIMONE DE BEAUVOIR

All of these works are published by Gallimard; dates
of first publication are given below.
References to *Quand prime le spirituel* are taken
from the original 1979 edition; and to each of the
other books from the currently available Gallimard,
'Folio' edition.

Quand prime le spirituel, 1979
L'Invitée, 1943
Le Sang des autres, 1945
Tous les hommes sont mortels, 1946
Les Mandarins, 1954
Les Belles Images, 1966
La Femme rompue, 1967

ALBERT CAMUS

Each work is published separately by Gallimard;
dates of first publication are given below.
References to *La Mort heureuse* are taken from the
original edition of 1971; and to the rest of the
fiction from *Albert Camus. Théâtre, Récits,
Nouvelles*, ed. R.Quilliot, Gallimard, 1967
('Bibliothèque de la Pléiade') - this edition
differs slightly in pagination from the 1962
edition.

La Mort heureuse, 1971 ('Cahiers Albert Camus I')

Bibliography

L'Etranger, 1942
La Peste, 1947
La Chute, 1956
L'Exil et le royaume, 1957

JEAN-PAUL SARTRE

Page-references in the body of my text are to
Jean-Paul Sartre. Oeuvres romanesques, ed. M.Contat
and M.Rybalka, Gallimard, 1981 ('Bibliothèque de la
Pléiade').
Each work is also published separately by Gallimard;
dates of original publication are given below.
L'Age de raison, *Le Sursis*, and *La Mort dans l'âme*
were the first three volumes of *Les Chemins de la
liberté*. 'Drôle d'amitié', the first set of
extracts from the intended fourth volume, *La
Dernière Chance*, was first published in *Les Temps
modernes* (no.49, Nov.1949, pp.769-806; no.50,
Dec.1949, pp.1009-39). Together with another set of
extracts, 'La Dernière Chance', it is now available
in *Oeuvres romanesques*.

La Nausée, 1938
Le Mur, 1939
L'Age de raison, 1945
Le Sursis, 1945
La Mort dans l'âme, 1949
Extracts from *La Dernière Chance*:-
    'Drôle d'amitié', 1949
    'La Dernière Chance', 1981

(b)   Other works cited

BEAUVOIR, S.de: *L'Existentialisme et la sagesse des
nations*, Nagel, 1948
                : *La Force de l'âge*, Gallimard, 1960
                : *La Force des choses*, Gallimard, 1963
                : *Tout compte fait*, Gallimard, 1972
CAMUS, A.: *Albert Camus. Essais*, ed. R.Quilliot and
L.Faucon, Gallimard, 1965 ('Bibliothèque de la
Pléiade')
        : *Carnets, mai 1936 - février 1942*,
Gallimard, 1962
        : *Le Mythe de Sisyphe*, Gallimard, 1942
        : *Noces*, Algiers, Charlot, 1939 (included
in *Essais*)

CHAMPIGNY, R.: 'Sens de *La Nausée*', *PMLA* LXXX
(1955), pp.37-46
FINGARETTE, H.: *Self-Deception*, Routledge & Kegan
Paul, 1969
FITCH, B.T.: *L'Etranger d'Albert Camus. Un texte,
ses lecteurs, leurs lectures*, Larousse, 1972
GIRARD, R.: 'Camus' Stranger Retried', *PMLA* LXXIX
(1964), pp.519-33
GOLDTHORPE, R.: 'The presentation of consciousness
in Sartre's *La Nausée* and its theoretical basis:
1.Reflection and facticity', *French Studies* XXII
(1968), pp.114-32; '...: 2.Transcendence and
intentionality', *French Studies* XXV (1971), pp.32-46
KEEFE, T.: 'The ending of Sartre's *La Nausée*', *Forum
for Modern Language Studies* 12 (1976), pp.217-35
            : 'Heroes of our time in three of the
stories of Camus and Simone de Beauvoir', *Forum for
Modern Language Studies* 17 (1981), pp.39-54
            : 'Marriage in the later fiction of Camus
and Simone de Beauvoir', *Orbis Litterarum* 33 (1978),
pp.69-86
            : 'Simone de Beauvoir and Sartre on
mauvaise foi', *French Studies* XXXIV (1980),
pp.300-14
OLAFSON, F.A.: *Principles and Persons. An ethical
interpretation of existentialism*, Baltimore, Johns
Hopkins Press, 1967
SARTRE, J.-P.:'Deux heures avec Sartre, entretien
avec Robert Kanters', *L'Express*, 17 Sept.1959
            : 'Entretiens avec Jean-Paul Sartre,
par Alain Koehler', *Perspectives du Théâtre*, no.3
(March,1960), pp.18-23; no.4 (April,1960), pp.5-9
            : *L'Etre et le Néant*, Gallimard, 1943
            : 'A qui les lauriers des Goncourt,
Fémina, Renaudot, Inter-allié? article-interview de
Claudine Chonez', *Marianne* 7 (Dec.1938)
            : *Situations IX*, Gallimard, 1972
WITTGENSTEIN, L.: *Philosophical Investigations*
(transl. G.E.M.Anscombe), Blackwell, 1963

INDEX

BEAUVOIR   1-3, 5, 6, 12, 13, 56, 76, 83, 87-8, 89,
    141, 163, 218, 234, 239
    Les Belles Images   163-235 passim, 245
    L'Existentialisme et la sagesse des nations   6,
    246
    La Femme rompue   163-235 passim, 245
    La Force de l'âge   7, 11, 12, 30, 56, 64, 84,
    246
    La Force des choses   6, 159, 175, 246
    L'Invitée   11-84 passim, 94, 179, 245
    Les Mandarins   2, 163-235 passim, 243, 245
    Quand prime le spirituel   11-84 passim, 245
    Le Sang des autres   87-159 passim, 167, 228,
    230, 241, 245
    Tous les hommes sont mortels   87-159 passim, 245
    Tout compte fait   235, 246

BOURGEOISIE   53, 54-5, 56, 58-62, 63, 95, 112, 113,
    120, 141, 156-7, 158, 182, 213, 233

CAMUS   1-3, 5, 6, 51, 56, 58, 62, 73, 78, 81, 82,
    83, 87-8, 89, 171, 213, 218, 231, 239
    Carnets 1936-42   11, 73, 84, 246
    La Chute   163-235 passim, 246
    Essais   84, 246
    L'Etranger   11-84 passim, 130, 157, 171, 179,
    182, 213, 231, 246
    L'Exil et le royaume   163-235 passim, 246
    'Introduction aux *Maximes* de Chamfort'   11, 73,
    84
    La Mort heureuse   11-84 passim, 171, 179, 213,
    245
    Le Mythe de Sisyphe   7, 246
    Noces   81, 246
    La Peste   87-159 passim, 204, 213, 230, 246

CHAMPIGNY, R.   84, 247

248

CHRISTIANITY   21-2, 41, 44-5, 46, 49, 65, 91,
   124-5, 127, 181, 185, 239-40

COMMUNIST PARTY   13, 14, 95, 99, 100, 103, 106,
   108-10, 113, 115, 117, 118-19, 134, 135-6, 145,
   146, 156-7

CONTINGENCY   20-1, 23, 24, 25, 31, 34, 40, 41, 61,
   65, 82, 102, 103, 112, 239

CONTROL   36-40, 42, 45, 47, 63, 66, 67, 70, 74, 77,
   79, 83, 127, 138-9, 158, 209

DANTE   209

DEATH   12, 18, 22-3, 23, 24-5, 30, 31, 33, 38, 41,
   44, 69, 76, 94, 155, 170

FAMILY   49, 105, 106, 109, 156, 175, 182-92, 193-4,
   203-4, 211, 229, 231, 232, 233, 239

FINGARETTE, H.   47, 247

FITCH, B.T.   30, 247

GIRARD, R.   64, 247

GOLDTHORPE, R.   30, 247

HISTORY   11-14, 87-100, 102, 120, 125, 127-9, 130,
   138, 145, 147, 150, 159, 163, 170, 171, 172, 179,
   188, 201, 204, 215, 221, 223, 230, 234, 239, 240,
   241

JUDGEMENT   28-9, 52, 201-6, 208, 210, 211

KEEFE, T.   47, 84, 192, 211, 247

LOVE   26, 154, 155, 177, 179-80, 191, 198, 239

LUCIDITY   31-47, 58, 63, 66, 70, 74, 77, 78, 79,
   82, 83, 131, 138-9, 159, 171, 208, 209, 223, 227,
   233

MARRIAGE   54-5, 58, 176-82, 183, 184, 185, 188,
   190, 191-2, 193-4

METAPHYSICS   19-30, 31, 32, 36, 40, 41, 42, 47, 63,
   73, 82, 88, 91, 94, 102, 138, 145, 159, 171, 172,
   174, 188, 223, 235, 237, 239, 240, 241, 242

OLAFSON, F.A.   244, 247

PERSPECTIVES   4-6, 92, 107, 149, 163-4, 170, 237, 240, 242, 243

RELATIONSHIPS   18, 25-30, 31, 49, 65, 73, 79, 101, 142, 153, 154-6, 172, 179, 190, 191, 192, 229-30, 231

RESPONSIBILITY   66-8, 82, 120-7, 129, 130, 234, 239

SARTRE   1-3, 5, 6, 12, 25, 40, 56, 74, 83, 87-8, 89, 141, 150, 163, 164, 171, 239
    L'Age de raison   11-84 passim, 97, 99, 179, 246
    La Dernière Chance   87-159 passim, 163, 246
    'Deux heures avec Sartre'   175, 247
    'Entretiens avec Jean-Paul Sartre'   6-7, 247
    L'Etre et le Néant   25, 30, 247
    La Mort dans l'âme   87-159 passim, 209, 230, 246
    Le Mur   11-84 passim, 130, 171, 246
    La Nausée   11-84 passim, 246
    'A qui les lauriers ...'   84, 247
    Situations IX   175, 247
    Le Sursis   87-159 passim, 247

SECOND WORLD WAR   1-2, 3, 6, 11, 12, 13, 83, 87-159 passim, 163-9, 172, 198, 201, 228, 234, 237

SELF-DECEPTION   31-47, 58, 61, 62, 63, 82, 138, 159, 174, 208, 222, 223

SEX   25-6, 43, 55-6, 179, 180-1, 221-2

SOCIETY   14, 48-64, 170-2, 174-5, 176, 182, 183, 188, 193, 194, 195-205, 210, 211, 212-35 passim, 237, 238-9, 240

SOLIDARITY   140-5, 150, 217, 227-32, 239, 242

SOLITUDE   15-28, 30, 32, 47, 56, 63, 65, 71, 77, 82, 83, 88, 91, 94, 112, 114, 130, 170, 228

SPANISH CIVIL WAR   12, 13, 14, 104, 106, 132, 134, 137

WITTGENSTEIN   2, 6, 247

WORK   15, 37, 49, 57, 175, 193-201, 204, 211, 230, 232, 233